# OUTSOURCING SOVEREIGNTY WITHDRAWN

This book describes the practice of using private contractors to perform essential or inherent functions in the
military and civilian sectors of government. It shows how
such practices undermine the capacity, effectiveness, and
morale of government officials, and it presents constitutional and statutory arguments to defend the public exercise of authority. While recognizing a proper role for
outsourcing and privatization, the book proposes safeguards against improper delegations. In our democratic
system, the executive branch is required to perform crucial
tasks directly unless Congress has permitted devolutions of
authority to others, such as private contractors. This anal-

ivate

of

# Outsourcing Sovereignty

## WHY PRIVATIZATION OF GOVERNMENT FUNCTIONS THREATENS DEMOCRACY AND WHAT WE CAN DO ABOUT IT

Paul R. Verkuil

CAMBRIDGE
UNIVERSITY PRESS

CAMBRIDGE UNIVERSITY PRESS
Cambridge, New York, Melbourne, Madrid, Cape Town, Singapore, São Paulo, Delhi

Cambridge University Press
32 Avenue of the Americas, New York, NY 10013-2473, USA

www.cambridge.org
Information on this title: www.cambridge.org/9780521867047

First published 2007

Printed in the United States of America

*A catalog record for this publication is available from the British Library.*

*Library of Congress Cataloging in Publication Data*

Verkuil, Paul R.
Outsourcing sovereignty : why privatization of government functions
threatens democracy and what we can do about it / Paul R. Verkuil.
  p.  cm.
Includes bibliographical references and index.
ISBN 978-0-521-86704-7 (hardcover) – ISBN 978-0-521-68688-4 (pbk.)
1. Contracting out – United States.  2. Privatization – United States.  I. Title.
HD3861.U6 .x V4 7  2007
338.973′05 – dc22                             2007013033

ISBN   978-0-521-86704-7 hardback
ISBN   978-0-521-68688-4 paperback

*For Judy, for everything.*

# CONTENTS

# ACKNOWLEDGMENTS

Some of the ideas that led to this project have been in my head for a while, others, the best ones really, were stimulated by colleagues in the academic and public sectors. My thinking on "private due process" was advanced at the January 2005 annual meeting of the Association of American Law Schools on an administrative law panel I shared with Michael Asimov, Gillian Metzger, and Ed Rubin. In February 2005, participants in the Cardozo Law School/Michigan Law School Conference on Contracting Out at the National Academy of Public Administration (led by Sally Anne Payton) proved indispensable in framing the issues. The participants in the March 2005 Harvard Law School Conference on Outsourcing the Government, organized by Martha Minow and Jody Freeman, broadened my thinking. That summer, I spent productive time at RAND's headquarters in Washington, where Bob Rich and Frank Camm tutored me in how contracting is done for the military at a high level.

A November 2005 faculty seminar at my old home, the University of North Carolina Law School (led by Michael Gerhart), refined my thoughts on the constitutional dimensions of the privatization process. A year later, in November 2006, a Cardozo faculty seminar with Laura Dickinson, David Epstein, David Lewis, Peter Lindseth, Gillian Metzger, Steven Schooner, and my colleague Kevin Stack helped me appreciate the significance of agency cost theory to the public sector. The Jacob Burns Institute for Advanced Legal Studies at Cardozo generously supported this meeting.

I am grateful also to Don Kettl and John DiIulio at the University of Pennsylvania, who invited me to visit the Fels Program in the fall of 2006 to share ideas (but these wonderful public administration scholars gave more than they received). Bernhard Schlink of Humboldt University, a sometime colleague at Cardozo, worked me through the intricacies of German and European Community law on privatization of security functions. Don Elliott and Richard Pierce offered me insights into the use by agencies of government contractors for policy making purposes, and Neil Eisner, a fine public servant at DOT, provided explanations for this largely unacknowledged practice. Jim Tozzi, of the Center for Regulatory Effectiveness, a former top civil servant at OMB, offered perspectives not easily found on government Web sites.

I benefited greatly from the work of P. W. Singer and Deborah Avant on the private military, and from Akhil Amar, Sidney Shapiro, Peter Strauss, and Cass Sunstein, on the constitutional and regulatory problems outsourcing creates. Dan Guttman's work in this regard and his efforts to locate sources and citations are also much appreciated. The most enjoyable exchanges occurred during the summer of 2006 with Gordon Wood at Bellagio on Lake Como, where we revisited fundamental assumptions about concepts of sovereignty at the Founding. I thank the Rockefeller Foundation for making that visit possible. I am indebted to Dean David Rudenstine for rearranging my schedule so I could finish this book and for supporting me with faculty research grants in the summers of 2005 and 2006. My colleagues Michael Herz, Arthur Jacobson, Michel Rosenfeld, and Kevin Stack were always available for consultation.

Ideas from my earlier articles appear in different form in Chapters 4 and 5: *Privatizing Due Process*, 57 Admin. L. Rev. 963 (2005) and *Public Law Limitations on Privatization of Government Functions*, 84 N. C. L. Rev. 397 (2006). Chapter 3 incorporates work from *The Publicization of Airport Security*, 27 Cardozo L. Rev. 2243 (2006). In addition, a chapter entitled "The Nondelegable Duty to Govern" will appear in a forthcoming Harvard University Press book *Outsourcing the U.S.* I thank each of these publishers.

J. T. Hutchens, Cardozo Class of 2007, went beyond normal research assistance to a degree of collaboration on aspects of the manuscript. Julie Rubenstein, Class of 2007, and Emily Posner and Cody Wright, Class of 2008, provided excellent assistance during the editorial process. Finally, my children, Tara, Gibson, and Alex, were always supportive.

# THE GOVERNMENT OF THE UNITED STATES

**THE CONSTITUTION**

## LEGISLATIVE BRANCH

**THE CONGRESS**

SENATE HOUSE

ARCHITECT OF THE CAPITOL
UNITED STATES BOTANIC GARDEN
GENERAL ACCOUNTING OFFICE
GOVERNMENT PRINTING OFFICE
LIBRARY OF CONGRESS
CONGRESSIONAL BUDGET OFFICE

## EXECUTIVE BRANCH

**THE PRESIDENT**
**THE VICE PRESIDENT**
**EXECUTIVE OFFICE OF THE PRESIDENT**

WHITE HOUSE OFFICE
OFFICE OF THE VICE PRESIDENT
COUNCIL OF ECONOMIC ADVISERS
NATIONAL SECURITY COUNCIL
OFFICE OF ADMINISTRATION

OFFICE OF MANAGEMENT AND BUDGET
OFFICE OF NATIONAL DRUG CONTROL POLICY
OFFICE OF POLICY DEVELOPMENT
OFFICE OF SCIENCE AND TECHNOLOGY POLICY
OFFICE OF THE U.S. TRADE REPRESENTATIVE

## JUDICIAL BRANCH

**THE SUPREME COURT OF THE UNITED STATES**

UNITED STATES COURTS OF APPEALS
UNITED STATES DISTRICT COURTS
TERRITORIAL COURTS
UNITED STATES COURT OF INTERNATIONAL TRADE
UNITED STATES COURT OF FEDERAL CLAIMS
UNITED STATES COURT OF APPEALS FOR THE ARMED FORCES
UNITED STATES TAX COURT
UNITED STATES COURT OF APPEALS FOR VETERANS CLAIMS
ADMINISTRATIVE OFFICE OF THE UNITED STATES COURTS
FEDERAL JUDICIAL CENTER
UNITED STATES SENTENCING COMMISSION

---

DEPARTMENT OF AGRICULTURE
DEPARTMENT OF COMMERCE
DEPARTMENT OF DEFENSE
DEPARTMENT OF EDUCATION
DEPARTMENT OF ENERGY
DEPARTMENT OF HEALTH AND HUMAN SERVICES
DEPARTMENT OF HOUSING AND URBAN DEVELOPMENT

DEPARTMENT OF THE INTERIOR
DEPARTMENT OF JUSTICE
DEPARTMENT OF LABOR
DEPARTMENT OF STATE
DEPARTMENT OF TRANSPORTATION
DEPARTMENT OF HOMELAND SECURITY
DEPARTMENT OF THE TREASURY
DEPARTMENT OF VETERANS AFFAIRS

---

## INDEPENDENT ESTABLISHMENTS AND GOVERNMENT CORPORATIONS

AFRICAN DEVELOPMENT FOUNDATION
CENTRAL INTELLIGENCE AGENCY
COMMODITY FUTURES TRADING COMMISSION
CONSUMER PRODUCT SAFETY COMMISSION
CORPORATION FOR NATIONAL AND COMMUNITY SERVICE
DEFENSE NUCLEAR FACILITIES SAFETY BOARD
ENVIRONMENTAL PROTECTION AGENCY
EQUAL EMPLOYMENT OPPORTUNITY COMMISSION
EXPORT-IMPORT BANK OF THE U.S.
FARM CREDIT ADMINISTRATION
FEDERAL COMMUNICATIONS COMMISSION
FEDERAL DEPOSIT INSURANCE CORPORATION
FEDERAL ELECTION COMMISSION
FEDERAL HOUSING FINANCE BOARD

FEDERAL LABOR RELATIONS AUTHORITY
FEDERAL MARITIME COMMISSION
FEDERAL MEDIATION AND CONCILIATION SERVICE
FEDERAL MINE SAFETY AND HEALTH REVIEW COMMISSION
FEDERAL RESERVE SYSTEM
FEDERAL RETIREMENT THRIFT INVESTMENT BOARD
FEDERAL TRADE COMMISSION
GENERAL SERVICES ADMINISTRATION
INTER-AMERICAN FOUNDATION
MERIT SYSTEMS PROTECTION BOARD
NATIONAL AERONAUTICS AND SPACE ADMINISTRATION
NATIONAL ARCHIVES AND RECORDS ADMINISTRATION
NATIONAL CAPITAL PLANNING COMMISSION
NATIONAL CREDIT UNION ADMINISTRATION

NATIONAL FOUNDATION ON THE ARTS AND THE HUMANITIES
NATIONAL LABOR RELATIONS BOARD
NATIONAL MEDIATION BOARD
NATIONAL RAILROAD PASSENGER CORPORATION (AMTRAK)
NATIONAL SCIENCE FOUNDATION
NATIONAL TRANSPORTATION SAFETY BOARD
NUCLEAR REGULATORY COMMISSION
OCCUPATIONAL SAFETY AND HEALTH REVIEW COMMISSION
OFFICE OF GOVERNMENT ETHICS
OFFICE OF PERSONNEL MANAGEMENT
OFFICE OF SPECIAL COUNSEL
OVERSEAS PRIVATE INVESTMENT CORPORATION
PEACE CORPS
PENSION BENEFIT GUARANTY CORPORATION

POSTAL RATE COMMISSION
RAILROAD RETIREMENT BOARD
SECURITIES AND EXCHANGE COMMISSION
SELECTIVE SERVICE SYSTEM
SMALL BUSINESS ADMINISTRATION
SOCIAL SECURITY ADMINISTRATION
TENNESSEE VALLEY AUTHORITY
TRADE AND DEVELOPMENT AGENCY
U.S. AGENCY FOR INTERNATIONAL DEVELOPMENT
U.S. COMMISSION ON CIVIL RIGHTS
U.S. INTERNATIONAL TRADE COMMISSION
U.S. POSTAL SERVICE

# 1 INTRODUCTION AND OVERVIEW – WHY OUTSOURCING THREATENS DEMOCRACY

## A. CONCERNS OF THIS BOOK

The government exercises sovereign powers. When those powers are delegated to outsiders, the capacity to govern is undermined. A government appointment creates a public servant who, whether through the oath, the security clearance, the desire to achieve public goals, or the psychic income of service, is different from those in the private sector. The office itself is honored. This is why many in our democratic system live in a dual reality, decrying the president, whether it be Bush or Clinton, Reagan or Roosevelt, but respecting the presidency, the office of George Washington, the first among the heroes of our Republic. Those offices that fall under the president deserve similar respect. Anyone who has served in government, from a buck private to a cabinet official, knows this feeling. And they also know that the public and private sectors have different boundaries. Outsourcing tests these boundaries. By doing so, it pushes government to justify delegations of public power to private hands.

One of the challenges of this book is to show exactly when public power has been transferred. By way of introduction, consider one statistic – security clearances. These are key indicators of public responsibility, reflecting the exercise of important duties and realized only after careful investigations by federal officials. Currently over eight hundred thousand contractors have security clearances at eleven thousand government facilities.[1] That may be more than exist on the civilian side of government. It certainly forces us to ask what it is these people do

1

for government and whether it is something that government should be doing for itself.

After many years of infatuation with the idea of privatization, the potential downsides of privatizing or contracting out government functions are being examined.[2] The perceived threat is to democratic principles of accountability and process in what has been a largely unexamined shift from public to private governance. On both a national and global stage, a "democracy deficit" may be emerging.[3] This book explores privatization and "outsourcing"[4] and sets itself against delegating the "sovereign"[5] powers of government to private contractors. The premises of this argument incorporate constitutional, statutory, administrative, and contractual sources. The argument builds on existing work in delegation theory and transactions cost analysis and contributes new ways of looking at constitutional provisions and bureaucratic behavior. Its conclusions should be of broad academic and public interest.

To date, strong public reactions against outsourcing sovereignty have been hard to locate. But that is changing. The recent exposé of shabby treatment and poor living conditions for wounded soldiers at Walter Reed Army Medical Center forced the resignation of the Secretary of the Army, Francis Harvey.[6] Private contracting of support personnel and maintenance workers, something Harvey (a former G.E. executive) encouraged, led to a reduction in force from 300 to 60 in 2006.[7] The House committee investigating the Walter Reed situation focused directly on the impact of outsourcing upon the performance of government functions.

In Iraq the implications of a "private military" have also been subjected to scrutiny. Ted Koppel, no isolated scholar, wrote in the op-ed pages of the *New York Times* about the "seductive . . . notion of a mercenary army."[8] The emergence of a private military is one consequence of the privatization movement. Koppel suggested the "inevitable" next step – a defensive military force paid for by energy corporations, such as Exxon Mobil, to be deployed in countries where their interests need to be protected. He then quoted officials at Blackwater USA, a leading provider of such services: Provide a battalion or two of troops to protect oil fields in Nigeria, they responded, no problem. They are ready to take on the "Darfur account." The idea of conducting foreign policy by contract – the idea that such a duty can be delegated in the first place – is certainly an arresting one.

Noting that the Pentagon was reluctant to have private armies outside its chain of command, Koppel mentioned issues of loyalty and accountability. But Blackwater's representatives did not flinch. "We are accountable. We are transparent." After all, they said, "If we were against the U.S. government's interests we would never get another contract."[9] Surely, this candid expression of economic interest from Blackwater and the many other private firms performing military work (which includes familiar names such as Halliburton and its subsidiary Kellogg, Brown & Root) satisfies stockholders' wishes. But it is not only stockholders whose interests must be served – it is citizens' interests as well. Blackwater and friends do not have the last word on whether they are doing too much, or whether they are transparent or accountable. This is where the government comes in.

Koppel, in terms Jonathan Swift would admire, next encouraged debate on the merits of mercenary regimes. And debate he got. Six days later, a remarkable series of letters appeared in the *Times* that raised many of the policy points this book will explore. Some said as a "democratic nation," sensitive to "fueling serious human rights abuses," the "frightening prospect" of mercenaries conducting our foreign intervention is not what America is all about.[10] One writer suggested, if the all volunteer army cannot staff the war in Iraq (or elsewhere), necessitating the use of private forces, perhaps that signals a vote against the war.[11] Yet another writer urged congressional oversight of private military contractors and called for the restoration of compulsory military service as an obligation of citizenship and patriotism. All of the letters decried Koppel's "dubious cause."[12] By doing so, the writers joined the issue publicly,[13] which surely is what Koppel was hoping for.

This exchange helps to establish the theme of this book: "Outsourcing sovereignty" occurs when the idea of privatization is carried too far. In an era of national and global privatization, the temptations are great to expand it to include governmental functions inherent in sovereignty.

The *New York Times* recently published a series of articles that label contractors as the "Fourth Branch" of government.[14] That term, coined in the 1930s to describe the independent agencies of government,[15] has now been appropriated to cover private contractors. If the fourth branch was "headless" when composed of independent agencies, think how more so it can be when it consists of private contractors performing government services.

Privatization demonstrates efficiency principles that can improve government performance. But when privatization encourages the outsourcing of political decisions, it exceeds its limits. John Donahue reminds us that democracy is not defined by efficiency alone.[16] Accountability is a countervailing principle of democracy. It may but need not be efficient. Indeed, as the Supreme Court has recognized, the Constitution is sometimes intentionally "inefficient."[17] Of cource, efficiency and accountability need not be in opposition – they can and do coexist. But when efficiency dominates – as is the case with outsourcing important aspects of public sector decision making – it clashes with accountability and undermines democratic values.

Moreover, although a dramatic example, the private military is in no way the exclusive setting for this problem. The urge to outsource affects many government programs, civilian as well as military. Recently, the Internal Revenue Service (IRS) decided to outsource delinquent tax collections to the private sector. The evidence was that the IRS could have done this important job itself more efficiently.[18] Outsourcing in the face of both accountability and efficiency objections is inexplicable. It amounts to, in Paul Krugman words, "a retreat from modern principles of government."[19]

Outsourcing failures have been highlighted recently in the Coast Guard's decision to turn over to Lockheed Martin and Grumman the responsibility to manage its $17 billion fleet modernization program.[20] The costs of this program now exceed $24 billion and the structural weaknesses in completed ships are rendering them unseaworthy. Many auditors and retired Coast Guard officials fault the privatization model, which "allowed the contractors at times to put their interests ahead of the Guard's."[21] This compulsion to delegate government responsibilities has earned President Bush the title of "Outsourcer in Chief."[22]

In both the IRS and Coast Guard examples, the outsourcing of management functions that are best performed in house undermines government performance in two ways: By utilizing second-best performers and by weakening or atrophying government's power to perform these functions in the future. Government managers cease to exist when they are not put to good use.

Some agencies, such as the Department of Defense (DOD), the Department of Energy (DOE), and the Department of Homeland Security (DHS), are outsourcing engines. The national security, public infrastructure, disaster relief, and border control missions these agencies perform are honeycombed with private contracts. And other agencies of government, when faced with personnel constraints or because of political preferences, increasingly turn to contractors to do policy formulation and implementation. The question becomes: Who is really in charge of government policy making? It is the burden of this book to show (1) that important work – labeled "significant" or "inherent" – is being contracted out to the detriment of democratic policy making; and (2) that this trend can be moderated, if not reversed, by feasible changes in the way government operates. When the public, "We the People" under the Constitution, call this a "dubious cause," as one of Ted Koppel's responders put it, we are commanded to listen.

The "era of privatization" has unintended costs as well as intended benefits. Outsourcing can lead to corruption of our bureaucracy, at least of its politically appointed members.[23] Political officials, who are appointed for short periods and enter service through the famous revolving door, sometimes utilize outsourcing both as a means of getting results and as a way of preserving later career opportunities.

Homeland Security seems to be the paradigm case. This multibillion-dollar agency, formed virtually overnight to meet a national security preparedness challenge, has been struggling to perform its complicated mission.[24] More than two-thirds of the Department's most senior executives, including its first Secretary, Tom Ridge, have moved to private positions, some with companies who receive lucrative contracts from the agency.[25] These companies are doing outsourced government work. Asa Hutchinson, a former undersecretary who ran for governor of Arkansas, allegedly had numerous private relationships with these companies, including one that sold him stock (Fortress America Acquisitions) that IPOed for a potentially generous return.[26] In the words of one critic, DHS itself seems to have become an IPO and "[e]veryone wants a piece of it."[27] Ethics rules control these activities to some degree, although they too seem to have been reduced in effectiveness.[28]

These activities reflect chronic problems with DHS itself [29] – problems that aggressive privatization exacerbates. In agencies with big budgets such as the DHS, in which the players are inexperienced and the programs are new, officials have enormous opportunities to benefit from the outsourcing process. But outsourcing also causes demoralization costs. Civil servants may be bypassed by outsourcing decisions and their purpose and commitment are frustrated. Given the aging of our bureaucracy and difficulty in finding qualified replacements, maintaining significant functions in-house is crucial to the preservation of our civil service. The Wall Street Journal puts it provocatively; Is government "outsourcing its brain?"[30]

## B. PERSPECTIVES AND PLAN

This book will explore public sector privatization, explain its roots, internal logic, and self-perpetuating nature, and propose ways to control it in the future. The perspective is not antiprivatization. The author has long favored deregulation and the values of efficiency,[31] and does not see government as the solution to all public problems. But it is surely the solution to some of them. The continued outsourcing of government functions has reached the point where limits on it must be addressed. There seems to be no consistent standard applied when the choice to privatize or retain government functions arises.[32] To avoid making outsourcing the default alternative, it should be checked by public law limits. These limits must be fixed for our democracy to work.[33]

The relationship of government to the private sector is very much in flux these days. The pressures to outsource more and more government functions are occurring at the same time as the federal bureaucracy is shrinking in alarming proportion to its oversight responsibilities,[34] and in relationship to the size of government itself. In these circumstances, the number of private contractors doing the work of government will inevitably accelerate to the limits of federal employees available to supervise them; and may be beyond.[35] Contractor oversight of contractors has become a routine proposition. The Government Accountability Office (GAO) now hires contractors to review contractors who have been suspended or barred for poor performance.[36] The surveillance of privatized activities is more difficult to achieve because of the reduction in key government personnel.[37] A disequilibrium is occurring between those in government who should oversee and those in the private sector who need to be overseen. Accountability is lacking.[38]

The gap is a by-product of two converging forces: the deregulation movement, which renders many government regulatory programs unnecessary, and the privatization movement, which transfers government activities to the private sector. Deregulation challenges the economic role of government over the economy. It seeks to end programs that are inefficient or counterproductive.[39] Even after its many successes, however, "the prevailing view still holds that government regulation is overzealous and needs to be reined in."[40] This view is not equally shared by the public or the academy,[41] but it often drives decisions at the White House, in Congress, and even before the courts. There is no need to challenge deregulation; the need is for government officials to make all significant decisions, whether they be regulatory or deregulatory in character.

Privatization's role is different from deregulation. It accepts the need for a government activity but sees advantages in shifting its operation to private hands. In the United States, at least,[42] privatization, unlike deregulation, is concerned less with the amount of government expenditures than with where to place responsibility for the activity. The size of government, viewed as a percentage of the Gross Domestic Product, could well grow in a privatized environment, as it has during the Bush administration.[43] But privatization and deregulation do share a belief that the market will improve the services provided by a monopolistic bureaucracy. A cornerstone of the reinventing government movement of the Clinton–Gore administration,[44] this commitment has become ideological under the Bush administration.

President Bush's vision of an "ownership society"[45] tries to build public support for reducing the size of government across the board. It has been used prominently to advocate private accounts as an alternative to Social Security, but it also has become a code word that signals more generally the private sector's role in the provision of traditional government services. Privatization, in this view, is a way to pass ownership of government on to the people, or at least some of the people.

But stating a preference for private over public solutions, as the term ownership society suggests, has unintended consequences. Government has been contracting out some of its services since the post–World War II period,[46] but its acceleration to the limits of accountability is a relatively recent phenomenon. The view that private enterprise provides a superior organizing principle to government monopoly puts the public sector on the defensive. It fuels the debate over whether Social Security should remain a public function or whether health care should become one. Indeed a central question arising from the privatization movement is whether the term "public sector" continues to be a viable social concept. Stated alternatively, is the public-private distinction, which has been reflected in law and political theory from the earliest times, still meaningful in an era of transcendent privatization? And if not, what replaces it?

This book explores the relationship of public law to privatization.[47] Chapter 4 elaborates on the public-private distinction and asks whether the values of responsibility and accountability behind the distinction still resonate. Accepting privatization, it is argued, need not be the end of public law; instead, public law limitations should be reformulated to restrict the outsourcing of significant government functions as a way to preserve democracy.

Chapter 6 discusses long-standing practices that forbid the contracting-out of "inherent government functions." These functions must be first understood and then preserved in the process of contracting-out. The privatization movement cannot ignore the limits that phrase implies. The application of both constitutional and statutory requirements, in particular the Take Care and Appointments Clauses and the Subdelegation Act, frame the analysis in Chapters 5 and 6. These provisions serve not only as grants of power to the Executive but also as limits on the exercise of those powers. The Constitution is largely about the delegation and sharing of powers among the three branches. The "fourth branch" (the administrative state, not the contractors) is central here, as contracting is largely done by the agencies.[48]

The Office of Management and Budget's (OMB's) Circular A-76 process also helps to define the limits of the contracting-out process. The realities of current practice under this circular show how improvements can be made in the way that contracting-out is usually conducted by agencies. OMB's role in contracting-out is crucial, and has the potential to preserve inherent functions in the hands of government officials.

Ultimately, the goal is to balance the two positives of the private and public sectors – efficiency and accountability – in ways that confirm rather than threaten our legal and political traditions. Accountability emerges from constitutional principles, from legal standards, and from administrative practices. New formulations that embrace an invigorated conception of the public sector are also needed. Therefore, Chapters 7 and 8 ask: How can public service – the dreaded bureaucracy – be reorganized and reinvigorated to meet the challenges that privatized government presents? For years, the bureaucracy has been neglected and derided. But we have reached a point where it must be given a renewed life.

DHS and FEMA's performance during Hurricane Katrina dramatically shows the dangers of excessive privatization. The proper balance between public and private solutions must be struck for mission-oriented agencies such as DHS to work effectively. Since 2001, government has been developing a new specialty in national security and disaster relief. These enormous responsibilities are the essence of inherently governmental; they cannot be shifted to the private sector. Yet contractors are expanding their roles in ways that make the shift increasingly inevitable. How did we get to the place where the proposition of who runs government admits of no easy answer?

## C. THE IRAN–CONTRA ROOTS OF THE OUTSOURCING CONTROVERSY

Under the American system, Government is accountable to the people.[49]

The administration of President Bush and Vice President Cheney has perfected the art of contracting-out key functions of government. The preference for private solutions has combined with a penchant for secrecy that began at the outset of the administration when the vice president met privately with leaders of private oil companies to formulate an energy policy.[50] Although the secrecy attempts ultimately succeeded, the policy itself has yet to be revealed, at least to the satisfaction of most observers.[51] Cheney, of course, had deep ties to the energy community through his service as CEO of Halliburton which (with its subsidiary KBR) has become the major contractor for services in Iraq.

But the desire to outsource was not born with this administration. It was nurtured through several prior administrations, including Clinton and Bush I. It was the Reagan administration, however, that seems to have grasped most fully what privatization of policy making was all about. Indeed, the Iran–Contra Affair provides a virtual textbook in how to establish a private foreign and military policy shop.

## 1. The Relevance of Iran–Contra to Outsourcing Sovereignty

It is well to remember what Iran–Contra was all about. The plot was convoluted, but the goals were deceptively simple, and eerily familiar. In order to help release American hostages in Lebanon, the White House sold missiles purchased from Israel to the Iranian government of Ayatollah Khomeni and used the profits to fund the Contras in Nicaragua, who were trying to destroy the Sandinista government of Daniel Ortega.[52] The plot was managed by Lt. Col. Oliver North in the White House basement on instructions from the National Security Advisor Robert McFarlane;[53] it was made necessary by the fact that Congress, through the Boland Amendment, had forbidden the expenditure of federal funds for support of the Contras. President Reagan denied involvement or even knowledge of the "affair." Given the fact that both houses were in Democrat hands, hearings were held and Reagan received a devastating blow to his administration.

There are many views of who should have been charged and convicted in the aftermath of this debacle.[54] But one thing is clear: It was the most outrageously creative use of privatized resources ever deployed for government purposes. Colonel North secured over $30 million from Saudi Arabia[55] and $10 million from private donors in addition to the profits made in the arms sales to Iran.[56] When North's operation threatened to draw public attention, Admiral Poindexter told North not to talk to anybody but him.[57] Thus did the president ultimately secure the deniability necessary to save his office (and earn the title of "hands-off" president[58]).

Appropriately the Iran–Contra Report had a section entitled "Privatization." In it, the following statement appears:

> The NSC staff turned to private parties and third countries to do the Government's business. Funds denied by Congress were

obtained by the Administration from third countries and private citizens. Activities normally conducted by professional intelligence services – which are accountable to Congress – were turned over to Secord and Hakim.[59]

The report concludes that, whatever his level of actual knowledge, the president was responsible because, under the Constitution, he has the duty to "take Care that the Laws be faithfully executed."[60] Whatever one's political views, it is hard to argue with this constitutional view of accountability. It holds that the president may not avoid responsibility by transferring policy functions to unaccountable bureaucrats or especially to private parties. The duty to govern, described in detail later, was the lesson of the Iran–Contra experience.

## 2. The Counterlessons of Iran–Contra and the Rise of Executive Privilege

The Iran–Contra Report has another dimension that connects Vice President Cheney to the themes of privatization and secrecy. In defeating attempts to learn about his energy advisors, the vice president successfully asserted executive privilege with respect to the Federal Advisory Committee Act (FACA).[61] But his attraction to secrecy hardly began there. It is reflected in the minority view to the Iran–Contra Report, written under the direction of Representative Dick Cheney of Wyoming.[62] Although admitting at the outset that "President Reagan and his staff made mistakes,"[63] the minority report saw them as the result of "[a] compassionate, but disproportionate" concern for the hostages held in Lebanon. Instead of a lack of accountability, it attributed the decisions taken by President Reagan as the product of two things:

A legitimate frustration with abuses of power and irresolution by the legislative branch; and

An equally legitimate frustration with leaks of sensitive national security secrets coming out of both Congress and the executive branch.[64]

Cheney may not have actually penned these words, but they certainly reflect his secretive executive take on the world. Given this jaundiced view of Congress, it must have given the vice president great pleasure to preside over the Senate and great frustration to see it end so abruptly by the loss of one seat in November 2006. The emphasis on secrecy is a prominent aspect of the current administration, where government officials are frequently kept in the dark.[65] And this desire for secrecy encourages the use of private contractors, who can do jobs for the government exempt from FOIA and FACA disclosures.[66]

The Iran–Contra minority report takes even stronger positions on the Constitution's view of executive power. It says that the Boland Amendment, by restricting the president's power to expend funds on behalf of the Contras, fails the Constitution's requirement that the president be the "Sole Organ" for diplomacy.[67] This legal analysis has fascinating echoes to the present. It relies on Justice Jackson's concurring opinion in the *Steel Seizure* case,[68] much as Attorney General Gonzales did in justifying the president's national security intercept program.[69] David Addington, Cheney's long-term aide and constitutional advisor,[70] served on the minority staff, which gives this legal memo a remarkable currency. It is hard not to conclude that the legal theories of executive power refined in the Iraq situation were first developed by Cheney and Addington in defense of Iran–Contra.[71]

## 3. Iran–Contra as a Preview to Iraq

The players are largely the same, but the sides have shifted. Now it is Iran that bears watching, not collaborating with. The frustrations the Reagan administration felt with Congress over the Boland Amendment were understandable because Congress changed its views on Contra support several times. But these frustrations are largely absent for the Bush administration in Iraq because both Houses had compliant Republican majorities until 2006. Even so, executive prerogatives were still jealously guarded. The torture legislation[72] – and the subsequent signing statement of President Bush[73] – demonstrate how distrustful the Executive Branch was of the Legislative.

Occasionally, Congress still acts to restrict executive prerogatives in ways that are reminiscent of the Boland Amendment. In 2005, Congress passed the Andean Counterdrug Initiative that provided $750 million for antidrug activities in Colombia. But it added this proviso: "That no United States Armed Forces personnel or United States civilian contractor employed by the United States will participate in any combat operation in connection with assistance made available by this Act for Colombia."[74] This proviso restricts executive policy making. It runs counter to the expansive view of executive authority staked out in the Iran–Contra minority report and the torture memo.[75] And it importantly identifies the use of private military contractors, who operate in Colombia, as an oversight problem.

The contractor approach to executive authority hides decisions from public view. Accountability for acts of government is difficult when duties are delegated to private hands and secrecy covers the tracks. Accountability is something that emerges when public acts are challenged or capable of being challenged. The Iraq war is being brought forth by an administration that distrusts Congress. The use of private resources has become central to the Iraq war effort. Although foreign policy has not been privatized in the Iran–Contra sense, private contractors in Iraq are surely performing inherent government functions.

## D. OUTSOURCING POLICY MAKING TO THE IRAQ STUDY GROUP?

You don't outsource the responsibilities of the Commander in Chief.
– Richard Perle[76]

In political terms, the Iraq Study Group Report, authorized by Congress, was a slap at the Bush presidency, or at least Iraq invasion supporters saw it that way. In the aftermath of the November 2006 elections, with the Iraq as a decisive factor in the shift to Democrat control of both houses, the report sought to define a new way forward. Although President Bush promised to study it before unveiling his own plans, many of its suggestions (e.g., direct negotiations with Iran and Syria[77]) were initially rejected out of hand. To undermine the report, some reactions characterized it as an outsourcing of the president's responsibilities. This was really a disingenuous attack – and ironic for an administration that has embraced outsourcing as a pervasive policy.[78] But just labeling the report as an inappropriate exercise in outsourcing allowed critics to ignore its true purpose and function. This reaction also offers an opportunity to distinguish proper from improper uses of outsourcing.

Unlike the Iran–Contra staffing, which employed private contractors and was hidden from view, the Iraq Study Group was created with bipartisan support from Congress. Its purpose, publicly embraced, was to analyze the situation in Iraq and offer alternatives. The Study Group had no power to implement its views or direct public officials to act. It simply made recommendations that had to be discussed and accepted by the relevant government actors. Perhaps this aspect of the report, by speaking to Congress and the president, caused the president's unitary executive power believers to balk. By bringing up the inappropriate outsourcing allegation they sought to discredit the "misadventure," in Richard Perle's words, from the outset. It mattered not at all that some of the advice might be useful or even wise.

Whatever the ultimate effect of the report, whether it gathers dust on the shelf or inspires new policy directions in Iraq,[79] it will not suffer from the charge of outsourcing sovereignty that has been leveled at many activities highlighted in this book. In fact, the report shows how the private sector (through distinguished former government officials) can play a legitimate role in advising government rather than an insidious one in transferring power. The report, in other words, had no confusion about the identity of the sovereign.

## E. A NOTE ON THE MEANING OF SOVEREIGNTY

The Magna Charta is such a fellow that he will have no sovereign.
– Sir Edward Coke[80]

This book approaches sovereignty from a traditional perspective. It accepts Weber's view that sovereignty is the exercise of power by the state.[81] Thus, notions of "new sovereignty"[82] in the international setting are outside its ambit, as are intriguing propositions of "disaggregated" sovereignty that invite various government institutions to act together internationally without the direct involvement of the states of which they are part.[83] But sovereignty is no easy concept to comprehend. Even under a traditional perspective, sovereignty has long been "shared," for example when government established corporations who acted with legal powers delegated by the state.[84]

Stephen Krasner usefully describes four kinds of sovereignty: international legal sovereignty, Westphalian sovereignty, domestic sovereignty, and interdependence sovereignty.[85] "New" sovereignty is concerned with definitions one and four. We are here concerned more with definition three.[86]

That said, however, sovereignty in the American setting needs further explanation. One must still consider Lord Coke's observation placing ultimate sovereignty not in the state, but in the Barons. American ideas about sovereignty later carried this idea to its logical conclusion by switching the People for the Barons.

The meaning of sovereignty was much debated during the creation of the Republic.[87] Gordon Wood teaches us that during the Constitution drafting period, antifederalists derided the notion of shared or "divided" sovereignty between the Congress and the states. They used this contradictory phrase to argue that the Supremacy Clause of the Constitution would annihilate the independent sovereignty of the states.[88] According to Wood, James Wilson resolved the impasse by arguing that sovereignty had not been divided but remained with the People, the true Sovereign. The People then delegated powers in such proportions as she thought necessary to the states and the three branches.[89] Wilson's concept of sovereignty triumphed when the Constitution shifted its emphasis from "We the States" to "We the People."[90]

Akhil Amar writes that Wilson believed the Constitution only to be a *private* document until it was ratified by the People.[91] The ratification process itself was "extraordinarily extended and inclusive," with ten states waiving property restrictions so as to permit a broader number of voters to participate.[92] Once ratified, of course, this private document became public. And the unique principle of American sovereignty was established.

Placing sovereignty in the People has two distinct advantages for the arguments presented here. First, it makes clear who the principal and agents are. The People is the sovereign and the Congress and president are her agents. The political branches receive delegated powers either directly or indirectly from the Constitution.[93] Whatever powers they in turn delegate are in fact subdelegated. It is in this context that the Subdelegation Act makes perfect sense.[94] Second, once the principal-agent relationship is established, the Constitution has a role in policing it. Thus when the Congress subdelegates to the president or the agencies or the president further delegates to private parties, the Constitution still umpires the relationships.

Thus, sovereignty is an essential force under our Constitution. When sovereign powers are delegated, it is with the permission of the People. Notions of dual sovereignty or diffused sovereignty may more accurately describe federal and state relations. But they only serve to obfuscate the question of where accountability and responsibility lie for performing the people's duties under the Constitution.

Once it is accepted where sovereignty is placed and how it is exercised, "outsourcing sovereignty" becomes a logical impossibility; unless of course the people concur and the agents faithfully follow her instructions. This is not some artificial construct. The Organization Chart of the United States, appearing in the front of this book, describes the government and its three branches. Note that it places the Constitution at the top. This chart symbolizes what it means to place sovereignty in the People and similarly what it means to demand faithful accountability to the Constitution by all three branches. The People, through popular sovereignty, established the Constitution, the document under which her agents are clearly identified and properly charged.

The metaphor of the People as sovereign also permits a (hopefully forgivable) literary flourish: the opportunity to personalize the constitutional connection. Arguments expressed here are made on behalf of the People. As Lady Liberty, she for they, the citizens delegates power under the Constitution and she sets the limits on delegations of power to private hands. In Chapter 9, therefore, her requirements are set out for the branches to follow. These requirements establish that this book's title, outsourcing sovereignty, is a constitutional oxymoron.

## NOTES

1. *See* Defense Security Service, *About DSS Homepage.* There are fewer than two million civilian, nonpostal service employees in government. *See infra* n. 32.
2. *See* Symposium, *Public Values in an Era of Privatization.*
3. *See generally* Aman, *The Democracy Deficit* at 3 (viewing globalization as a problem in public accountability). Similar concerns are expressed about privatization within the United States. *See* Freeman, *Extending Public Law Norms Through Privatization* (using public law norms to "publicize" the privatization movement).
4. Privatization and outsourcing will be used interchangeably, except where the term privatization's broader meaning (i.e., denationalization) is intended. *See infra* n. 6. Also, outsourcing is defined in terms of contracting-out government services within the United States; thus, the outsourcing of jobs abroad is

not the focus. *See* Gross, *Why "Outsourcing" May Lose Its Power as a Scare Word* (observing that outsourcing references have declined as the number of domestic jobs has increased).

5. Sovereignty is a much debated concept. Its philosophical roots, going back to Locke and Hobbes, will be discussed later in this book. A definition of sovereignty is offered in Part E of this chapter.

6. *See* Priest & Hull, *Soldiers Face Neglect, Frustration At Army's Top Medical Facility.*

7. Cloud, *Army Secretary Ousted in Furor on Hospital Care* (Harvey did not help his cause by blaming enlisted personnel rather than contractors for the deplorable conditions in the rehabitation facilities).

8. Koppel, *These Guns for Hire*. Koppel lists five points in favor of mercenaries:

> Growing public disenchantment with the war in Iraq; The prospect of an endless campaign against global terrorism; an over-extended military backed by an exhausted, even depleted force of reservists and National Guardsmen; the unwillingness or inability of the United Nations or other multinational organizations to dispatch adequate forces to deal quickly with hideous, large-scale atrocities (see Darfur and Congo); the expansion of American corporations into more remote, fractious and potentially hostile settings.

   *Id.*

9. *Id.*

10. Letters to N.Y. Times, *Waging War with Private Forces.*

11. *Id.* The paradox is that America may have been more democratic when its military was conscripted. Vietnam demonstrated the connection between a service obligation and belief in cause. The volunteer military has weakened that connection. With the advent of a private military, of course, it disappears altogether. The question of a revival of national service is addressed in Chapter 8 Part C.

12. *Id.*

13. Admittedly, letters published in the *New York Times* reflect a limited slice of the public. Still, even conservative publications might produce similar calls for pride in the military.

14. Shane & Nixon, *In Washington, Contractors Take on Biggest Role Ever* (discussing how expenditures for contractors have gone from $200 billion to $400 billion from 2000 to 2005, and labeling them the Fourth Branch).

15. Pierce, Shapiro & Verkuil, Adminstrative Law and Process, at 2.3.

16. *See* Donahue, *The Privatization Decision: Public Ends, Private Means* at 10–11 (efficiency is only one dimension of the larger societal (democratic) issue of accountability).

17. Much of the Constitution is concerned with preserving political values, an exercise that may be inefficient in an economic sense. In *INS v. Chadha*, Chief Justice Burger, in holding the legislative veto unconstitutional, famously

declared: "the fact that a given law or procedure is efficient, convenient, and useful in facilitating functions of government, standing alone, will not save it if it is contrary to the Constitution." 462 U.S. at 944. Although his opinion has been attacked as unduly formalistic, it contains an essential truth – economics and politics often reside in separate realms.

18. The national taxpayer advocate at IRS has criticized the private debt collection program as economically inefficient and prone to abuse. *See* Browning, *I.R.S. Use of Private Debt Collectors Is Criticized.*

19. *See* Krugman, *Tax Farmers, Mercenaries and Viceroys* (discussing IRS outsourcing and noting the accountability problems of privatization).

20. *See* Lipton, *Billions Later, Plans to Remake the Coast Guard Fleet Stumbles.*

21. *Id.*

22. Krugman, *Outsourcer in Chief.*

23. Career officials are less likely to be corrupted because they have a long-term commitment and have less ability to take advantage of outsourcing opportunities. But they are more likely to suffer the demoralization costs of having significant decisions transferred from them to contractors by political appointees. *See* Chapter 7.

24. Secretary Chertoff's performance in the aftermath of Katrina demonstrates an agency unable to respond. *See* Hsu, *Messages Depict Disarray in Federal Katrina Response*; *see also* Chapter 2; *cf.* Ervin, *Open Target* (former Inspector General at DHS documents wasteful spending on private contracts).

25. *See* Lipton, *Former Antiterror Officials Find Industry Pays Better.*

26. *Id.* (stating that Mr. Hutchinson's two hundred thousand shares, which originally cost him $25,000, are reportedly worth over $1.2 million).

27. *Id.* (Scott Amey, general counsel of the Project on Government Oversight).

28. *Id.* (noting that contacts are restricted during a former official's first year outside government, but suggesting loopholes requested by senior DHS officials have diminished the effectiveness of those rules).

29. The first DHS Inspector General documents the many bureaucratic turf problems with starting a new agency and the resulting lack of institutional competence and pride that can overcome them. *See* Ervin, *Open Target* at 4–9, 17 (noting that he "was forced to step down" as Inspector General for uncovering incompetence).

30. Wysocki, *Is U.S. Government 'Outsourcing its Brain'?*

31. *See generally* Harrison, Morgan, & Verkuil, *Regulation and Deregulation*; Verkuil, *Is Efficient Government an Oxymoron?*; Verkuil, *Reverse Yardstick Competition.*

32. Ironically, as this book shows, this lack of consensus on standards can lead both to over- and underoutsourcing. The Transportation Security Agency may be an example of the latter. *See* Chapter 3.

33. The democratic deficit caused by the use of private military in Iraq is aptly alluded to in one of the *Times*' letters. If the all-volunteer army can not meet its

goals to staff the war effort, one writer suggests, perhaps that is an indication of the democratic response to that effort. *See* note 11.

34. There are currently fewer than 1.9 million civilian employees of the federal government (excluding the post office). In 1990, there were over 2.25 million. At the Department of Defense, civilian employment was nearly cut in half during the 1990 to 2003 period. *See The Fact Book* at 8–9. Of course, not all employees are equally important, but the downsizing trend is also reflected in the Senior Executive Service, the top public managers. *See* Chapter 2.

35. *See* Light, *The True Size of Government* at 1 (stating that the "'shadow of government' . . . consisted of 12.7 million full-time-equivalent jobs" in 1996). The ratio of private contractors to public employees is now over six to one, but the more significant deficit is in the reduction of top level government officials, such as contracting officers and the Senior Executive Service, who have seen their numbers drop as their contracting oversight responsibilities have grown.

36. *See* Shane & Nixon, *In Washington, Contractors Take on Biggest Role Ever* (describing how CACI International, itself a challenged contractor who provided interrogators in Iraq, has been conducting "inherently governmental" contract oversight for GAO).

37. The Government Accountability Office (GAO), for example, has reported that DOD oversight was insufficient in about one-third of its contracts, a deficiency it attributes at least partially to declining personnel levels. *See GAO Report on Improving Surveillance* at 2–3.

38. A useful definition of accountability in the bureaucratic setting is provided by Dean Ed Rubin: "accountability refers to the ability of one actor to demand an explanation or justification of another actor for its actions and to reward or punish that second actor on the basis of its performance or its explanation." Rubin, *The Myth of Accountability and the Anti-Administrative Impulse* at 2119 (arguing for the accountability advantages of the administrative state).

39. For example, airline regulation by the Civil Aeronautics Board. Of course, not all deregulatory actions involve program termination, and "reregulation" often follows deregulation. *See* Harrison, Morgan, & Verkuil, *Regulation and Deregulation* at 16–19; *see also* Aman, *The Democracy Deficit* at 93–96 (describing various kinds of legislative delegation to the market).

40. Parker, *The Empirical Roots of the "Regulatory Reform" Movement* at 360.

41. *Id.* at 360 n. 1 (labeling those groups as "sharply divided").

42. Privatization in European countries has a broader connotation – the denationalization of government programs. By transferring assets to the private sector (airlines, television stations, and public utilities are good examples) some nations can reduce the size of the public sector. *See generally* Petretto, *The Liberalization and Privatization of Public Utilities and the Protection of Users' Rights* at 99–106 (describing public utility deregulation).

43. *See* Norris, *In the Bush Years, Government Grows as the Private Sector Struggles* (describing how the government's share of GDP has risen under the Bush administration, and stating that under President Bush "17.4 percent of all wage and salary payments came directly from the government" versus sixteen percent at the end of President Clinton's second term); *see also* Brooks, *How to Reinvent the G.O.P.* at 32–35 (explaining how Republicans abandoned the ideal of small government).

44. Total Quality Management and reengineering were favorite concepts. *See* Osborne & Gaebler, *Reinventing Government* at xix, 21–22, 159–60; Verkuil, *Reverse Yardstick Competition* at 4–9 (documenting government efforts to privatize during the Reagan, Bush I, and Clinton administrations); Verkuil, *Understanding the "Public Interest" Justification for Government Actions* at 147.

45. *See* Rosenbaum, *Bush to Return to 'Ownership Society' Theme in Push for Social Security Changes.*

46. *See* Guttman, *Inherently Governmental Functions and the New Millennium* at 40–46.

47. In doing so, it does not challenge creative attempts to involve the private sector in the regulatory process. *See e.g.* Ayres & Braithwaite, *Responsive Regulation* at 3–4 (proposing participation by the private sector in shaping regulations); Lobel, *The Renew Deal: The Fall of Regulation and the Rise of Governance in Contemporary Legal Thought* at 376–79 (describing how regulated parties should be able to help shape the regulation that controls them).

48. *But see* note 15, describing a new fourth branch - the contractors themselves.

49. *Iran–Contra Report* at xvi.

50. *See Cheney v. U.S. Dist. Court,* 542 U.S. 367, *on remand, In re Cheney,* 406 F.3d 723 (*en banc*) (strictly construing the Federal Advisory Committee Act (FACA) because of separation of powers considerations and holding that a presidentially convened committee consists of federal officials and private industry members are exempt from the Act if only the public officials have voting power).

51. *See* Means, *Bush's Credibility Tank is on Empty*; Friedman, *A New Grip On 'Reality'.*

52. *See Iran–Contra Report* at 4–8. If all this still sound familiar, it is because Ortega was recently elected president of Nicaragua; Ollie North campaigned against him. *See* Kinzer, *The Marxist Turned Caudillo.*

53. The plot secured the release of one hostage. *Id.*

54. *See e.g.* North, *Under Fire* (defending the deed); Abrams, *Undue Process* (challenging the prosecution); Walsh, *Firewall* (justifying the prosecution).

55. *See* Walsh, *Firewall* at xiv (documenting Saudi Arabia's contributions of over $1 million per month for two years to the Contras).

56. *See Iran–Contra Report* at 4–8. These funds were sequestered in Swiss bank accounts.

57. *See The Tower Commission Report* at 467.
58. *See* Greenstein, *The Hidden-Hand Presidency* at ix n. 2.
59. *See Iran–Contra Report* at 15–16 (noting that Secord and Hakim managed the private accounts in Swiss banks).
60. *Id.* at 21.
61. Pub. L. No. 92–463, 86 Stat. 770 (1972); Pub. L. No. 105–153, 111 Stat. 2689 (1997). *See supra* n. 46.
62. At this point in his career, Cheney had already served as a staffer in the Nixon White House and after his congressional tour was to become Secretary of Defense in the Bush I administration, from there he transferred to Halliburton and then back to Bush II as the vice president.
63. *Iran–Contra Report* at 437.
64. *Id.*
65. *See* Woodward, *State of Denial* at 230 (describing marginalization of Secretary Powell and the State Department by the White House and Defense).
66. *See* Chapter 4.
67. Boland Amendment, Pub. L. No. 97–377, §793, 96 Stat. 1833, 1865 (1982). *See Iran–Contra Report* at 473.
68. Youngstown Sheet and Tube Co. v. Sawyer, 343 U.S. at 635–38.
69. *See NSA Spying Memo* at 19–20.
70. *See* Mayer, *The Hidden Power* (profile of David Addington, "an ally of Cheney"s since the nineteen-eighties").
71. *See id.* While Addington does not go back to the Nixon years, Cheney does, and to Jane Harman, ranking Democrat on the House Intelligence Committee, "they're focused on restoring the Nixon Presidency." *Id.*
72. *See The Torture Papers – The Road to Abu Ghraib* (collecting the "torture memos" written by Bush administration officials).
73. *See* Savage, *Bush Could Bypass New Torture Ban.*
74. Pub. L. No. 109–102, 119 Stat. 2172, 2186, 2188 (2005).
75. *See supra* n. 65 and accompanying text; *see also* CRS Report to Congress, Colombia: Plan Colombia Legislation and Assistance at 10 (discussing Clinton administration programs and the use of private firms in Plan Colombia program).
76. *See* John M. Broder and Robin Toner, *Report on Iraq Exposes a Divide within the G.O.P.* (Mr. Perle was referring to the Iraq Study Group, which he characterized as a "misadventure.").
77. The Iraq Study Group Report at 50.
78. Krugman, *Outsourcer in Chief.*
79. *See* Shane, *Latest Blue-Ribbon Panel Awaits Its Own Ultimate Fate* (noting that Robert M. Gates, the new Secretary of Defense, is one of the Group's members, which may help its reception in the White House).
80. On the Lords' Amendment to the Petition of Right, Rushworth's Hist. Coll. 1659, i.

81. To Max Weber, the definitive quality of the state is its monopoly on the legitimate use of force. *From Max Weber: Essays in Sociology* at 78.
82. *See* Chayes & Chayes, *The New Sovereignty: Compliance with International Regulatory Agreements.*
83. *See* Slaughter, *A New World Order* at 34–35.
84. Jacobson, *The Private Use of Public Authority: Sovereignty and Associations in the Common Law* (reflecting the notion that sovereignty cannot be reconciled with a broad decentralization power and viewing corporations as sovereign entities under the common law).
85. *See* Krasner, *Sovereignty: Organized Hypocrisy* at 3–4, 20–21 (Krasner is concerned primarily with Westphalian sovereignty, loose international political organizations that do not compromise domestic sovereignty, except when they do – which then becomes an example of "organized hypocrisy").
86. To some extent also with definition one, when international legal regimes question the proper use of force by the privatized military, for example. *See id.* at 14–15.
87. *See* Wood, *The Creation of the American Republic* at 344–89.
88. Id. at 528.
89. *Id.* at 530–32.
90. *See* Wood, *The American Revolution* at 160–61.
91. Amar, *America's Constitution: A Biography* at 7–8.
92. *Id.*
93. The president has authority both under Article I (directly) and Article II (delegations from the Congress).
94. *See* Chapter 6.

# 2 THE OUTSOURCING OF SOVEREIGNTY

The use of private contractors to do the work of government has been going on since the post–World War II period. And concern about the negative consequences of these activities has been expressed for just as long. We need only to remember the prescient words of President Eisenhower in his farewell address: "In the councils of government, we must guard against the acquisition of unwarranted influence . . . by the military industrial complex."[1] Spending on federal contracts has now reached over $381 billion annually, which means 40 percent of every discretionary dollar is spent with private companies.[2] Obviously, the military-industrial complex has had a good run.

But in the last decade the transfer of public power to private hands has expanded in new directions.[3] The military-industrial complex President Eisenhower warned us against has entered new territory. No longer limited to the production of military equipment, it now seeks to provide personnel for military-style incursions in a variety of foreign settings and it proposes to secure our borders.[4]

This chapter will describe situations in which the transfer of government power to private contractors is most pronounced. Some situations are cutting-edge, some traditional and relatively well accepted, and some are hardly even recognized as sovereignty transfer situations. But each stems from the same basic problem – an emptiness at the center. Private contractors are necessary because government is often inadequately staffed to do its job directly. By the 1970s, in agencies such as the National Aeronautics and Space Administration and the Department of Energy private contractors proved the bulk of their workforce.[5] In fact, at these agencies, government officials are in such short supply that they are virtually limited to serving as figureheads rather than operating officials.[6]

Use of the private military is a post-Vietnam phenomenon that has grown to startling proportions. President Eisenhower warned us about the effect the private production of military equipment and weapons systems had on the creation of public policy and its encouragement of a military state. Today's concerns are with the creation of a private army that supplements and in some settings even replaces what now must be called our "public" military. Should the Pentagon (or State or Interior) be able to farm out military force to private contractors without subjecting those transfers to policy debates in Congress, or even with other agencies of the executive branch?

Privatized services and capacity issues are not just spawned by the military. Military conflicts are only one kind of cataclysmic event. We are contracting out public service obligations when civilian disasters occur – Katrina being the most prominent recent example. In the wake of September 11, agencies such as the DHS are delegating significant duties to private hands. Disaster relief, border control, and port security are just some of the possibilities. The names of many of the players are familiar, but new entities have been created to fill new demands. When wars, disasters, and security deployments become overwhelming responsibilities, outsourcing has become the inevitable response.

A third kind of outsourcing happens largely at the state level – the private prison and its relative, the private police. These are established activities that supplant traditional public services. When we accept the private alternatives in these settings, the reasons for our degree of comfort are largely structural.[7] State governments with legislative approval have set contractual requirements. Contracts are entered into after competitive bidding, they follow specifications, and state oversight and control are provided for. But even here the private alternative must be compared to public solutions at the state and federal levels.

A fourth kind of private contracting brings together disparate activities engaged in by many agencies of government. Agencies contract with regularity for a variety of private management services, such as decision writing, speech preparation, document summary and review, and "draft" decision making. Some of these functions are innocent enough. But some of these activities are governmental in purpose and effect. Their use by government officials raises questions about the ultimate responsibility and performance of the public task. The fear is that nameless consultants are becoming the "hidden hand" of government.

Use of these less noticeable delegations seems to have grown with downsizing. When officials are stretched thin, they are forced to turn to alternatives that potentially undermine the effectiveness and possibly even the integrity of government decisions. Such activities are hard to rectify for this reason. Still, open-ended management services contracts raise institutional questions about the protection of public decision processes.

These examples are just one cut at the outsourcing problem. Other examples of privatized activities could have been chosen.[8] But these are sufficient to state the case against outsourcing sovereignty. The goal is to ask whether, in the vernacular of the reinventing government movement, we have a government that outsources services in order to "steer" but not row,[9] or a government that has lost both its oars and its tiller?

## A. THE PRIVATE MILITARY

...provide for the common defence

–Preamble to the U.S. Constitution[10]

Frankly, I'd like to see the government get out of war altogether and leave the whole feud to private industry.

– Major Milo Minderbinder, Catch-22[11]

"Mercenary" was once a pejorative term, associated with George III's despised Hessians who fought our Continental militias.[12] Today, however, mercenaries can be on our side. We have met the enemy, as Pogo reminds us, and they are us. In today's world, the term "private army" has ceased to be a negative. Is this a good thing for America? Drawing from a diverse literature,[13] this chapter explores that question.

## 1. The New Private Military: Blackwater and Friends

The "private military," a concept largely unknown a decade ago,[14] is apparently here to stay. It is an industry with $100 billion in annual sales and bold designs on the future.[15] The companies involved[16] are highly professional; some are publicly traded. Blackwater proudly states on its Web site: "We have established a global presence and provide training and operational solutions for the 21st century in support of security and peace, and freedom and democracy everywhere."[17]

This sounds more like the mission statement of a United Nations agency than a private company. One might wonder how carefully Blackwater's clients are screened for their democratic and "peaceful" intentions before contracts are negotiated. But one needn't wonder who its preferred first client is – the United States.[18] Blackwater is the company that protected Paul Bremer in Iraq on behalf of the United States and guarded the streets of New Orleans after Katrina on behalf of FEMA.[19] Blackwater is well networked. It is a member of the Private Security Company Association of Iraq (PSCAI), an industry lobbying group. This group has over forty members and works closely with the government of Iraq.[20] Welcome to the world of the private military.

Much of what private companies do in Iraq is uncontroversial. Companies such as Halliburton perform logistical and support services that, although criticized for inefficiency and worse,[21] are not in themselves problematic. Kellogg, Brown & Root has been providing logistical support to the Pentagon on many fronts for many years.[22] Some believe that Halliburton and its subsidiaries "cashed in" during the Iraq War. Christian Miller claims that one half of the value of all contracts issued in Iraq went to Halliburton – a $22 billion bonanza that quadrupled its stock price.[23] But they also performed necessary services.

When the war in Iraq commenced, DOD turned to Halliburton for support and logistical services that the military was not capable of providing. Private contractors can provide the "surge capacity" necessary to prepare for war. It makes sense for the military not to keep its force level at peak capacity, as to do so would build costly redundancies into the system. But the question of whether the costs associated with creating this private capacity relate to military rather than nonmilitary (support) services is one that should trouble policy makers. Contractors such as Blackwater, M.P.R.I., CACI and others offer a different kind of service. They provide battlefield personnel for escorting convoys, protecting civilian leadership (e.g., Paul Bremer), and even interrogating prisoners. These services are hard to distinguish from military ones. The only limitation is that they are not meant to be offensive. The euphemistically named International Peace Operations Association (IPOA) recently testified before Congress that its members only provide defensive operations support.[24] But in Iraq, of course, offensive and defensive may be a distinction without a difference. Keeping operations defensive in a setting where there are no front lines or combat zones is a virtually impossible task.[25] Once the decision is made to permit the private military to enter the battlefield, combat support services devolve into combat services. Thus, to an increasing extent, the private military in settings such as Iraq are part of the combat mission. Over twenty thousand strong, private military contractors are the second largest force in Iraq, larger than the British contingent and other members of the "coalition of the willing" combined.[26] This amounts to over 15 percent of U.S. forces on the ground.[27]

The Department of the Army has issued a field manual dealing with contractors on the battlefield.[28] Field commanders are cautioned about their use of contractors, and their preference is to use military personnel because of command and control issues.[29] But field commanders are in absolute control of the battlefield. Sometimes they use private military contractors in combat-related situations as a necessity. This may be how military functions such as the interrogation of prisoners got assigned to contractors at Abu Ghraib. Seymour Hersh reported that CACI International, a private company, not only participated in but facilitated abusive interrogations.[30] Its employees were later disciplined although, according to the CACI website, none has been indicted.

Private contractors might have a role to play in the interrogation process, perhaps through the provision of translation services,[31] but when they use force, and instruct military officials to do the same, their private role has crossed into the public arena.[32] The military condemned the actions of its soldiers at Abu Ghraib and prosecuted some of them.

The fact that private contractors were involved and largely escaped punishment further reveals the accountability weaknesses surrounding the use of contractors in battlefield situations.

In addition to conducting interrogations, assignments such as securing convoys or protecting Paul Bremer or even the Secretary of State often involve indirect or even direct combat confrontations. Indeed, sometimes contractors cause military actions even if they are not assigned to carry them out. The four Blackwater employees who were dismembered and mutilated in Fallujah, where they ended up while guarding a convoy,[33] is a grim reminder of how the military must react to contractor actions. The Marines had to secure that city after that gruesome event, which was not in their plans beforehand.[34]

These contractor actions violate express restrictions at DOD requiring government officials to perform tasks of "warfighting."[35] In these circumstances, as Martha Minow has said, "reliance on contractors . . . risks jeopardy to the quality of military activities, the national interest, and democratic values."[36] But once contractors are accepted on the battlefield, it is very difficult to manage or limit their services appropriately.

## 2. Managing the Public-Private Military

Why are these contractors on the battlefield in the first place? There are several reasons. First, in a theater of war such as Iraq, it is difficult to know where the battlefield is or was after the invasion ended. Restricting contractors in this manner might therefore overexclude them. But, second, the military has a growing personnel crisis; it has difficulty meeting recruitment goals. The percentage of the population in the military today is less than one-half of 1 percent, the lowest since before World War II.[37] Without the draft, the ready source of personnel provided from World War II until the end of Vietnam no longer exists.[38] The volunteer service alternative has significant consequences for the numbers and costs of troops.[39] The high-tech military requires well-trained troops and the market price for them continues to go up. When conflicts such as Iraq convert from attack mode to insurgency response, understaffing results.[40] Because fewer are willing to serve when the stakes and risks are highest, the staffing gap widens.[41] The National

Guard, not the active army, now represents over one-half of the billets in Iraq. At this point, the idea of a true volunteer military evaporates. National Guard members are under contract to serve in theaters of war when the president calls them up, so they have no legal complaint. But one tour in Iraq may be expected, whereas two or even three tours is hardly what they signed up for. Without the draft,[42] however, pressures on enlistment will not abate and neither will the need to overuse these troops and to outsource as many military functions as possible.

The Pentagon is also actively studying what military roles can be turned over to civilian hands. Private contractors are one source of personnel for filling some military roles. But they are not the only source of civilian personnel; military jobs also can be transferred to the civilian side of the federal government. DOD enlisted RAND to assist in deciding when and how far either to outsource or to "civilianize" the military.[43] RAND looked at the question in two stages: what jobs (billets) are "militarily essential" or "inherently governmental" and what jobs can be contracted out. In drawing this dichotomy, RAND follows the requirements of the FAIR Act and OMB Circular A-76.[44] The first stage involves billets that must be governmental, either military or civilian; the second stage (those that can be competitively sourced) is determined based on relative cost advantage.

"Militarily essential" positions are those that are part of a formal military command and control structure; "inherently governmental" positions involve "discretionary application of lawful coercion or violence."[45] These are use of force positions; they exclude contractors. Contractors are limited to nonforce assignments that can be engaged on a cost advantage basis only.

RAND's dichotomy is legally correct, but it does not reflect reality on the ground. For example, convoy protection and interrogation are roles that involve "lawful coercion or violence." Private contractors would not qualify for these roles under the RAND guidelines, yet Blackwater's Web site proudly advertises them.[46] There is a disconnect between rule and reality here. In effect, Iraq has broken the mold. The United States went to war with a level of force that made contractors necessary. Contractors are now so entrenched they have become indispensable. Now they even negotiate directly with Iraqi and U.S. military forces.[47]

The field commander must have total control over the combat sector. If contractors are within that sector, they will be drawn on to perform whatever tasks are needed.[48] The field commander is not in a position to employ RAND's careful distinction between proper roles for military, civilian, and contractor personnel. When the need is acute, necessity overrides prudence.[49] DOD seems to ignore these implications.

DOD is faced with a dilemma. By issuing a field manual that contemplates the use of contractors on the battlefield,[50] it introduces a situation in which field commanders may be compelled to use private contractors for inappropriate missions. If the DOD wants to stop contractors from performing military roles, they need to be removed from the "battlefield" (assuming that term can be defined). It is hard to believe RAND is naïve about this situation. Indeed, in its report RAND seems to acknowledge the realities of using contractors in combat roles when it says "legal formalities aside."[51] But policy makers cannot ignore legal formalities forever; they must shape government policy in ways acceptable to the public. The contractor role at Abu Ghraib is a cautionary tale in this regard. The DOD seems unsure how to proceed. Using contractors on the battlefield may not be the field commander's first choice,[52] but he or she is given limited options by a Pentagon hamstrung by shortages in military personnel and missions with fluid battlefields.

## B. PRIVATE SOLUTIONS TO NATURAL DISASTERS AND NATIONAL SECURITY

Brownie, you're doing a heck of a job.

– President G.W. Bush[53]

In the military setting described earlier, the outsourcing problem revolves around the contracting-out of "military essential" or inherent governmental functions.[54] Although military situations involving the use of force present the most dramatic choices between government officials and contractors, this book's inquiry is not limited to the military. On the civilian side of government equal inroads upon public deciders are also occurring, often with less public scrutiny.

In the natural disaster setting, the outsourcing problem revolves around inherent government functions. Agencies such as the DHS (which oversees FEMA) were created by Congress to meet a national security mission.[55] But when a new agency such as the DHS is created, its personnel have to adjust to the tasks assigned. Jobs may be outsourced for competency reasons, because of personnel ceilings, or because the political leadership of the agency is more comfortable with contractors. In these situations, the use of private contractors becomes instinctive.

Controlling natural disasters at the federal and state levels is much like conducting a military campaign. During Katrina, the Gulf Coast resembled a battlefield; controlling it was in some ways no easier than dealing with Iraq. Under stress, public authorities welcome help from all parties. This "any port in the storm" mentality often means public-private lines are crossed. The question is, however, are there still lines to be crossed.

## 1. DHS, FEMA, and Natural Disasters

Katrina tested governmental agencies like never before. And many were found wanting.[56] The reasons were threefold: inadequate advance planning, poor coordination during the crisis, and a lack of qualified government personnel.[57] These deficiencies were heightened by intergovernmental rivalries and the failure to coordinate with nonprofit entities such as the American Red Cross.[58] Private contractors of goods and services were employed without adequate consideration given to the roles they would play. Blackwater was awarded contracts to patrol the streets of New Orleans because police were apparently not available.[59] Governor Kathleen Blanco hired James Lee Witt to organize Louisiana's relief efforts because she had an inadequate staff.

The federal and state civilian response teams were definitely short-handed during Katrina. They turned not only to private contractors but to military resources to assist in natural disaster relief. The National Guard was a vital part of Mississippi and Louisiana's recovery effort.[60] But the military seems to have been part of the federal response as well. Remarkably, in the aftermath of Katrina, President Bush stated: "It is now clear that a challenge on this scale requires greater federal authority and a broader role for the armed forces – the institution of our government most capable of massive logistical operations on a moment's notice."[61]

This observation is puzzling given the degree to which our forces are stretched thin in Iraq, and Secretary Rumsfeld fought the president on this issue.[62] The president seemed to be urging the commitment of military personnel to natural disaster relief over civilian personnel, like FEMA or state officials, or even National Guard, who have traditionally handled these assignments. Moreover, the president may have ignored the fact that "logistical operations," which Katrina relief would largely consist of, had already been contracted-out by the military in Iraq.[63] The president's message seemingly dismissed the capacities of civilian agencies such as the DHS and FEMA to do the job of disaster relief.

President Bush's comments may have reflected his tussle with Governor Blanco over federalizing Louisiana's National Guard in the wake of Katrina.[64] The president's perceived indifference to Katrina may have led him to try taking over the recovery effort after the fact. But his suggestion of using the military to secure the country against natural disasters, given the severe limits Iraq imposed on military resources, seems quixotic. It was hardly the answer either to recovery or military problems.

The one federal service that did have a positive effect on the Katrina recovery process was the Coast Guard. It was credited with rescuing thousands and saving many lives,[65] and has been lauded for its effective management in New Orleans. The Coast Guard is not the "military" in a federalizing sense – it operates as a part of the DHS. Its mission is to work with state and local agencies, not to supplant them, which is part of what makes the Coast Guard successful. It really performs much as the National Guard does – a local force that knows the terrain and challenges and is composed of people committed to the region.[66]

It is hard to defend the performance of DHS or FEMA, or their leaders, in the Katrina disaster. Secretary Chertoff failed to call for disaster relief until twenty-four hours after Katrina hit, and FEMA's Michael Brown seemed more concerned with his image than with results.[67] FEMA, which had conducted and participated in prior hurricane planning exercises (Hurricane Pam) with the help of private contractors, allowed bureaucratic formalities to affect results.[68] Leadership at these agencies was clearly inadequate. Chertoff (who is a smart and talented former judge) was just not up to speed when Katrina hit; Brown seems not to have had the speed to get up to. But this does not mean these agencies are meant to fail. FEMA had been led by an effective professional, James Lee Witt, in the years before Katrina.[69] And the DHS, properly chastised by Congress and the public, has since shown the ability to improve its performance.[70]

Privatization and outsourcing are both part of the problem and part of the solution. FEMA entered into numerous contracts for goods and services (e.g., buses to evacuate and mobile homes to house victims). These were traditional contracts for which competitive sourcing was entirely appropriate. Unfortunately, these resources sat on the sidelines throughout the disaster, but that was not the contractors' fault.[71] Properly used, private contractors and resources are essential to disaster relief. Like the military, disaster relief agencies need "surge capacity" when storms, earthquakes, or other national disasters occur. The Red Cross also has staff and volunteers who can be effective if properly used. As with the situation in Iraq when battlefield commanders use private contractors for military-type missions, field commanders at the federal and state levels could have used some inherently governmental help during Katrina. Governor Blanco decided as much when she employed James Lee Witt to coordinate recovery efforts at the height of the storm.[72]

The next disaster should be better handled by federal agencies if some hard lessons are learned. First, disaster relief cannot be conducted by unprepared and uninspired public officials. Second, political appointees may be inadequate for the task. Third, no organization can succeed without committed public officials (the best public servants at FEMA had left the agency when it was reorganized[73]). Fourth, operational and policy jobs cannot be contracted-out. Proper planning and execution of responses to disasters or terrorist attacks are core government functions. They require government officials to perform them.

## 2. Contracting-Out National Security at the Border

The DHS has many critical missions – natural disasters are only one dimension of an overall approach to managing risks in our society.[74]

National security risks are equally challenging. Indeed, in many respects, natural disasters are more amenable to public management than terrorist attacks because they are predictable, offer some advance warning, and have private market analogues.[75] For example, private insurance can interact with government-subsidized flood insurance to reduce the degree to which persons are at risk in hurricane-plagued areas of the country.[76] DHS has viable options to pursue in the disaster situation. Weighing options and searching for a range of policies is what Richard Posner calls a "tolerable-windows approach."[77] The job for Congress and the DHS remains complicated, but the tools to do the job are available.

Controlling terrorist attacks, by contrast, is a far more entangled task. Clear warnings are not usually provided (as with hurricanes[78]), and planning is not as easily accomplished.[79] National security is hard to manage because so many authorities intersect. Although virtually all observers support public solutions,[80] so many variables are at play (intelligence, target opportunities, time frames) that planning is a daunting prospect. In these circumstances, private contractors are often turned to for creative solutions. This is the case with securing our borders.

### a. *Contracts to Secure Borders*

The Secure Border Initiative (SBI) announced by President Bush requires the DHS to plan for heightened control over our Mexican border.[81] One point of SBI is SBInet, an attempt to move from "simply buy[ing] an amalgam of high-tech equipment to help it patrol the borders" to a unitary technological system.[82] The DHS describes the program thus: "The goal of this program component of SBI is to field the most effective mix of current and next generation technology, infrastructure, staffing, and response platforms. . . . SBInet will integrate multiple state of the art systems and traditional security infrastructure into a single comprehensive border security suite for the department."[83] Michael Jackson, DHS Deputy Secretary, described the program to a group of potential bidders: "Those people who sell gizmos think about infrastructure. Those of you who are in infrastructure talk to people in gizmos. We're asking you to come back and tell us how to do our business."[84] This kind of encouragement to private contractors in a competitive market for ideas and services should produce new ways of thinking and implementation.

The government received bids from Boeing Co., Lockheed Martin Corp., Northrop Grumman Corp., and Raytheon Co. (all four among the fifteen largest federal technology, especially defense-related, contract-holders), and Ericsson Inc.[85] In responding, the contractors took up the Deputy Secretary's motivation to be expansive. Lockheed Martin's proposal "recommends using Customs and Border Patrol's existing systems augmented with new and upgraded capabilities that will provide interoperability with their state and local partner police agencies."[86] The major defense contractors, already well positioned, are eager to participate. President Bush authorized approximately $100 million for SBInet for 2006, but industry analysts estimate that the program will cost $2 billion over three to six years,[87] a figure that could turn out to be conservative.

### b. *Challenges to Public Control of Border Contractors*

This privatized program raises significant issues about the DHS's ability to supervise, oversee, and control. The winning contractor will seemingly coordinate the entire approach. Indeed, private contractors will direct deployment of patrolmen, the equipment they will use, and the processing and disposition of captured illegal immigrants.[88] Some of these functions are undoubtedly inherently governmental under existing standards.[89]

Critics note that the government is committing to employing a program without knowing what shape the program will actually take.[90] Supporters at the DHS and in Congress respond that the department will maintain oversight and is not required by the program to actually implement any particular aspect of the consultant's recommendations.[91] Moreover, according to the DHS, the contractors are in the best position to evaluate the suitability for SBI's needs for rapidly changing technology.[92]

Private contractor involvement in this project raises a complicated issue. For one thing, there is the question of contractor competence. The teams from Boeing, Ericsson, and Northrop Grumman have ties to L-3 Communications Corp., which is the successor to L-3 Government Services. L-3 Government Services was a contractor for the prior program, which had audit problems including "lax government over-sight, incorrect cameras and improper installments."[93] This program was cancelled in 2004 and replaced an interim one; SBInet is intended to replace both programs.[94] Difficulties of implementation have also surrounded attempts to integrate technology with border patrols. Seven years into its ten-year startup plan, the $10 billion US-VISIT program, intended to automate the collection of data from border entries and exits, has not yet been control-tested.[95] But these difficulties may be manageable if the competitive bidding process is scrupulously followed, as it has not been in Iraq.[96]

The bigger problem, and the one highlighted throughout this book, is the effect of such comprehensive private contracts on the govern-ment's ability to manage and control the outcomes. As noted, the win-ning bidder(s) will direct deployment of border patrol officers and process captured illegal immigrants.[97] The DHS must have known that inherent government functions are involved in these assignments, yet there has been no review of whether these duties have been properly delegated to contractors. When such a broad assignment is outsourced, government functions get caught in the web of delegations; it is up to the agency to guard against this possibility.[98] Especially for an agency such as the DHS, with a reputation for flawed leadership after Kat-rina, care should be taken in delegating assignments to contractors. It is notable that the military, when faced with this kind of challenge, engaged RAND to determine how best to utilize – and limit – private contractors.[99]

The DHS is a new agency. Formed quickly with a collection of managers from disparate backgrounds. In many respects it is an agency without institutional memory. It needs stable and creative leadership that is wary about delegating government functions. But it lacks conti-nuity at the top. Indeed it appears instead to have created a "revolving door" problem of major proportions.

## 3. Homeland Security, Inc.

Many of the top officials of the DHS left for lucrative jobs before Katrina hit. Often these jobs are with private companies who are bid-ders on potential contracts.[100] Rather than stability in leadership, we have excessive turnover. The founding secretary Tom Ridge, for example, allegedly owned stock in Savi Technology. Lockheed Martin, the SBInet bidder, has apparently purchased Savi.[101] If this occurred, it surely does not inspire confidence either in the bidding process or in the conflict of interest rules. It seems that DHS officials lightened lobbying restrictions on their former colleagues[102] just as they put themselves on the market. Clark Kent Ervin, former Inspector General of DHS, has called attention to this ethical gap:

> People have a right to make a living, but working virtually immediately for a company that is bidding for work in an area where you were just setting the policy – that is too close. It is almost incestuous.[103]

If not incestuous, it is certainly uncomfortable government. Here we have a new agency, with limited institutional resources, whose top leadership transfers virtually *en masse* to the private sector and openly markets its influence.[104] Who is minding the store? No one has asked questions about the appropriate use of private contractors. And the presence of former top DHS officials in the private contractor community will likely increase the use of consultants. This is an agency with the potential for good leadership.[105] But delegating vast amounts of public authority to private hands does not build public trust and confidence. In fact, for an administration that has suffered credibility problems because of Vice President Cheney's connections to Halliburton,[106] the heavy use of consultants at DHS only raises deeper misuse of power issues.

## C. THE ADVENT OF PRIVATE PRISONS AND PRIVATE POLICE

Up to now, the examples of outsourcing have been controversial and even unprecedented.[107] But the privatization movement is far more pervasive than those examples suggest. It is, in fact better established than it has been given credit for. Private prisons and the use of private police are ready examples. Although these efforts should not be uncritically accepted,[108] they provide established alternatives to "public security." By exploring privatization in these other contexts, some perspective on military, natural disaster and national security privatization can be achieved.[109]

Private prisons constitute a relatively small portion of the total prison market (about 5 percent of prisoners),[110] whereas the number of private police exceeds the number of federal, state, and local "public" police combined.[111] This is a significant base from which to compare public and private solutions to security problems.

## 1. Distinctions between Private Regimes

Private police and private prisons involve different phenomena. Private police are not usually contracted for by government;[112] they are instead employed by private parties who use them to protect their property and lives. Private prisons, by contrast, are by definition contracted for by governments, who delegate the authority to incarcerate persons convicted by the criminal justice system.

The absence of contractual connections to government may deny the application of the state action doctrine to private contractors. The doctrine applies to private prisons[113] but is inapplicable to private security personnel, unless they work for government.[114] State action imposes due process requirements upon those incarcerated in prison; but detention by a security guard at a convenience store is outside the ambit of these protections.[115] This state action disequilibrium is significant. When private contractors perform what are otherwise public functions, as in the policing situation, the lack of due process protections may mean a public injury goes uncompensated by government. By contrast, in the private prison setting, the responsibility of government for injuries by its private delegees is not conveyed away.[116]

This aspect of the private prison setting is relevant in several respects. Employees of the private military in Iraq (Blackwater, for example) are not covered by the Uniform Code of Military Justice, but they are responsible for their criminal actions under the Military Extraterritorial Jurisdiction Act (MEJA)[117] and potentially under suits in Iraqi courts.[118] But when Blackwater patrols the streets of New Orleans, as it did after Katrina, are its agents private or public police?[119] Because they have contracts either with the city or with FEMA and not with private businesses seeking security services, state actor liability could attach to their actions.[120] The state action doctrine has meaning in terms of excluding evidence under the Fourth Amendment or under Color of Law requirements of Section 1983.[121] The presence of a contract with the government to police the streets (or to run the prisons) should be enough to invoke the doctrine. And this fact alone ensures some public control over private contractors.

## 2. Contracting for Prisons by the State

The contractual process can transform the relationship between the state and its private partners. Unlike the private military and other open-ended outsourcing arrangements entered into by DHS in situations such as border control, the private prison relationship is established by contracts. Although outsourcing questions still arise,[122] they seem more manageable because of contractual assumptions and commitments.

### a. *The Prison Contract and Public Accountability*

The typical prison contract between the state[123] and a private provider results from set practices and protocols. Requests for Proposals (RFPs) defining the assignment are issued to competing firms, and competitive bids are usually submitted before contracts are awarded.

Corrections Corporation of America (CCA) is the largest private prison provider with sixty-nine thousand beds (inmates) managed in sixty-three state and federal facilities, or more than 50 percent of all private prisons.[124] This is a publicly traded corporation whose Web site, like Blackwater's discussed earlier,[125] is a model of corporate communication and promotion. Companies such as CCA enter into contracts with governments that are the result of detailed demands and expectations.[126] Their performance is often benchmarked against similar public facilities,[127] and renewals come only after public oversight.

Contractual accountability occurs in this setting, unlike the no-bid, no-oversight, Iraq version. But John Donahue has observed that, for private prisons, "full, effective monitoring is a tall order"[128] and Sharon Dolovich has noted that actual monitoring appears to be a hit or miss situation.[129] Still, the threat of monitoring and the concern over losing contracts in the future has a disciplinary effect. In addition, private prisons have their own accrediting agency, the American Correctional Association (ACA), which sets standards for penal facilities and provides monitoring services. Even if one is skeptical about the value of private accrediting agencies the fact is that all private prisons meet ACA standards, whereas some public ones do not.[130]

Another form of oversight is also provided by the courts. After *Richardson v. McKnight*,[131] private prison inmates can bring Section 1983 actions.[132] These actions have many limitations that make them less than ideal oversight mechanisms,[133] but they are more effective against private prison officials than their public counterparts, as defenses based on qualified immunity are not permitted. Availability of judicial relief constrains private prison behavior, since successful cases can be costly and affect contract renewals. For all the limitations of Section 1983, private prisons may be more effectively disciplined by the courts than public prisons, or even public police.[134] The consequences of tort actions against employees are more likely to be taken into account in the contracting process than with many police departments where union rules preclude direct discipline of offending officers.

### b. *Lingering Doubts about Private Prisons*

Constructing efficiency measures that favor private prisons (or at least do not disqualify them) does not satisfy the commitment to public control over those who exercise force. Prison officials must exercise force over inmates in some circumstances. With the private military the use of force is an inherent government function that is meant to disqualify private contractors.[135] As a contractual matter, exercises of force by prison officials are far more controlled than the unconstrained and unpredictable exercises of force by the private military in Iraq.[136] Federal and state prison authorities[137] have the ability to draft contracts that reduce or eliminate exercises of unreasonable discretion or force. In these circumstances, the private prison contractor seems a far more stable candidate for delegation of force than does the private military provider.

Sharon Dolovich also postulates humanity and integrity considerations that cannot be satisfied in the private prison setting.[138] The humanity condition requires adequate safeguards against prisoner abuse.[139] The integrity condition requires that public officials supervise the work of the criminal justice system. For example, how can public officials know whether private officials will give inmates proper credit for time served so that those eligible for parole are properly recognized? These decisions are arguably made by those who have an inherent conflict of interest, since they want to retain prisoners for financial reasons.[140] Assuming that such motivation exists, can it be controlled by audits and contractual review? This question is not irrelevant to public prisons where jobs are also at stake, but the financial incentives may be less clear. The truth is prison populations continue to be a growth industry due to mandatory sentencing laws.

Perverse economic incentives will always be present, but it is hard to use them to disqualify all contracts with private prison companies. Private prisons may pose additional risks caused by the presence of private rather than public governance, but public control can reduce them. Experimenting with a private market seems a sensible risk for state legislatures to take. The benefit of benchmarking performances that might otherwise be hidden on the public prison side is a valuable byproduct. Monopoly, whether public or private, tends to be self-serving, costly, and unimaginative. Thus, competition with oversight by public authorities over inadequate entities has its merits.

## 3. A Note on Rendition and Private Prisons

The practice of rendition, taking prisoners from one country to a third country for incarceration and interrogation, has been a source of controversy since the Iraq war began. International law forbids the rendition or forced return of any person to a foreign locale where there is a risk of torture.[141] Still, several countries, including Sweden[142] and Canada,[143] engage in the practice. The United States, although reluctant to admit that it uses the practice,[144] ultimately justifies it on an efficiency basis: "The transfers were portrayed as an alternative to what American officials have said is the costly, manpower-intensive process of housing them in the United States or in American-run facilities in other countries."[145]

This is an interesting justification. If secret jails are like private prisons for suspected terrorists, are they created pursuant to contracts that reflect terms used in private prisons generally? If Guantanamo is the public prison for terrorists, how are the private alternatives chosen and what are the efficiencies involved in that choice?

These questions risk trivializing the human rights concerns justifiably involved in the practice of rendition,[146] but they do help illuminate the importance of contractual terms and protections for the use of force in the prison setting. The constitutional protections afforded citizens in U.S. prisons, exemplified by Section 1983 actions, are not available to foreigners or even to U.S. citizens[147] caught in the terrorism network.

The delegation of this public responsibility to private hands (which foreign governments are for this purpose) surely fails accountability requirements, even if it satisfies efficiency ones. In this sense, the rendition experience highlights the reason for public control in the first place and offers another example of how the private prison model is ignored in comparable settings.

## D. CONTRACTING-OUT THE ANALYSIS FUNCTION: THE HIDDEN HAND OF ADMINISTRATION

It's the President who creates the foreign policy around here, not some hidden hand.

– Stephen J. Hadley[148]

The fear that someone other than the president is making policy is not unique to the Bush administration. Indeed, the "hidden hand" reference mentioned by Stephen J. Hadley was coined during the Eisenhower administration. But it had a different purpose then. It was used to praise President Eisenhower's ability to make it appear that others were doing work he actually directed.[149] In Eisenhower's case, the metaphor was used to compliment his leadership style.

In President Bush's case, Hadley is using it negatively in an effort to defend the president against charges that someone else (either the vice president or some unnamed consultants) was doing the policy making. The concern is that Bush is a "hands-off" president[150] who lets others make decisions for him. Administration officials (especially Cheney and Hadley) are at pains to show that they give the president the widest range of input but that the president actually makes decisions.[151]

The hidden hand metaphor can also be used to describe how consultants work. They operate under vaguely worded contracts to provide advice and analysis. And many government officials, not just the president, rely on consultants for policy advice and counseling on critical issues. In fact, the use of consultants in this regard is an increasingly problematic venture in government, as the number of policy officials is shrunk by headcount limitations, and an army of analytical contractors stands ready to assist those who remain.

The earlier examples of outsourcing dealt with functions of government involving the exercise of force and authority.[152] The situation considered here is more subtle. The contractor is not asked to perform a government function directly (whether "inherent" or not), but for help in making decisions. If the contractor does all the work to prepare a decision, has the decision line itself been crossed? When an official rubber-stamps a contractor's recommendation, who is performing the government function?

## 1. Deciding as Public Management

How the decisional processes of government work is a question at the heart of public management. We expect sound and even wise decisions from our public officials. But to achieve that level of competence, how much of the actual work must be done by those who share the governance function? To decide well, officials have to analyze. Analysis precedes sound decision making.

Good decisions emerge from a process of careful analysis, an exchange of views, and the commitment to sustained thought. Decisions mature or "ripen" over a period of time and produce ingrained habits of thought that recognize familiar and distinguishable contexts. Obviously, we want President Bush to consult widely before he goes to war and to change his mind on learning new views or different facts. It often is the case that the decider's initial conclusion fails the test of sustained scrutiny. Like judges who have one view before an oral argument, deciders may find that their initial views will not hold up when they go to write the opinion.

It is difficult for the public to know whether the official decider is actually engaging in this kind of decision processing. Judicial scrutiny is limited, as the courts rely on a "presumption of regularity"[153] to protect the decision process. Still, every judge or administrator knows when he or she has properly analyzed a problem before deciding it. Judges, for example, hire law clerks[154] to help with research and even the drafting of opinions, but judges write the opinions and make decisions; moreover, these clerks are public employees, not private contractors. Judges may read articles by or have discussions with academics or others who are not public employees. But the published opinion is the work of *that* judge.

The public does not expect all government officials to live up to the decision standards of judges. But people do expect that decisions will be made by officials. This is why the inherently governmental function definition includes the exercise of discretion and judgment.[155] Reasoned decision making, however, remains a particularly elusive concept. It is easier to identify a function as off limits to privatization (e.g., use of military force or protection of national security) than it is to place a process of thought or action as beyond the power to delegate.

And consultants are valuable resources. Think tanks help produce better government solutions and government should not be deprived of their input. RAND has long stood for this proposition.[156] But government officials, entrusted by the public to make decisions, should limit the role of consultants to advice-giving only. The RAND model of improving analysis and research is carefully tailored to incorporate these limits on government decision making.

In the business setting, consultants often play roles that may not be appropriate in government. McKinsey, the well-known consulting firm, says it works *with* its business clients, not *for* them.[157] This conjures up a picture of the consultant coaching the decider or even supplanting the decider altogether. As a business strategy this may work well, and many McKinsey partners go on to be chief executives themselves. But it is too intrusive a strategy for the government setting. In government, public officials have a more complex decision matrix. They are appointed to make decisions and must consider a complex range of factors. In addition to data or analysis, they must make in political calculations.

McKinsey thrives on data-driven rather than political decision making. In some ways this makes private sector decision making easier than public decision making.

The making of public decisions has long been a matter of public concern. In 1962, a cabinet report to President Kennedy known as the Bell Report[158] recognized that the contracting-out of military research and development has "inevitably blurred the traditional dividing lines between the public and private sectors of our nation."[159] But the conclusion was: "We regard it as axiomatic that policy decisions must be made by full time Government officials clearly responsible to the President and Congress."[160] These cautionary words were a recognition of the temptation to delegate analysis to others. This is why, as Dan Guttman has explained,[161] decision making has been explicitly connected to the inherent government function requirement.

## 2. Examples of Delegated Decision Making

The Bell Report did not make the problem go away. It came to the fore in 1989 when Senator David Pryor asked Comptroller General Bowsher whether the DOE could rely on contractors to prepare security clearance determinations and also the Secretary's own testimony before Congress.[162] The Comptroller's response to the Senator was equivocal. Although not approving of the practices, the Comptroller relied on the "degree of discretion" a government official like the DOE Secretary must retain and the "value judgments" such decisions involve.[163]

But even this warning seems lost on some agencies. Under the Superfund Program, the EPA appears to have readily transferred decisional power. Charles Goodsell records the situation: "Contractor personnel drafted regulations and memos, recorded decisions and filed reports, trained other contractor personnel, evaluated their performance, responded to Congressional inquiries, and wrote annual reports."[164] Goodsell has described an agency that seems to have abdicated its decisional responsibilities for a given program to the private sector.

These propositions can be expanded even further: Should, for example, EPA be allowed to contract-out the reading and summary of the record in substantive rulemaking proceedings? Or, more pointedly, should the EPA be able to contract-out the drafting of the concise statement of basis and purpose that accompanies the final rule?[165] These are the intellectual underpinnings of the rule. If the administrator or her delegate merely signs off on these documents, the government's job has not been performed. If thinking through the problem before decisions are made is the essence of decision making, then it must be a nondelegable duty. Rational decision making is a government function.

Some agencies better anticipate the problem of contracted decision analysis and limit its effect. At the Department of Transportation (DOT), contractors are specifically limited in their role. They are used to summarize comments and only provide analysis if the agency is short-handed or if the decision must be made on a rush basis. In the usual situations, consultant task orders make it clear that the agency is making "the reasoned determination." But often the task orders, which are brief and vague, do not rule out the analysis function. In this circumstance, at least at the DOT, the practice is to ignore any policy recommendations that come from contractors.[166] Not all agencies behave the same way, of course, and in those strapped for decision personnel the temptation to let the contractors do the thinking for them may be too hard to resist.

These kinds of delegations are difficult to cabin or control. As Chapter 4 explores, it is hard for the courts to intervene because of separation of powers and judicial management concerns. But if the delegation of the analysis function becomes acceptable government management because of downsizing effects or political choices, our government is in more trouble than we realize. There must be thousands of open-ended consulting contracts in agencies across government.[167] The contracts themselves are not the problem. Good decision making involves prudent use of consultant reports, subject always to careful review and independent analysis. But rubber-stamping is not the exercise of an inherent government function. A downsized government in which officials have fewer colleagues to rely on internally and in which political appointees are often incented to use private contractors[168] not only makes the problem harder to solve, it gives a whole new dimension to privatized government.

## NOTES

1. *Farewell Radio and Television Address to the American People* at 421.
2. *See* Office of Mgmt & Budget Watch Home Page; Federal Spending Organization Home Page.
3. Spending on federal contracts has jumped from $173 billion in FY 2000 to $381 billion in FY 2005. *See id.*
4. The largest military contractor, Lockheed Martin, has now become a supplier of border security services. *See* Press Release, Lockheed Martin, *Lockheed Martin Delivers Secure Border Initiative Proposal.*
5. *See* Guttman, *Inherently Governmental Functions* at 43–44; *see generally* Guttman & Wilner, *The Shadow Government* (describing NASA and DOE's workforce).
6. *Id.*
7. The term "comfort" is used advisedly, since there are dissenters from these practices (who will be heard from). Still, private prison providers have established relationships with states that are better defined than the ones private military contractors have with the federal government.
8. Some of the most notable outsourcing services are in the Medicaid and welfare decision making fields. *See generally* Smith & Lipsky, *Nonprofits for Hire: The Welfare State in the Age of Contracting.*
9. *See* Osborne & Gaebler, *Reinventing Government* at 26–28.
10. *See* U.S. Const. art. I, §8, granting to Congress the power to provide for the common defense.
11. Singer, *Corporate Warriors* at 230, used this quote, but I couldn't resist it.
12. The Declaration of Independence lists as a grievance against the King the use of "foreign mercenaries to complete the works of death, desolation and tyrannies...." *See id.* at 33–34 (describing how the brutality of Hessians fighting in New York galvanized the colonists against the British).
13. Two leading books are Singer, *Corporate Warriors*, and Avant, *The Market for Force*. Singer is in general critical, or at least cautionary, in tone; Avant is more ambivalent or even supportive of the idea.
14. Singer, *Corporate Warriors* at 242.
15. *Id.* at 78 (predicting a doubling of revenue for the industry by 2010).
16. For a list of the private military companies in the United States, *see* Avant, *The Market for Force* at 10.
17. Blackwater USA Home Page.
18. Blackwater is a contractor with the United States, not a "front company" for the CIA or other security agencies. Front companies still exist, however. *See* Singer, *Corporate Warriors* at 48.
19. Press Release, Blackwater USA, *Blackwater Continues to Support Katrina Devastated Areas.*

20. The PSCAI is a nonprofit organization maintained to lobby for and provide information to military contractors in Iraq. It receives "up-to-date information from the highest levels of government" (U.S., Coalition, and Iraq). *See* Blackwater USA Home Page. If this is so, its members presumably have appropriate security clearances, although that fact is not addressed on the Web site.

21. Cost overruns by Halliburton and its subsidiary KBR are largely the result of nonbid, single sourced contracts. *See* Teather, *Halliburton Accused of Not Justifying £1 Billion Army Bills* at 17; *see also* Editorial, *Sharing the Riches of War in Iraq*, N.Y. Times at A16 (Halliburton's logistical contracts have been worth $15 billion in Iraq).

22. *See* Singer, *Corporate Warriors* at 80 (noting lucrative contracts for Halliburton in the Balkans).

23. *See* Miller, *Blood Money – Wasted Billions, Lost Lives and Corporate Greed in Iraq* at 72–75 (also discussing Vice President Cheney's connection to Halliburton).

24. *See Hearings on Private Security Firms Operating in Iraq*, 109th Cong. (testimony of IPOA president Doug Brooks).

25. *See* Singer, *Corporate Warriors* at 235 ("...wherever possible private contracting should be kept out of critical battlefield areas."); *see also* Michaels, *Beyond Accountability* at 1020–24 (discussing combat-related privatization and its democratic deficiencies).

26. *See* Singer, *Corporate Warriors, id.*

27. Of course not all, or even most, of the private military are in combat roles, but then neither is more than half of the 130,000 United States military in Iraq.

28. *See* Army Field Manual No. 3–100.2.

29. RAND has done a comparative risk study of private contractors that focuses on the principal-agent problems with their use versus military officials. *See* Camm & Greenfield, *How Should the Army Use Contractors on the Battlefield* at 26–28.

30. *See* Hersh, *Chain of Command* at 32–33.

31. Finding Arabic speakers willing to serve in the Army is, however, no easy task. *See* Elliot, *For Recruiter Speaking Arabic, Saying 'Go Army' Is a Hard Job* at A1.

32. *See* Schooner, *Contractor Atrocities at Abu Ghraib* at 555.

33. *See* Avant, *The Market of Force* at 22; *see also* Santora & Glanz, *Five American Security Employees Killed in Baghdad Helicopter Attack* (describing how Blackwater employees were killed while monitoring convoys).

34. *See* Woodward, *State of Denial* at 296–97 (describing how the deaths of the Blackwater employees forced Paul Bremer to change plans for pacifying Fallujah and order a full military attack, and how this decision reached all the way to the President).

35.  U.S. General Accounting Office (GAO), *Commercial Activities Panel: Improving the Sourcing Decisions of the Government: Final Report* at 7 (also included as government functions were "judicial, enforcement, regulatory, and policy making functions").

36.  Minow, *Outsourcing Power* at 1016; *see also* Michaels, *Beyond Accountability* at 1020–22.

37.  *See* Freedberg, *How We Fight* at 36.

38.  The draft ended in 1973. *See id.* at 34–36.

39.  The pay, pension, and benefits needed to attract volunteers amounts to over $350,000 per soldier, versus $50,000 (in 2005 dollars) during World War II. *Id.* at 34.

40.  Understaffing the Iraq war has been a steady criticism directed at the president and (former) Secretary Rumsfeld ever since they removed General Shinseki for challenging manpower needs. *See* Kirchgaessner, *Powell 'Gave Warning' on Iraq Troops* at 4; Galloway, *Army Shake-Ups Clear Path for Rumsfeld's Vision* at A3.

41.  The Pentagon has known since 2003 that keeping 150,000 troops in Iraq would stretch its resources too thin and require short-term expedients like extended tours, short rotations, and the excessive use of the National Guard. *See* Editorial, *America's Army on Edge*, N.Y. Times at A9. The Iraq war has now gone on longer than World War II.

42.  Chapter 8 will take up in greater detail the prospects for a draft or national service. As discussed in Chapter 1, it is well to remember that the draft, although compulsive, is in many ways democratic. If the military were forced to raise troops by conscription, those conscripted (and their families) might exert political pressure on the government to end the adventure in Iraq. *See* Vennochi, *A Military Draft Might Awaken Us* at A11.

43.  *See* Camm, *Policy Issues Relevant to Civilianizing Billets in the Department of Defense*; Camm, *Thinking Strategically about Military to Civilian Conversion.*

44.  *See* Camm, *Thinking Strategically about Military to Civilian Conversion* at 2. *See* Chapter 5 for a full discussion of these provisions.

45.  *See* Camm, *Policy Issues Relevant to Civilianizing Billets in the Department of Defense* at 4.

46.  *See* discussion at nn. 17–19.

47.  *See* discussion of PSCAI, n. 20.

48.  Moreover, if the contractors are former military personnel, the field commander may be more comfortable using them. The RAND report captures this reality: "Legal formalities aside, a government or contractor civilian with former military service is generally expected to have a closer cultural affinity with military command and control, enhancing a commander's control over such a person." Camm, *Policy Issues Relevant to Civilianizing Billets in the Department of Defense* at 5. Blackwater, of course, hires ex-military personnel just for this reason.

49. Blackwater's Web site is careful not to reflect any discriminatory standards in employment; it mentions nondiscrimination based on "federal, state or *local* discrimination laws" (emphasis added). This sets up the possibility that gays and lesbians, dismissed from the military based on don't ask, don't tell grounds, might find a home at Blackwater supporting the military effort. *See* Niejelow, *The Derivative Effects of Don't Ask Don't Tell* at 28–29. Blackwater requires an honorable discharge, however, which may disqualify some candidates who have been dismissed.

50. The use of civilian billets to replace military ones is appropriate even if the use of force is involved. But, of course, that will add to head count, which is another constraint on government that pushes decisions in a private contractor's direction. *See* discussion at Chapter 6.

51. *See* quote at n. 48.

52. Contractors, after all, cannot be ordered to perform nor disciplined for refusing to do so.

53. Hsu & Glasser, *FEMA Director Singled Out by Response Critics* at A1.

54. *See* Camm, *Policy Issues Relevant to Civilianizing Billets in the Department of Defense.*

55. The structure and mission of DHS are explained in Chapter 1.

56. *See* Horne, *Breach of Faith* at 91–99 (discussing failures of DHS, FEMA, and President Bush, as well as Governor Blanco and Mayor Nagin); *see also* Ervin, *Open Target* at 179–87 (a critique of the DHS by its former inspector general).

57. *See generally* Daniels et al., *On Risk and Disaster: Lessons from Hurricane Katrina* (describing through individual essays various causes of the Katrina "breakdown" in authority).

58. *See* Horne, *Breach of Faith* at 90 (FEMA ordered the Red Cross not to perform rescue services during evacuation).

59. *See* Blackwater USA Home Page.

60. The Governor of Louisiana had to call her National Guard back from service in Iraq (some of whom were due to rotate anyway). This suggests that the personnel crisis in Iraq has an even deeper dimension. If National Guard troops are demanded back home for other duties (including not only hurricanes but possibly even border patrol), how can they provide half of the personnel in Iraq or other foreign theaters of operation?

61. Press Release, The White House, *President Addresses Hurricane Relief in Address to the Nation.*

62. *See* Woodward, *State of Denial* at 427–28 (describing how Rumsfeld refused to take Andrew Card's word that the president wanted troops assigned to Katrina and called the president directly to object to the idea).

63. Of course, turning disaster relief over to the military would permit that institution to hire contractors like Halliburton to do the logistical jobs.

64. The president pushed the governor to federalize Louisiana's National Guard so that he could assume control of the Katrina recovery. The Posse

Comitatus Act, 18 U.S.C. §1385 (2006), forbids federal troops from getting involved directly. Governor Blanco refused the president's request to federalize the National Guard, a position Governor Barbour of Mississippi had not been asked to take. Almost half of Louisiana's 13,268 National Guard troops were in Iraq when Katrina hit. *See* Horne, *Breach of Faith* at 96–97.

65. *See* Bier, *Hurricane Katrina as a Bureaucratic Nightmare* at 252–53 (Coast Guard responsible for twenty thousand rescues in the Gulf area in the weeks after Katrina hit).

66. The Corps of Engineers is also local in this sense, but its performance in levee control, which did not include rescue attempts, has been subject to severe criticism. *See* Horne, *Breach of Faith.*

67. *See* Bier, *Hurricane Katrina as a Bureaucratic Nightmare* at 248–50.

68. For example, FEMA required "originals" of requests from Governor Blanco before it would process them. *Id.*

69. *See id.* Governor Blanco decided to privatize a government function by contracting with Mr. Witt to head up the Louisiana recovery effort. *See Horne, Breach of Faith.*

70. In fact, the signs are that it is doing better. *See* Goodnough, *Chertoff Pushes for More Hurricane Readiness* at A16.

71. As to the FEMA busses that never arrived in New Orleans, *see* Horne, *Breach of Faith* at 95. As to the eleven thousand unused trailers, *see* 152 Cong. Rec. H612 (daily ed. Mar 7, 2006) (Remarks of Mr. Ross) (discussing eleven thousand trailers purchased by FEMA for $431 million that sit in a pasture in Hope, Arkansas).

72. *See* n. 69.

73. *See* Chapter 8 Part A. (discussing the status of career officials at FEMA after it was combined with the DHS).

74. *See generally* Harrington, *Rethinking Disaster Policy after Katrina* at 203–10.

75. *See* Trebilcock & Daniels, *Rationales and Instruments for Government Intervention in Natural Disasters* at 89–103.

76. *See* Kunreuther, *Has the Time Come for Comprehensive Natural Disaster Insurance?* at 175–202.

77. *See* Posner, *Catastrophe: Risk and Response.*

78. Earthquakes are harder to anticipate and pandemics even more difficult to predict. *See id.* at 21–24, 29–30.

79. The Hurricane Pam planning exercise directed by FEMA aided the Katrina relief effort by installing the contraflow exercise, for example. But its full implications seem to have been lost on FEMA. *See* Horne, *Breach of Faith* at 51, 147.

80. *See* Trebilcock & Daniels, *Rationales and Instruments for Government Intervention in Natural Disasters* at 89–103 (discussing libertarian approaches).

81. *See* Lipton, *Seeking to Control Borders, Bush Turns to Big Military Contractors* at A1.

82. *Id.* The House is currently considering legislation that would require the President to certify the border secure before allowing a guest worker program. *See* Swarns, *House G.O.P. Planning Recess Hearings* at A20. Presumably, SBInet would allow the president to meet the certification requirement, should it become law.

83. U.S. Customs and Border Protection Home Page, *About SBInet.* A release to companies by DHS described the solicitation of bids as "a fundamentally new approach to procurement for [Customs and Border Protection]." U.S. Customs and Border Protection, *SBI Industry Overview.*

84. Yoest, *Procurement for Secure Border Initiative Should Be Finished in September, Officials Say.*

85. Lipowicz, *Teams Vie for SBInet* at 11; SBI Industry Overview at 4.

86. Press Release, *Lockheed Martin Delivers Secure Border Initiative Proposal.*

87. Lipton, *Seeking to Control Borders, Bush Turns to Big Military Contractors* at A1; Hsu & Pomfret, *Technology Has Uneven Record on Securing Border* at A1.

88. Lipton, *Seeking to Control Borders, Bush Turns to Big Military Contractors* at A1.

89. *See* discussion at Chapter 6.

90. Lipton, *Seeking to Control Borders, Bush Turns to Big Military Contractors* at A1; Hsu & Pomfret, *Technology Has Uneven Record on Securing Border* at A1; *see* Strohm, *Appropriators Skeptical of Promised Secure Border Initiative.*

91. Lipton, *Seeking to Control Borders, Bush Turns to Big Military Contractors* at A1.

92. Hsu & Pomfret, *Technology Has Uneven Record on Securing Border* at A1. The companies that submitted bids have varied experience. Northrop Grumman was involved in the America's Shield Initiative (ASI), which was a technology program intended to replace the 1990s' Integrated Surveillance Intelligence System (ISIS) but that ended when the Initiative was included in SBI. Lipowicz, *Teams Vie for SBInet* at 11. Lockheed has worked with the Coast Guard on surveillance, and Raytheon has contracts for surveillance in Brazil and for border security in Ukraine and the Middle East. *Id.*

93. Lipowicz, *Teams Vie for SBINet* at 11. Close to half of the nearly five hundred cameras ordered for that program were never installed; sensors that were buried in the ground were prone to activation by wild animals and passing trains, as evidenced by the fact that 92 percent of responses were to false alarms, and only 1 percent of responses led to arrests. Lipton, *Seeking to Control Borders, Bush Turns to Big Military Contractors* at A1; Hsu & Pomfret, *Technology Has Uneven Record on Securing Border* at A1.

94. Strohm, *Department Moving on Massive Border Security Project.*

95. Hsu & Pomfret, *Technology Has Uneven Record on Securing Border* at A1. In April 2006 a $6.5 million unmanned plane crashed seven months after it began surveillance flights along the U.S.-Mexico border. *Id.*; Lipton, *Seeking to Control Borders, Bush Turns to Big Military Contractors* at A1.

96. *See* discussion at n. 21.
97. *See* Lipton, *Seeking to Control Borders, Bush Turns to Big Military Contractors* at A1.
98. GAO could well be called on to make an evaluation of inherent governmental functions. *See* discussion at Chapter 6.
99. *See* discussion at nn. 43–46
100. *See* Lipton, *Former Antiterrorism Officials Find Industry Pays Better* at A1.
101. *Id.* There are many other examples of questionable dealing by officials, including the undersecretary, Asa Hutchinson, who are consultants or lobbyists for companies doing billions of dollars of business with the government. *See* discussion at Chapter 1.
102. *Id.*
103. *See* Ervin, *Open Target.*
104. Consider how likely it is that a GS-14 contracting officer will be able to stand up to a private contractor represented by the agency's former secretary or undersecretary.
105. Clark Ervin, who was replaced as IG at DHS, has considerable praise for the leadership abilities of Secretary Chertoff. *See id.* at 228.
106. *See* Miller, *Blood Money – Wasted Billions, Lost Lives and Corporate Greed in Iraq* at 73–75 (referring to the "shadow" cast over Halliburton's contracts in Iraq due to its connections to Cheney).
107. The use of private military is unprecedented; the delegation of inherent government functions by DHS is controversial, but not unprecedented.
108. *See, e.g.,* Dolovich, *State Punishment and Private Prisons* (discussing the failure of private prisons to meet integrity and humanity conditions).
109. *See* Rosky, *Force, Inc.* at 879.
110. There are over two million persons incarcerated in the United States, about one hundred thousand of whom are in private prisons. *See* Harrison & Karberg, *Prison and Jail Inmates at Midyear 2003.*
111. *See* Sklansky, *The Private Police* at 1168.
112. There are exceptions to this rule, as the Defense Department and GSA employ private guards and military and other government properties.
113. *See Richardson*, 521 U.S. 399.
114. *See* Sklansky, *The Private Police* at 1240 (citing cases); *see also id.* at 1253–54 (discussing a "public functions" test for state actions).
115. *See id.* at 1253.
116. *See also* Chapter 4, discussing the public-private distinction.
117. 18 U.S.C. § 3261 (2006). The DOJ investigated private contractors involved in Abu Ghraib under MEJA. *See* Avant, *The Market for Force* at 234.
118. *See* Coalition Provisional Authority Order No. 17 (Revised) at 4 (contractors in Iraq are immune from Iraqi law in matters pertaining to their contractual work); *see generally* Carney, *Prosecuting the Lawless: Human Rights Abuses and Private Military Firms* at 330–36 (suggesting that the modern private military operates almost outside of any law).

119. *See* discussion at n. 19. The presence of combat-ready soldiers, who are more comfortable on the streets of Baghdad, patrolling New Orleans streets surely gives pause to looters, as well as ordinary citizens.

120. *See* Sklansky, *The Private Police* (arguing that policing (keeping the King's peace) is the original public function, but later admitting that the public function distinction is moribund).

121. *See id.* at 1187–88.

122. *See* Dolovich, *State Punishment and Private Prisons* at 5.

123. "State" here refers both to federal and state authorities. Prisons are run by both sovereigns and detention facilities run by the Immigration and Naturalization Service are a growing factor. *See id.* at 8 (citing statistics).

124. *See* Corrections Corp. of Am. Home Page. CCA provides both security and health care, basic education, and substance abuse treatment. It boasts a 95 percent contract renewal rate. Its mission is to form a partnership with government by providing a public service. Its 2005 annual report shows revenues of $1.2 billion. It has shown considerable earnings growth. Its 2005 annual report notes an imbalance between demand and supply of prison beds that should provide a "meaningful opportunity."

125. *See* discussion at n. 17.

126. Harding, *Private Persons and Public Accountability* at 2–3.

127. *See* Dolovich, *State Punishment and Private Prisons* at 8.

128. *See* Donahue, *The Privatization Decision* at 171.

129. *See* Dolovich, *State Punishment and Private Prisons* at 29 (describing empirical studies).

130. *See id.*

131. *Richardson*, 521 U.S. 399.

132. 42 U.S.C. §1983 (2006) provides a remedy for citizens who suffer deprivation of constitutional rights.

133. Proving constitutional violations, such as those arising under the Eighth Amendment, presents high burdens of proof. *See, e.g., Estelle*, 429 U.S. at 106 (must show "deliberate indifference" to a serious medical need).

134. There is no necessary connection between the prevalence of §1983 suits and the discipline of public officials. Indeed, in New York City, for example, tort claims against police officials are rarely causes to discipline the officials themselves. *See* Treaster, *Mollen Panel Says Buck Stops With Top Officers* at A21; Mollen, *Report of the Commn. to Investigate Allegations of Police Corruption and the Anti-Corruption Procedures of the Police* Dept. *But see* Bandes, *Patterns of Injustice: Police Brutality in the Courts* at 1275 (arguing that generally courts inappropriately treat police abuses not as systemic problems in a department but as the result of a small number of "bad apples").

135. *See* discussion at n. 45.

136. Certainly military operations in Iraq are at the extreme end of unpredictability, as the horrible image of the dismembered four Blackwater employees in

Fallujah reminds us. *See* n. 33. But prison situations also can be unpredictable where riots and other emergencies call for the use of force or, contractually, for the discretion to use it.

137. For example, although the use of force is defined as inherently governmental under Circular A-76, *see* Chapter 6, federal prisons are still contracted out to private contractors. Thus, there must be a distinction drawn in the two uses of force that satisfy the inherent government function refinement.

138. *See* Dolovich, *State Punishment and Private Prisons* at 35–42.

139. *See id.* at 35–36 (describing prisoner abuses at CCA-run prisons).

140. *See id.* at 43, 46; *see also* Ratliff, *The Due Process Failure of America's Prison Privatization Statutes* (describing financial "incentives" private prisons face on parole denials).

141. *See* Hersh, *Chain of Command* at 54–55.

142. *See id.*

143. *See* Shane, *Torture Victim Had No Terror Link, Canada Told U.S.* at A10 (describing how Canada cooperated in sending one of its citizens, Maher Azan, with U.S. involvement to Syria, where he was tortured).

144. The United States officially denies that it engages in the practice, but also says that it does not permit torture in countries where prisoners are (or are not) sent. Secretary of State Rice also says secret jails for terror suspects have led to information that saved lives. *See* Brinkley, *U.S. Interrogations Are Saving European Lives, Rice Says* at A3; Woodward, *State of Denial* at 80–81 (describing a meeting after 9/11 where President Bush asked Prince Bandar for help in interrogating prisoners).

145. *See* Jehl & Johnston, *Rule Change Lets C.I.A. Freely Send Suspects Abroad* at A11 (remarks attributed to a senior U.S. official).

146. The CIA has broad authority to transfer suspected terrorists to foreign countries for interrogation purposes. The CIA seeks assurances that suspects will not be tortured, but admits that "nothing is 100 percent unless we're sitting there staring at them 24 hours a day." *See id.*

147. *Hamdi*, 542 U.S. 507.

148. Sanger & Schmitt, *Cheney's Power No Longer Goes Unquestioned* at A1 (Stephen J. Hadley is President Bush's National Security Advisor).

149. *See* Greenstein, *The Hidden Hand Presidency—Eisenhower as Leader* (unpublished presidential memos show that Eisenhower, not Secretary of State John Foster Dulles or Chief of Staff Sherman Adams, was the architect of his presidency).

150. Professor Greenstein in the preface to the 1994 edition calls President Reagan a "hands-off" president who during Iran–Contra wanted to know nothing about what was going on. *See id.* at ix, n. 2; Chapter 1 Part C.

151. *See* Sanger & Schmitt, *Cheney's Power No Longer Goes Unquestioned* at A22.

152. A fourth example is the Internal Revenue Service's outsourcing of delinquent taxpayer debts to private debt collectors. The IRS has outsourced because

Congress (and the Administration) denied it the additional personnel to do so directly, even though the government solution was more cost effective. *See* Johnston, *I.R.S. Enlists Outside Help in Collecting Delinquent Taxes, Despite the Higher Costs* at A1.

153. *See, e.g., Chem. Found.*, 272 U.S. at 14 ("The presumption of regularity supports the official acts of public officers...." ); *Gregory*, 534 U.S. 1 (same); *see also* discussion of the *Morgan* cases in Chapter 6.

154. And even the use of law clerks can be controversial in some settings. In England, the judges do not use law clerks, who in their view might compromise the judge's duty to decide and analyze independently.

155. *See* discussion at Chapter 6 Part B.

156. RAND's mission: "The RAND Corporation is a nonprofit institution that helps improve policy and decisionmaking through research and analysis." RAND Home Page.

157. *See* McKinsey & Co. Home Page. McKinsey works with the business sector primarily and the nonprofit sector, but its government work is less significant. RAND is primarily a government and nonprofit consultant.

158. *See* Executive Office of the President, *Report to the President on Government Contracting for Research and Development* (David Bell was Director of the Budget Bureau.).

159. *Id.*

160. *Id.*

161. *See* Guttman, *Inherently Governmental Functions* at 2–10 (describing how these concerns led to the "inherently governmental" restrictions placed in the Federal Activity Inventory Reform (FAIR) Act).

162. *See id.* at 13–15.

163. *See Letter from Charles A. Bowsher, Comptroller General, to Hon. David Pryor* (Dec. 29, 1989).

164. Goodsell, *The Case for Bureaucracy* at 147; *see also* Kettl, *Sharing Power* at Chapter 5 (citing other examples).

165. Discussion by author with Don Elliott, former general counsel at EPA, Jan. 31, 2007.

166. Neil R. Eisner, Assistant General Counsel of DOT, communication with author.

167. These are not easy to uncover through FOIA requests and the like since general support contracts may be so open ended as not to reveal the true extent of a contractor's participation in the decision process. *See* Guttman, *Inherently Governmental Functions*.

168. *See* Chapter 2 Part B3.

# 3 CASE STUDY: PUBLIC AND PRIVATE APPROACHES TO TRANSPORTATION SECURITY

The previous chapter set out a variety of situations in which contractors have been doing work that government officials should perform themselves or at least that Congress should expressly permit to be delegated to the private sector. It may seem that all public activities are moving from government to contractors. But sometimes it is in the other direction. This chapter looks more closely at public and private solutions to transportation security.

## A. AN INTRODUCTION TO TRANSPORTATION SECURITY

A major aspect of national security involves transportation to, from, and within U.S. borders. The events of September 11 cruelly highlighted weaknesses in our airport security system. And port security remains an ongoing problem, even though no catastrophic event has yet occurred.[1] In both situations, the private sector plays or has played important security roles, whether as owners of facilities or as contractors directly managing security services.

National security sweeps far more broadly than transportation security, of course, but it shares with transportation security the use of public officials and private contractors to achieve security goals. Privatization of military functions,[2] for example, raises troubling questions about converting vital security functions to private control. The transportation security function has similar implications for privatization.

Privatization of airport security also raises comparative questions because there are marked differences in approach between the United

States and its European allies. In European countries, security inspections themselves are often done by private contractors. But in the United States, government control of airport security has become the norm after 9/11. The terrible fact that terrorists were able to board flights and turn airliners into instruments of mass destruction focused attention on the weaknesses of our airport security system. This system had been staffed by private employees hired by airlines and regulated by the Federal Aviation Administration (FAA).[3] Airlines treated the security function as a cost-control item and forced the quality of services downward.[4] In these circumstances, it should have been no surprise that the airport security system failed in its essential purpose.[5]

When it created the Transportation Security Agency (TSA),[6] Congress made the decision to "publicize"[7] airport security personnel.[8] The reasons that Congress took this action reflect concerns with public values and inherent government functions, essential considerations that are often left out of the debate over privatization.[9] The TSA decision was part of Congress's overall intention to provide public control of security through the Department of Homeland Security.[10]

The issue of port security in the United States provides intriguing comparisons. In this setting private and public controls intersect. Many of the ports are privately owned and contractors and the Coast Guard share security responsibilities relating to them. Port security also has a political dimension. The Dubai Ports World controversy raises a variety of security and foreign policy issues.

## B. THE ROLE FOR GOVERNMENT IN AIRLINE SECURITY IN THE UNITED STATES

Before 9/11, private airliners were assigned the task to screen passengers and baggage at airports as part of an overall service responsibility that included ticket agents, pilots, flight attendants, and maintenance personnel. They operated under FAA oversight.[11] The airlines did not actually employ the screeners as they did flight and maintenance staff; instead they entered into contracts with private security firms.[12] Not surprisingly, these contracts went to the lowest bidders. As a result, the private security firm employees were poorly trained, lacking

language skills, and otherwise unqualified (they were sometimes convicted felons).[13] The Department of Transportation Inspector General
found in the years before 2001 that undercover agents could pene-
trate security at major airports.[14] Indeed, just days after 9/11, seven
of twenty people carrying knives passed through security at Dulles
Airport.[15]

It was against this background that Congress confronted the need
to improve airport security after 9/11. Senators John McCain and Fritz
Hollings introduced a bill to federalize the airport security workforce,
which passed the Senate unanimously.[16] The bill required new training
and performance standards for the public employee screeners and
also required law enforcement personnel to be stationed at airport
checkpoints.[17] After initially supporting the Senate Bill, President Bush
shifted to an alternative House bill designed to limit the federal role.[18]
The bill would have installed federal supervisors at baggage and passenger screening checkpoints, but left the security workforce itself – the
inspectors of passengers and baggage – in private hands.[19] Ultimately,
however, support for complete federalization in Congress was so overwhelming[20] that the president backed off the partial privatization bill.

## 1. The New Consensus

The Aviation and Transportation Security Act (ATSA)[21] was passed
by Congress and signed by the president on November 19, 2001. It created a new department, the Transportation Security Administration,
within the Department of Transportation, and gave the TSA responsibility for aviation security.[22] The TSA was to federalize airport security
screeners within one year. All screeners were to speak and read English,
be U.S. citizens,[23] have no criminal records, and have graduated from
high school.[24] Screeners were also required to complete forty hours of
classroom instruction and sixty hours of on-the-job instruction.[25] The
act also provided for a pilot program to test private security personnel
in up to five airports across the country.[26] In addition, airports were
to be allowed to apply to reprivatize (as part of the Security Screening
Opt-Out Program) after November 19, 2004.[27]

The public employment status of airline security personnel coun-
ters recent trends toward privatization of government functions and

deserves careful study. Both Democrats and Republicans realized that some change in the status of airport security personnel had to be made, but the scope of that change led to contentious debate. The Senate Democrats pushed for full federal employment.[28] The House Republicans responded by proposing a bill that only partially publicized the security personnel.[29] The White House sought to avoid what it saw as a needless increase in bureaucracy.[30] Given the Bush administration's commitment to privatization,[31] and the Republicans' general belief that federal employees, once unionized, would become constituents of Democrats,[32] it is not surprising that they disfavored full federal employment.

Ultimately, Congress, in passing a public employment bill, succumbed to Democrat arguments that U.S. airports, like borders, should be patrolled by federal personnel. Over sixty thousand new federal employees were created.[33] Despite existing counterexamples,[34] the notion of private contractors conducting safety inspections struck both legislators and the public as a distortion of government responsibilities. When it equated airport security officials with customs officials, Congress in effect endorsed the necessity for public service.

This step has intriguing consequences. Federal officials are different from private contractors because they take oaths, wear badges, and have the power to arrest and detain.[35] Although TSA inspectors do not in fact wear badges or have the power to arrest, they are still uniformed public officials. The public perception is one of government control, even though the cost of airport security officials is paid by air travelers through a ticket surcharge,[36] not by the federal treasury. This status had enough symbolic value to counter the trend in the United States toward privatization of government services. It also bucked trends in other countries with greater commitments to public sector solutions.[37]

## 2. The Values of Public Employment – Loyalty and Reliability

The preference for public officials to provide security at airports reflects unease about the competence of private alternatives. Indeed, Representative Roy Blunt observed that it even raised questions about the loyalty[38] of those employed by private firms to perform the inspection task. The statutory requirements of no criminal records and higher educational and training levels were meant to assure more reliable employees; the requirement for U.S. citizenship was meant to enhance loyalty. Loyalty is a difficult concept to quantify in our society. At one extreme, it brings to mind "loyalty oaths," which during the 1950s had a dampening effect on freedom of expression.[39] By contrast, from a principal-agent perspective,[40] the loyalty of an agent is an essential requirement of effective contracting. It may be, as Clifford Rosky has suggested,[41] that loyalty is a strength of public providers in the military setting. But whether public sector loyalty is best obtained by requiring citizenship is another matter. If that requirement is so crucial, one might wonder why it does not also apply to members of the United States military.[42] Indeed some soldiers serve in Iraq with the hope of becoming citizens.

In the TSA setting, could loyalty and reliability have been achieved contractually?[43] Because the privatization trend has already encompassed prison guards, military contractors, and others who are as much a part of the security network as TSA employees,[44] to curtail privatization in this setting requires more explanation.

President Bush, in his signing message, noted that "For the first time, airport security will become a direct federal responsibility, overseen by [a] new undersecretary of transportation for security."[45] This was an uncharacteristic commitment to public solutions by a president known for his downsizing and outsourcing. It was necessitated by the need to assure the public that airlines were secure and it was safe to travel. Sometimes even committed privatizers recognize the value of public solutions. By providing assurances to a skeptical and even fearful traveling public, the government showed it was in charge. The public status that Congress and the president ultimately subscribed to was reassuring for the moment, whether or not its long-term effects were superior.

Converting to public status does not by itself assure superior performance. Public employees need proper training and oversight to be effective. As a conceptual matter, carefully supervised private employees can be as capable of effective inspections as their public counterparts.[46] The government could have approached the issue differently. It could have looked at the nature of the duties involved and determined how to train and prepare the inspectors. A careful analysis of the nature of the functions involved might have asked whether they were "inherently governmental" or eligible for "competitive sourcing."[47] Although the DHS did not employ the OMB A-76 competitive sourcing process in the TSA situation, Congress could have asked whether these jobs were governmental or eligible to be contracted-out.[48] At that stage, the airport security function would have been divided into separate components. Inspectors closest to the traveling public who have limited roles would likely be eligible for outsourcing; those who supervised would have been reserved for government service.[49]

However, the goal of reassuring the public might not then have been achieved. Public status – the presence of an inspector with government authority – was deemed necessary to calm the public and achieve the overall goals of the program. In this case, government status reflected values that transcended the individual nature of the jobs being analyzed. Symbols of authority and accountability cannot be delegated to private contractors.

It is hard to know how much to emphasize this symbolic value.[50] Certainly, the objective evidence does not rule out the private sector. And five years later, the traveling public, tired of having its lip glosses, shaving creams, and other toiletries confiscated by eager TSA inspectors, might not believe that the uniform makes a positive difference. Still, these employees have come to represent the face of government. Although their jobs are not inherent in sovereignty, shifting to private contractors at this stage could have its own costs in terms of public support.

## C. PRIVATIZATION AND AIRPORT SCREENERS IN EUROPE

During the debate over the airport security bill in the United States, House members favoring private inspectors noted that European countries used private inspectors at airports.[51] This was a surprising debating point. Because European countries are more comfortable with public employment than the United States,[52] the accuracy of this assertion is worth exploring.

## 1. Privatization in Europe

It turns out that privatization of government jobs is a significant development in Europe. In many countries, the jobs of inspectors are no longer governmental. In the European Community (EU), the choice to employ public or private airport security personnel varies by country or state. But the EU's role is still crucial because it sets common standards for airport security each state must follow.[53] These standards permit the employment of private contractors in the airport security setting, so long as they are subject to public oversight and control.

The EU standards cover use of airport security equipment, the requirement of background checks for security personnel, and provision for unannounced inspections of individual airport security arrangements.[54] The choice between public or private providers of security is not determined by those standards. But in some countries, the function of baggage and passenger inspections has been delegated to private actors. German law, for example, embraces a concept of "functional privatization," which allows entities to receive assistance from private parties.[55]

These delegations to private hands are not absolute. German law imposes several important limitations: (a) the delegation must be supervised by a public official; (b) administrative procedures necessary to protect individuals must remain in place; and (c) decisions that affect individuals must be taken by public officials.[56]

These procedural protections reflect public oversight of the airport inspection process. The use of private screeners in European countries is explainable on grounds readily understood in the United States. These member state and EU common control standards help determine when public officials should be required to perform "public" functions. They act much like the OMB A-76 process might in the United States.[57] The European experience reflects the growth of what Professor Alfred Aman has called the "nonstate public sector,"[58] which increasingly acts for the government. Although a "democracy deficit"[59] occurs if accountability to the public is ignored, the EU and member states such as Germany seem to be aware of that concern, and their regulations anticipate accountability problems. In addition to supervision by public employees, audits and unannounced inspections of member state airports[60] help ensure that private contractors are performing well. Presumably, the use of contractual obligations and competitive bids are also available as monitoring devices.

## 2. The Right to Travel as a Privatizing Incentive

The privatizing of airport inspection jobs in European states also may be based on factors that are not relevant to the United States. The EU is focused on the creation of open markets, a subject we long ago addressed under the interstate commerce clause.[61] In order for the EU to work, both capital and labor must flow freely across member states.

To encourage labor availability, the EU limits the number of jobs for which state citizenship can be required. If Germany requires citizenship for teachers, for example, no non-Germans need apply to teach. The citizenship requirement creates barriers to entry into state employment. A counterprinciple – the free movement of persons – is designed to prevent states from exploiting the citizenship requirement. Under the Treaty of Rome,[62] free movement of persons is a fundamental principle. Jobs in member state bureaucracies may only be limited to state citizens if they constitute employment in a state's "public service."[63] Public sector employees must have a "special relationship of allegiance to the state."[64] Many public employees, such as secondary school teachers and perhaps also inspectors at airports, are excluded from this definition. Presumably, a similar restriction prevents states from expanding the "public sector" standard to encompass airport inspectors.

If a member state must employ nonnationals as well as its own citizens to perform the airport inspection function, the advantages of preserving government employment are diminished and private contracting becomes a more viable alternative. The United States does not limit public employment in this way; indeed, the federal government can make citizenship a job requirement, as the ATSA requires.[65] The principle comparable to the EU's free movement of persons in the United States arises under the First Amendment.[66] It is only if states were to require jobs to be held by their "citizens" that the right to travel would constrain public employment in ways similar to the EU.

In Europe, the preference for public sector solutions has been trumped by a higher principle congenial both to community integration and the world of privatization. The United States has made the employ-ment of airport screeners a public decision for symbolic reasons. And in both settings the question of public or private employment of airport screeners seems to be one of choice, not necessity. At some higher level of authority, however, both systems agree that public employment is nondiscretionary. The question of where to draw that line brings us back to the inherent government function discussion.

## D. THEORIES OF PUBLIC AND PRIVATE CONTROL IN AIRPORT SECURITY

The United States sets limits in the kind of government jobs that can be privatized, not the kind that can be publicized, as is done in Europe. Officials performing "inherent government functions" are explicitly excluded from the privatization calculus. The distinction between com-petitive and inherent functions drawn by the government's A-76 pro-cess, discussed earlier,[67] provides the basic breakdown, but the dis-tinction is not easy to apply. Indeed, in its indeterminacy, the process shares some of the ambiguities surrounding public service jobs under EU law.[68]

Still, the process itself offers a framework for making decisions about jobs that may be appropriately outsourced. The TSA might put pub-lic inspectors up for competitive sourcing under A-76, if more airports sought exemptions from the current rules. How should the agency pro-ceed, and what would be the outcome? The TSA would first determine whether the inspectors' positions are inherent or subject to competitive sourcing. TSA employees would be expected to argue that they per-formed inherent government functions or that, even if competitively sourced, they were superior providers.[69] If this hypothetical challenge were commenced, the government providers would not find it easy to prevail.

First, the fact that security is a government role begs the question. As private security guards on military bases demonstrate,[70] the gov-ernment delegates inspections or policing to private contractors.[71] So something more must be shown. The level and degree of that dele-gation is what tests the proposition. The act of screening passengers or baggage is a limited and discrete assignment; properly supervised,

it would not seem to require government actors.[72] Certainly, that is
the outcome in Europe. And Congress came very close to privatizing TSA officials – at least as to the inspection function performed by
those officials.[73] So it speaks too broadly to call the inspection function
inherently governmental.[74]

However, placing public oversight and control as well as inspections
in private hands (outsourcing the entire process) is a different matter.
Under current legislation, the undersecretary of Homeland Security[75]
is required to perform oversight functions. As this assignment involves
judgment and discretion it is inherently governmental and thus nondelegable. This would be the outcome under an A-76 competition and
under statutory and even constitutional principles.[76]

The requirements of supervision and control are indicators of inherent functions. Although the actual inspections are discrete assignments
and may be delegated, the responsibility to search and detain[77] or to
ensure proper performance by those officials remains a governmental
one. The EU rules are instructive here as well. They permit private
airport inspectors, but only if they are controlled, trained, and overseen by public officials. Our traditions would reach the same conclusion. Moreover, the ATSA confirms this stance. In the limited opt-out
context, the Undersecretary of Homeland Security still oversees the
private contractors who operate the five airports that were excepted
from the act.[78] Expanding the number of privately contracted airports
is contemplated by the act and would be acceptable on a public-private
responsibility scale so long as the oversight remained in public hands.

If one were doing a simple make-or-buy choice,[79] the question of
outsourcing airport security would be limited to which program performed better and at what cost. This choice also might include the oversight function. So long as the private performance could be measured,
the case for privatization would satisfy this transactions cost approach.
In terms of inspector quality, recent airport security studies do not con-
fer a performance edge on government over private inspectors.[80] But
even if private contractors have an efficiency advantage, it would not
extend beyond the actual inspectors themselves. The oversight function, which involves subjective qualities of judgment and discretion, is
harder to quantify and less susceptible to effective contracting. On this
view, determining whether privatized employees are adequately supervised and trained remains a governmental function. Public officials

oversee the inspection process in the United States and Europe for a reason. The management requirement involves qualities that are difficult to describe in contractual terms. The harder they are to describe, the harder they should be to privatize.

In setting up the Transportation Security Administration, Congress gave the DHS capacity to achieve the necessary level of public oversight, even if decisions were later made to privatize the airport security function. Whether or not public oversight is effective is another matter,[81] but there is no doubt where the responsibility lies. Professor Williamson's view that outsourcing should be favored so long as transactions costs are reduced[82] helps focus the inquiry on institutional structures.[83] The government is a peculiar kind of structure; it cannot be freely manipulated by contract. The Constitution ultimately limits government delegation and organizational freedom.[84]

Assuming that airport screeners perform delegable duties, how far up the chain of command can the public role be delegated without abandoning the government's responsibility to govern? John Donahue has answered this question in efficiency and public management terms that echo the transactional cost concerns of Professor Williamson.[85] Donahue argues for government to choose the best structure (public or private) necessary to assure accountability.[86] He grants the accountability criterion priority over efficiency in public decision making.[87] Accountability, in the form of process and oversight, has long been recognized as the necessary condition for effective privatization.[88] Delegations of government functions to private hands that ignore Donahue's accountability criterion are inherently suspect, whatever their efficiency advantages. Under his approach, efficiency concerns can never supplant the need for accountable government.

Because security is a traditional public good,[89] privatization must be integrated into that framework, not the other way around. In terms of airport security, this requires a careful analysis of the various functions performed by the officials involved. The physical inspections of passengers and baggage, outsourced to private providers in Europe but not in the United States, are discrete assignments subject to privatization.

The crucial accountability-efficiency question is not whether these specific arrangements can be outsourced, but whether those performing the inspection functions are properly supervised. As long as the delegated assignments are clearly limited by contract,[90] and the oversight function is publicly performed, the private contractor approach can be accommodated. In the United States, the ATSA is reassuring on this note. Even if it is assumed that the exceptions to public inspectors become the rule in the future, protections remain in place through contractual limitations and public oversight (including clearly defined administrator responsibility at DHS[91]), to assure that public accountability is not lost.

Unlike many other situations in government today, most prominently the private military in Iraq,[92] airport security has been properly structured as a public function. Even when privatization has a role to play, the national security interest is still protected through accountability mechanisms that reflect the inherent role of government. This makes one wonder why total public control has been exercised over one aspect of transportation security and others have been left to incomplete solutions. It was only by chance that airport security captured our attention on 9/11; if America's ports had been hit instead, the public-private arguments addressed above would have been equally or even more central to the debate.

## E. THE POLITICS OF PORT SECURITY

Port security is in many ways the DHS's continuing nightmare. Since 9/11, we have been inundated with examples of lax oversight and control,[93] but little seems to have been done. Containerized shipments from abroad continue to enter U.S. ports with inadequate screening of cargo at the place of embarkation or disembarkation.[94] The Container Security Initiative (CSI), which operates in foreign ports, has been less than successful in inspecting cargo.[95] The distinction between public and private solutions is less well understood in this context.

The DHS, largely through the U.S. Coast Guard and Customs and Border Protection, is responsible for cargo screening functions. But the port operator – a private owner – is responsible for controlling cargo coming in and out of the port. The owner secures the facility and employs security personnel. By analogy to airport security, where many airports are also in public hands, inspection personnel are private contractors. Given the earlier discussion, this fact does not by itself undermine security. As the airport security situation shows, properly supervised, private contractors can perform the actual inspections of persons and cargo in either situation. Of course, proper supervision is the big question. The DHS (without the aid of a TSA) must exercise oversight of port security. It can call on the Coast Guard and Customs for assistance in this role. But it also has to worry about the nature of private port ownership itself. Ownership of the ports has become a public security issue.

## 1. The Dubai Ports Debacle

Unlike airports, which are owned by a mix of public and private entities,[96] ports frequently are owned or operated by private parties. This distinction aroused little concern until a United Arab Emirates (UAE) government-owned company (Dubai Ports World) sought to purchase several ports in New York and New Jersey and other cities from a British-controlled company.[97] Port security, long seemingly overlooked, then became a front page event.

The Committee on Foreign Investment in the United States concluded that the acquisition presented no national security concerns, and President Bush initially approved the deal.[98] The president emphasized that the U.S. Coast Guard and Customs would still have oversight of port security, but that did little to mollify the critics. Surprised by the move, members of Congress in both parties raised strenuous objections.[99] Questions were raised about the UAE and its connections to terrorists, including Osama bin Laden himself.[100] The administration responded by viewing the security question in a broader light. It was more concerned about the consequences for U.S. military access to UAE ports in the Gulf region than with the effect of the acquisition on U.S. ports.[101]

It was not entirely clear what security risks the DP World transaction posed.[102] The deal may have been caught up in the political objections to outsourcing to foreign countries more generally. But Congress ultimately demanded that the deal be restructured.[103] Later, DP World sold its U.S. holdings to A.I.G. and the problem went away.[104] Still it is hard to comprehend the lessons of this debate. Surely private ownership was an issue, but was it only private ownership by a Middle Eastern country? If the objection was to private ownership more generally, it is hard to establish standards that could apply equally to all situations. The government cannot own all port facilities. Ultimately, some combination of joint responsibility and private ownership in the form of public-private partnerships will be necessary for the security system to work.[105]

## 2. The Present State of Public Control

The larger issue this confrontation illuminated, however, has continuing relevance and concern. In defending the deal, supporters noted that American longshoremen, not Arab terrorists, would be handling cargo.[106] But longshoremen are private contractors to the DP World subsidiary, not public employees, and certainly not security officials such as TSA employees. Public controls at the cargo handling level are still in short supply. DHS has issued final rules for 250,000 port workers who in the next eighteen months will be required to apply for tamper-proof identification cards.[107] Even when implemented, these identity cards will be less than fully effective.[108]

The presence of Coast Guard oversight is helpful to allay fears, but the structure of oversight and accountability seems less clearly articulated than in the airport security context. Whereas these concerns have been raised because the UAE[109] was involved in the transaction, the question of port security remains largely where it was before the DP World incident. Private employees who work for private companies who own our ports are still waiting to be adequately supervised and controlled by public authorities. DHS through its branches has overall responsibility. The protection of critical infrastructure remains an area of public vulnerability that can only be reduced by a combination of public and private initiatives.

National security is achieved through public and private institutions under public norms. In terms of transportation systems, a key aspect of our critical infrastructure, government officials sometimes utilize private contractors to perform these security functions.[110] This occurs more readily in the port security setting than in the airport security one. As to airport security, the United States has chosen different roles for the private and public sectors.

But whatever choice is made, the crucial variable is accountability. If oversight remains in public hands, national security goals can still be achieved. That requirement should be made clear by statute, as it has with the ATSA. Port security is the general responsibility of DHS, but it is less well articulated legislatively.

Whether or not public oversight is in fact achieved, however, is a managerial problem. If public authorities have adequate regulatory authority to perform the oversight function, the legislative function then becomes one of oversight as well. Are these agencies performing their missions properly? When implementation is lacking, as it obviously was with the DHS's failures in natural disasters such as Katrina,[111] government management remains problematic. In the port security context, now highlighted by the DP World debacle, the lines of authority and control also need to be strengthened to avoid a management breakdown.

To some extent, the privatization problem is less extreme now that the public has been brought into the debate. Democratic processes will determine the success of our security efforts. The publicization of airport security by Congress dispelled some myths about the dominance of privatized government. It reflected deep-seated values about public service. Even if specific jobs do not themselves require a badge or oath of office to be performed, the perception of the public (as interpreted by Congress) is that government has the essential role in securing against terrorism. Any potential solutions, whether in the ports or the airports, cannot succeed if that perception is ignored.

## NOTES

1. *See The 9/11 Commission Report* § 12.4, at 357–58 ("Millions of containers are imported annually through more than 300 sea and river ports served by more than 3,700 cargo and passenger terminals. . . . Opportunities to do harm are as great, or greater, in maritime or surface transportation [as in commercial aviation]."); Scott, *Slipping Through the Net and into Our Ports*; *infra* nn. 93–95 and accompanying text.
2. *See* Chapter 2; Singer, *Corporate Warriors* (documenting the use of private military in a variety of foreign settings).
3. Dempsey, *Aviation Security* at 721.
4. *See* Ervin, *Open Target* at 110 (suggesting private contractors cut corners in providing airport security).

5. Viewed as an ancillary mission, airline-sponsored security services were subjected to rigorous cost controls with many of the jobs being of the minimum wage variety. As the events of 9/11 ultimately showed, failure of performance by these employees was borne by the government.

6. Aviation and Transportation Security Act, 115 Stat. 597 (2001) (Codified at 49 U.S.C.A. § 114).

7. *See* Freeman, *Extending Public Law Norms through Privatization* at 1285 (using the term "publicization" as a counterpoint to "privatization").

8. Five airports were allowed to retain private employees supervised by the TSA. See *infra* n. 26.

9. *See* Verkuil, *Public Law Limitations on Privatization of Government Functions.*

10. *See* Treverton, *Governing the Market State* at 104–05 (calling TSA a national security exception to the privatization movement).

11. 14 C.F.R. § 108.9 (2001) (specifying airlines' security responsibilities).

12. *See* Dempsey, *Aviation Security* at 721.

13. Hessick, *The Federalization of Airport Security: Privacy Implications* at 46.

14. *Id.* (referring to a 1999 DOT report).

15. *Id.* at 47.

16. S. 1447, 107th Cong., 2d Sess. (2001).

17. Shesgreen, *Bush Offers Compromise on Aviation Security Bill; It Stalls on Provision to Make All Screeners Federal Employees.*

18. H. R. 3150, 107th Cong. (2001). The House bill permitted private screeners but section 3 said that "[a]ll screenering must be supervised by uniformed Federal employees of the TSA." 147 Cong. Rec. H7631, H7632 (Nov. 1, 2001) (available at 2001 WL 1347343).

19. *Id.*

20. A *Washington Post* poll found 82 percent of Americans in favor, along with the U.S. Conference of Mayors and the entire U.S. Senate. Hessick, *The Federalization of Airport Security: Privacy Implications* at 50.

21. *See supra* n. 6.

22. Branum & Dokupil, *Security Takeovers and Bailouts* at 459.

23. The U.S. citizen requirement essentially prevented rehiring of former airport security personnel, many of whom were immigrants. And it imposed a hiring requirement that does not even apply to the U.S. military. *See* Michael Hayes, *Improving Security* at 60–61 (viewing the TSA as an antilabor bill).

24. Hessick, *The Federalization of Airport Security: Privacy Implications* at 53.

25. Baggage screeners were subjected to extensive background checks by TSA, which it had difficulty implementing. *See* DHS, Office of Inspector General, *A Review of Background Checks for Federal Passenger and Baggage Screeners at Airports.*

26. The public employment requirement permitted five airports to opt out: San Francisco, Kansas City, Rochester, Jackson Hole, and Tupelo. *See* Transportation Security Administration, *TSA Releases Performance Report On Contract Screeners At Five U.S. Airports.*

27. Branum & Dokupil, *Security Takeovers and Bailouts* at 461.
28. Sen. 1447, 107th Cong. (Sept. 21, 2001).
29. H. R. 3150, 107th Cong. (Oct. 17, 2001).
30. *See e.g.* White House Off. of the Press Sec., *Press Briefing by Ari Fleischer* (Nov. 6, 2001) ("the best system is a mix of public and private screeners, so long as the federal government plays a very vigorous role in enforcing standards and setting much higher standards").
31. *See generally* Verkuil, *Public Law Limitations*, at 401–02.
32. *Cf.* NPR Talk of the Nation: Federalizing Airport Security Personnel, 2001 WL 4190170, Oct. 25, 2001 (Senator McCain defends full federal employment by giving president the right to fire employees at will).
33. *See* Hayes, *Improving Security* at 59 (64,000 new TSA employees).
34. *See e.g.* Part C, *infra.*
35. *See* Verkuil, *Public Law Limitations* at 428–31 (discussing historical importance of oath requirements). A third symbolic requirement, that of U.S. citizenship, also was added. See discussion at n. 23, *supra.*
36. Pub. L. No. 170–71, § 118(a), 115 Stat. 597, 625 (2001); 49 U.S.C. § 44940(a)(1)(A).
37. The Administration sought to counter the full public employment requirement by referring to the use of private contractors at European airports. *See* n. 32, *supra* (comments by Roy Blunt (R)).
38. *See* Rosky, *Force, Inc.* at 979–81 (connecting the problem of loyalty to the choice between the public and the private use of force).
39. *See* Corwin, *The President: Office and Powers* at 107–10 (discussing loyalty oaths set by executive order).
40. *See* discussion at Chapter 7.
41. *See* Rosky, *Force, Inc.*
42. *See* Singer, *Corporate Warriors.*
43. Indeed, in the private opt-out program that is part of the act, qualified private screening companies are defined as those that employ the same contractual requirements for screeners as are applied to public employees. *See* 49 U.S. C. §§ 44919–20. Qualified companies must also be owned and controlled by U.S. citizens. 49 U.S.C. § 44920(d)(2).
44. *See generally* Rosky, *Force, Inc.* (describing the private use of force and comparing it to public use, including airport security).
45. Federal Document Clearing House, *President George W. Bush Signs the Aviation Security Bill.*
46. The TSA employees are not exactly the gold standard of inspections. *See* Kocieniewski, *El Al Asks U.S. to Let It Do Extra Screening at Newark* (reporting that El Al inspectors received permission from TSA to do a second screening of baggage going on its planes).
47. *See* Exec. Off. of the Pres., Off. of Mgt. & Budget, OMB Circular A-76, at A-2. *See also* Chapter 6 (describing OMB's A-76 process in detail).
48. *See id.*

49. This decision is close to what the House bill imposed. *See* n. 29, *supra*.
50. We cannot discount the consequences of 9/11 on the public's opinion of public servants. In New York City, for example, police and fire officials have enjoyed the status of heroes, and skeptical New Yorkers now wear FDNY/NYPD hats and t-shirts. *See The 9/11 Commission Report* § 9, at 260 ("Heroism and Horror").
51. *See* n. 32, *supra* (Rep. Blunt asserted that every European country had a system that was "largely private sector based, but with federal rules"), *id.*
52. Statist solutions may be more congenial in Europe, after all, and governments typically fight privatization of public enterprises. *See generally Public Services and Citizenship in European Law* 2–10 (describing the privatization and third way – public/private – movements in Europe).
53. *See* Regulation (EC) No. 2320/2002 (Dec. 16, 2002) (establishing common rules for civil aviation security).
54. *See id.* at arts. 7–9.
55. *See* Metz, *Simplification of the Public Administration: The "Lean State" as a Long-Term Task* at 651–54 (describing the role of privatization in Germany's Lean State program).
56. *Id.* These requirements also apply to a variety of other privatized activities, such as motor vehicle inspections, individual safety inspections, and traffic control. *See* n. 52, *supra*.
57. *See supra* n. 47 and accompanying text.
58. Aman, *Privatization, Prisons, Democracy, and Human Rights* at 514.
59. *See* Aman, *The Democracy Deficit* at 1–3.
60. *See* Regulation (EC) No. 2320/2002 art. 7 (Dec. 16, 2002).
61. *See e.g. Gibbons v. Ogden*, 22 U.S. at 1 (Marshall, C. J.). The Chief Judge of the European Court of Justice once told the author that with respect to interstate commerce, the Court was in its "John Marshall phase." Cases such as *Gibbons* are of much interest to the Court.
62. *See Treaty Establishing the European Economic Community*, art. 48 (describing the free movement of persons and the exception for "employment in the public service").
63. *See e.g. Commission v. Belgium*, [1982] E. C. R. 1845 (holding various municipal officials, e.g., night watchmen, not entitled to be Belgian nationals); *Bleis v. Ministere de l'Education*, [1991] E. C. R. I-5627 (secondary school teachers not restricted to French citizens).
64. *Bleis v. Ministere de l'Education*, [1991] E. C. R. I-5627.
65. *See supra* n. 23.
66. Free movement of persons from state to state is part of the liberty branch of due process in the U.S., enforced through the Supremacy Clause. *See The Passenger Cases*, 7 How. [48 U.S.] at 492 ("We are all citizens of the United States; and, as members of the same community, must have the right to pass and repass through every part of it without interruption, as freely as in our own States.").

67. *See supra* n. 47 and accompanying text.

68. *See* discussion at nn. 63–64, *supra*. Of course, in the United States, inherent government functions may not be delegated to private contractors, whereas jobs designated to be in the public service might be delegated to private contractors if the member state preferred to do so.

69. *See* Chapter 6 for greater detail on how the process works.

70. *See* Singer, *Corporate Warriors*.

71. *See* discussion of private police in Chapter 2, Part C.

72. It does not, for example, involve the search or restraint of passengers; that function is performed by public officials. *See* n. 77, *infra*.

73. Indeed, Congress did approve of private inspectors at five airports. *See supra* n. 26.

74. If the inherently governmental challenge fails, TSA employees would then be able to "compete" in stage two. But here the record of performance, as well as comparative costs, would be decisive. There is no clear edge for the current system on these measures. *See* discussion n. 46, *supra*.

75. *See* n. 22, *supra*.

76. *See* Chapter 5.

77. Searches are intrusive and privacy depriving. We ordinarily expect police officials to do searches and seizures. But these are criminal contexts, whereas most airport searches are not. However, when drugs are found during an airport search, it can become a criminal matter. *See e.g. United States v. Ramsey*, 81 Fed. Appx. 547.

78. *See* n. 26, *supra*.

79. *See* Williamson, *Public and Private Bureaucracies: A Transactions Cost Economics Perspective* at 308–26 (favoring outsourcing if transactions costs are reduced).

80. *See* Ervin, *Open Target* at 110 (acknowledging TSA employees have not done a better job of screening than private contractors, but still favoring public control).

81. Statutory directives do not always translate into effective oversight. DHS and its subsidiary FEMA mishandled the Katrina disaster despite abundant authority to oversee the events. But at least congressional hearings and subsequent legislation can help place the responsibility where it belongs. *See* Neuman, *Report Details Katrina Communications Fiasco. But see* Varney, *Fact-Finding Senators Feel Stiffed by FEMA*.

82. *See supra* n. 79.

83. *See also* Williamson, *The Economic Institutions of Capitalism* at 398–402 (discussing the relationship between governance structures and contract law).

84. *See* contract/delegation discussion in Chapter 7 Part A.

85. *See* Donahue, *The Privatization Decision*.

86. *Id.* at 38 (chapter 1 is entitled The Architecture of Accountability).

87. Donahue describes accountability as "fidelity to the public's values." *Id.* at 12. Efficiency is defined so as to incorporate these values. *Id.* Donahue's premise

is that privatization decisions are not made simply by comparing private and public forms of behavior, but by recognizing that "[p]ublic tasks are different, and mostly harder." *Id.* at 215.

88. *See* Verkuil, *Public Law Limitations* at 424–25; Metzger, *Privatization as Delegation* (requiring procedures to accompany private delegations).

89. *See* Verkuil, *Public Law Limitations* at 455–59 (discussing security and defense as public goods, citing authorities).

90. *See* Donahue, *The Privatization Decision* at 78 ("when a well-specified contract in a competitive context can enforce accountability").

91. *See* n. 22, *supra.*

92. *See* Chapter 2 Part A.

93. *See e.g.* Walsh, *For Coast Guard, Priorities Shifted on September 11; Focus Is on Defense Against Terrorism*; Sweeney, *New York Harbor 'Ripe' for Al Qaeda-Style Attack*; Clendenning, *Most Ports Dawdle Over Beefing Up Security; Few Nations Likely to Meet July Deadline.*

94. *See* Ortolani & Block, *Keeping Cargo Safe from Terror – Hong Kong Port Project Scans All Containers; U.S. Doesn't See the Need.*

95. *See* Ervin, *Open Target*, ch. 4 (the former DHS Inspector General documents inadequacies in the CSI foreign ports inspection system).

96. For example, the Port Authority of New York and New Jersey owns the three airports in the Metropolitan New York area, Newark, LaGuardia, and Kennedy. *See* The Port Authority of NY & NJ, *Homepage.*

97. The Peninsular and Oriental Steam Navigation Co. is the world's fourth-largest port operator, with eighty-five ports in nineteen countries. *See* Off. of Sen. Charles Schumer, *Press Release: Multi-Billion Dollar Company that Operates NYC Port to be Taken Over by United Arab Emirates Government-Owned Firm Today.*

98. The White House released the following statement from President Bush on February 21, 2006:

> If there was any chance that this transaction would jeopardize the security of the United States, it would not go forward. The company has been cooperative with the United States government. The company will not manage port security. The security of our ports will continue to be managed by the Coast Guard and Customs. The company is from a country that has been cooperative in the war on terror, been an ally in the war on terror. The company operates ports in different countries around the world, ports from which cargo has been sent to the United States on a regular basis.

White House Off. Of the Press Sec., *Fact Sheet: The CFIUS Process and the DP World Transaction.*

99. *See* CBS News, *Coast Guard Warned of Ports Deal Gaps* ("With the deal under intense bipartisan criticism in Congress, the Bush administration agreed

Sunday to DP World's request for a second review of the potential security risks related to its deal.").

100. Senator Lautenberg noted that members of the UAE royal family had secretly met with bin Laden in 1999 near his camp in Afghanistan. 152 Cong. Rec. S1936–S1937 (2006).

101. *See* 152 Cong. Rec. S1941–S1942 (2006) (floor statement of Senator John Warner, reading letters from Generals Peter Pace and John P. Abizaid, describing the strategic value of UAE military access).

102. *See* Samuelson, *The Dangers of Ports (and Politicians)*.

103. DP World transferred its U.S. operation to a U.S. subsidiary. *See* Press Release, DP World, Statement by H. Edward Bilkey, Chief Operating Officer, DPWorld.

104. *See* Timmons, *Dubai Port Company Sells Its U.S. Holdings to A. I. G. – Political Hot Potato Handed Off.*

105. *See* Chapter 8, discussing the need for public-private partnerships.

106. *See* Samuelson, *The Dangers of Ports (and Politicians)*.

107. *See* Lipton, *U.S. Requiring Port Workers to Have ID's and Reviews* (noting that the program will cost $1.8 billion).

108. For example, background checks are not done on longshoremen, as they are on TSA employees. *See* n. 43, *supra.* The port workers, particularly truck drivers, need not be U.S. citizens, but they cannot be illegal aliens, which may cause severe distractions as drivers are rejected during port deliveries. *See id.*

109. Later, in fact, DP World purchased another British firm, Doncasters Group Ltd., which supplied parts used in aircraft and tanks. Even Senator Schumer raised no objection to this deal because it involved products, not services. Blustein, *Dubai Firm Cleared to Buy Military Supplier.*

110. *See* Auerswald et al., *Where Private Efficiency Meets Public Vulnerability: The Critical Infrastructure Challenge.*

111. *See* Hsu, *Messages Depict Disarray in Federal Katrina Response; On Risk and Disaster: Lessons from Hurricane Katrina; cf.* Ervin, *Open Target* (former Inspector General at DHS documents wasteful spending on private contracts).

# 4  THE PUBLIC-PRIVATE DISTINCTION

The distinction between public and private law thus varies in meaning depending upon whether it is criminal law or administrative law that one wishes to separate from private law. The distinction is useless as a common foundation for a general systematization of law.

– Hans Kelsen[1]

If the law is a jealous mistress, then the public-private distinction is like a dysfunctional spouse – you can't live with it and you can't live without it. It has been around forever, but it continues to fail as an organizing principle. Still, as Ronald Moe urges us to remember, it was "the Framers' intention that the governmental and private sectors be kept separate and subject to distinct theories of jurisprudence."[2] In fact, the distinction makes an enduring point for democratic societies: The separation of public from private creates the space necessary for individualism to flourish. And, in case we forget the lesson, the definition of fascism confirms it by assuming the dominance of the community or the hegemony of the public.[3] It is the presence of public law, what the great English legal thinker A.V. Dicey called the law of the Constitution,[4] that mediates the line between the two regimes in the democratic, rule of law-bound, state.

The public-private distinction and democratic political theory have an inevitable role to play in the context of privatization. In the examples explored in Chapter 2, the activities contracted-out are questionable because they either usurp public authority (as is the case with the private military), operate outside public checks on accountability, or do both. In Chapter 3, the "publicization" of airport security reminds us that the distinction still matters and in the proper case can be a decisive consideration. No study of the proper role of government can avoid confronting the public-private distinction.

## A. AN OVERVIEW OF THE PUBLIC-PRIVATE DISTINCTION

The words "public" and "private" are commonplace in American law and society. In society generally, these words can be politically charged. For example, they have been invoked to separate public discourse from private conversation in an effort to foster civic engagement.[5] Civic engagement is a way to express political ideas and opinions which are meant to be controversial. Neil Smelser has noted that "the private-public distinction constitutes a political strategy in and of itself."[6] The distinction has been used for centuries to defend or attack the public order. Michael Taggart suggests that it "has its roots in liberalism."[7] Liberalism not only underpins our social order: it provides the force behind the Constitution.

The distinction predates most political movements. Calling an activity "public" has legitimated governmental action since the time of Justinian.[8] In Continental jurisprudence, which traces its roots to Roman law, public law carries with it substantive obligations of the state to the citizen.[9] Although Anglo-American law is indebted to these earlier traditions, the public law concept is less well developed.[10] Yet expressions of the "public interest" have, since the nineteenth century, been used to justify the role of government in our liberal democratic state. Agencies were empowered to protect the "public interest, convenience, and necessity."[11] But that phrase is contested as offensively self-fulfilling. Classical liberals believe with Adam Smith that the exercise of self-interest is the best way to represent the public interest.[12] Indeed, it is the public interest.

This debate raged in the early years of the New Deal period, but ultimately agencies with public interest mandates were given wide sway.[13] Later, the conservative counterreaction to Roosevelt's public interest government culminated with the Reagan presidency.[14] The Reagan spirit still animates our deregulation and privatization movements. The current administration, in its focus on an "ownership society," continues this challenge to earlier visions of the public order. Indeed, that phrase may be meant to end one of the enduring programs of the New Deal itself.[15]

Privatization's association with deregulation also redefines the public interest. By placing some regulatory decisions in private hands, deregulation seeks to remove what Cass Sunstein calls "regulatory paradoxes."[16] But deregulation does not make the public-private distinction disappear.[17]

As the definition in Justinian's Digest suggests[18] and as history demonstrates, the line between public and private shifts over time,[19] but it ultimately endures. Public law is inseparable from government. Private law traditionally encompasses the common law of contract, torts, and property that regulates relations among individuals.[20] But the term "private" is no more self-evident (or any less self-fulfilling) than the term "public." If law and its enforcement are public acts, all legal regimes, even those ostensibly private at common law, are in essence public.[21] Additionally, otherwise private relations are often umpired and regulated by government.[22]

The malleability of the distinction is demonstrated when the Constitution expands or contracts the private category through definitions of liberty or property. Protections of the privacy interest, for example, use the concept of liberty to restrain the state from legislating morality.[23] Each time the First Amendment is applied, the role of government is expanded or inhibited accordingly.[24] To the extent that America is a "deliberative democracy,"[25] the legal definition of private and public will ebb and flow based on the preferences of interest groups, the agendas of political parties, and the views of the judiciary.

When government delegates public powers to private hands, as when it privatizes regulatory activity, the impact on the public interest is hard to measure.[26] To some degree, making public actions "private" subtracts from the public side. But it is not a dichotomous choice. The transfer of power to private hands sometimes comes with procedural controls, involving oversight and accountability. For example, the term "enforced self-regulation" implies public control.[27] These rule-of-law–based considerations help maintain a dividing line between public and private.

Fairness in procedures, indeed legalism itself, defines the liberal state. For Stuart Hampshire, process is not only a basic condition of the liberal state but of human nature as well.[28] Delegations of government authority to private hands are not simple transfer decisions. They are decisions that potentially transfer sovereignty. They should come with strings attached that ensure fairness at the individual level and accountability at the political level. The debate about public versus private, therefore, becomes a meditation on our constitutional values.

## B. CONSTITUTIONAL CONNECTIONS TO THE PUBLIC-PRIVATE DISTINCTION

The public-private distinction underpins both common law and constitutional traditions. It was central to the natural rights liberalism of John Locke,[29] who transmitted the values of the Glorious Revolution to the Constitution's drafters.[30] Locke saw the emergence of separate realms of public and private as essential conditions of the liberal democratic state.[31] To some extent, Locke and his followers[32] (including our Constitution's drafters) made liberal democracy a theory about what can be made public.

The Constitution employs the words "public" and "private" in a variety of ways worth exploring here.[33] But it was the decision, discussed in Chapter 1, to place sovereignty in the People that united liberal theory and the Constitution. Once the political sovereign was fixed, the three branches became the source of delegated, not inherent, powers. And the powers not thereby granted remained with the People as private rights.[34] Public law justifies itself through the Constitution and, by extension, through the administrative state that undergirds it.[35]

### 1. The Fifth Amendment's "Public Use" Requirement

The Just Compensation Clause of the Fifth Amendment,[36] a focal point of the public-private distinction, both guarantees the existence of private property and limits the extent to which government may commandeer (or "publicize") it. The "public use" requirement mediates the boundaries between the two concepts. In theory government is constrained by this clause from transferring private property. It must show a public need for transfer, especially if the transfer is to other private hands.

Despite this conceptual purpose, however, the "public use" doctrine has not often been interpreted in an authoritative way.[37] The Supreme Court has usually left the interpretation of public use to the states, which do not move in consistent directions.[38] This is a difficult doctrinal subject to capsulize, but some recent uses illustrate the argument. In *County of Wayne v. Hathcock*,[39] the Michigan Supreme Court articulated a public use test that put limits on the transfer of private property to private rather than public hands.[40] *Hathcock*'s limitations on the forced transfer of private property for public use both preserved the public-private distinction and supported a process-based limitation on the privatizing of public functions.[41] But other state courts took different positions. In *Kelo v. City of New London*,[42] the Connecticut Supreme Court, in permitting transfers of public property to private developers for economic development purposes,[43] glossed over the distinction. The Supreme Court until recently was content to let these competing views coexist. As Stewart Sterk has argued, the only consistent thing about the public use cases is that the Supreme Court honors the underlying federalism values behind state court interpretations.[44] But the "consistency" of its federalism approach to public use has recently been challenged by some members of the Court.

In *Kelo* (a 5–4 decision), the pro-federalism Justices of the Court dissented. They balked at further dilution of "public use"[45] and sought to restore the public-private line. Justice Stevens's majority opinion reflected the Court's dominant view by equating public use with the vague and all-justifying "public purpose" test. This test, like the "public interest, convenience and necessity" standard in administrative law, justified virtually any use of eminent domain proceedings for economic development purposes.[46]

Justice O'Connor's biting dissent sought to infuse "public use" with constitutional content.[47] Accusing the majority of trying "to wash out any distinction between private and public use of property," she refused to defer to state legislative judgments or to equate public use with the broad exercise of police power. For Justice Thomas, also in dissent,[48] the limitations upon public use were even clearer; he found that the

Constitution elsewhere defined "use" in the narrow sense of government ownership or control.[49]

These dissents made headlines and generated Congressional interest. They may signal a revival of classical property law limitations upon public use.[50] Whether or not this groundswell for legislative intervention is sustainable, it surely highlights the public-private distinction elucidated here. The public use requirements of the Just Compensation Clause, if revived, would connect directly to the Lockean concept of limited government discussed earlier.[51] The vigor with which the dissenters in *Kelo* supported a fixed meaning of public use makes these historical sources all the more relevant. Employing them to frame the idea of public use, however, may not yield any more consistency than the current federalism-based approach. As with the "affected with a public interest" category discussed next, the application of principle to specific facts inevitably produces disagreement.

## 2. The Rise and Fall of "Affected with a Public Interest"

The public-private distinction is often associated with the nineteenth-century rise of capitalism. Public charters, earlier granted by government to create and protect established monopolies, were challenged by new private enterprises eager to enter those restricted markets.[52] The Supreme Court provided Contracts Clause protection for these enterprises.[53] The corporate form (through the expanded concept of limited liability) made capital formation easier and more accessible. As Richard Epstein explains, the legal act of incorporation conferred "upon corporations and their shareholders a privilege against the rest of the world that they could not obtain under the usual rules of property, contract, and tort."[54] Thus, public law improved on the common law in facilitating the expansion of private enterprise.

But public law also constrained this expanded private power. State regulatory control over private monopolies introduced the concept of businesses "affected with a public interest." In *Munn v. Illinois*,[55] the Court traced the affected with a public interest concept back to English common law,[56] which equated "common carriers" with monopoly power and controlled them from the earliest times.[57] This connection gave states substantive regulatory power over private entities which the Court defended under the Due Process Clause. But tying the fate of common carriers to the shifting sands of monopoly power often made no economic sense.[58]

Regulation of the abusive exercise of economic power has deep roots. Even during the era of *Lochner v. New York*,[59] when regulation based on the conclusory notion of "public interest" was successfully challenged, the monopoly-based theory underlying *Munn* managed to survive.[60] In otherwise constitutionalizing the private interests protected by liberty of contract,[61] *Lochner* relied on the notions of liberalism inspired by Locke. Its premises were tied to deeply felt ideas of individualism and economic liberty.[62] Later, a more skeptical Court, inspired by Justice Holmes's *Lochner* dissent,[63] rejected these premises. Ironically, the Court also threw out *Munn*'s monopoly-based definition of "affected with a public interest" that had survived during the *Lochner* period.[64] Perhaps, as Professor Horwitz has argued, rejection of the public interest test was the fault of the Legal Realists, who, in debunking the idea of a truly private sector, also undermined the notion of a truly public sector.[65] Once freed from its historical moorings, the public interest concept became just another legal fiction, which made it fair game for later critics of government regulation.[66] The focus today is more on the procedural side of regulation because the public interest rationale is less able to serve as a justifying or limiting principle.[67]

When substantive control of enterprise was accepted, private grievances shifted to the acts of regulatory overseers, the bureaucracy itself. The "spoils" system of government, emblematic of the administrations of Presidents Jackson and Grant,[68] served private interests initially, but soon came under attack for undermining the effectiveness of the regulatory process. To regulate in the public interest, government had to bring integrity, if not competency and efficiency, into the public service.[69] Civil service reform was intended to reshape the political process into a public interest regime.[70] In fostering oversight and accountability through professional management, government sought to remove process deficiencies from the existing regulatory state.[71] By subjecting the administrative process to the rule of law, regulation became a more rational exercise.

The "affected with a public interest" theory of regulation, the formation of the civil service,[72] and the rule of law are related concepts.

Professional administration coupled with legal process defined public interest by adding fairness, transparency, and accountability to regulation. The convergence of these events marked the beginnings of public management. And it contained a necessary truth: The definitional vagueness of the "affected with a public interest" concept could be ameliorated by its connection to the rule of law, which forced rationality on the regulatory process.[73] The presence of a professional civil service removed some degree of politics from the process. In our pluralistic society, in which agreement on ends is never assured or expected, justice as process provides agreement on means. Indeed, for Stuart Hampshire, who stipulates substantive disagreements over concepts of justice in society, the common commitment to procedural justice is what permits a just society to emerge.[74]

## 3. Public Functions and Process Limits

Unmoored from its monopoly-based definition, and liberated from the constraints of the *Lochner* court,[75] the public interest concept flourished. During the New Deal, many kinds of previously unregulated private enterprises were subjected to government control.[76] An invigorated bureaucracy transformed government's relationship to the private sector. Not since the trust-busting days of the first Roosevelt administration had government service been such a creative enterprise.[77] The second Roosevelt administration acted through agencies (often independent and newly created, such as the Securities and Exchange Commission) and the extensive use of governmental corporations.[78] The notion of "yardstick" competition[79] gave government an entrepreneurial role, with major projects like the Tennessee Valley Authority.[80] But these efforts also suggested an arrogance – government can not only regulate better, it can compete better – that would prove to be politically unsustainable. The privatization movement may be government's way of doing penance for this earlier entrepreneurial hubris.

Greater calls for procedural regularity accompanied the New Deal's regulatory regimes. The private sector feared that administrative regulations would overwhelm the rule of law and jeopardize the premises of the liberal democratic state.[81] Therefore, conservatives, outflanked on the substance of New Deal legislation, turned to process as a means of defense.[82] The Administrative Procedure Act (APA)[83] ultimately emerged to accommodate the role of process in regulation. The APA remains the primary method for achieving procedural justice in the federal administrative state.[84]

The Due Process Clause was also invoked, but in its procedural, not substantive (i.e., *Lochner*ian), sense. The "public function" doctrine subjected some private activities to government control. In cases such as *Smith v. Allwright*[85] and *Marsh v. Alabama*,[86] the Supreme Court extended "state action" status to private entities, such as company towns, that by their monopoly positions inevitably performed public functions.[87] Echoing *Munn*, these cases essentially designated dominant private entities as affected with a public interest. The exercise of monopoly power by these private entities became the justification for due process regulation. These cases overcame limits on state action earlier declared under the Fourteenth Amendment.[88] In reconnecting due process to the exercise of private power, the Court in the public function cases achieved a broader level of public accountability and oversight.

Over time, the public function test waned in influence. The Court may have come to see it as the procedural equivalent of *Lochner*'s substantive due process test. Although continuing to recognize that public function tracks the monopoly concerns behind regulation,[89] the Court has abandoned the quest for defining state action through the public function test.[90]

The "public function" and "public interest" tests suffer from the same definitional weaknesses, so it is not surprising that the Court is hesitant to give them legal force. Along with "public use," these tests share a checkered history as legal concepts.[91] But since they still capture broad social concerns, they will not go away. To varying degrees, these phrases express the underlying public-private distinction that continues to demand judicial controls reflected in our political traditions.

## 4. The Overlap between State Action and Due Process

Two cases best illustrate the overlap between state action and due process: *Jackson v. Metropolitan Edison Co.*[92] and *Memphis Light, Gas & Water Division v. Craft*.[93] Both involved utilities (one private, one public) and the procedures required when a relatively minor property interest is transgressed – the termination of a customer's utility service for delinquency in payments. In *Jackson*, the Court found no state action despite the fact that the private utility was regulated as a natural monopoly, a circumstance that has traditionally signaled state involvement.[94] Chief Justice Rehnquist's majority opinion shows a Court looking for a state action escape route to avoid engaging in the unrewarding task of prescribing adversary-type procedures for new property claims.[95]

Later, in *Craft*, when the state action requirement could not be avoided because of public ownership, the Court exercised its "process is due" powers sparingly.[96] But even this concession did not satisfy Justice Stevens. He argued, in dissent, that the Court "trivializes" due process by not finding the existing termination procedures procedurally adequate.[97] This decision, and others like it,[98] narrowed the procedures mandated by due process. The unfortunate part of the *Jackson* decision is that it used the state action concept to achieve this goal. Either the majority's or the dissent's due process arguments in *Craft* could have achieved same result without narrowing state action. As a result, *Jackson* has become a major obstacle to applying due process to privatized activities, the setting that is of most concern here.

It is understandable that the Court did not want to become, in effect, the drafter of a code of procedures for state functions. This was a role it had earlier embraced in *Wong Yang Sung v. McGrath*,[99] then rejected, pursued again in *Goldberg v. Kelly*,[100] and finally abandoned with *Jackson*. By seeking various exit strategies, including a redefinition of state action, the Court has brought the era of procedural due process in the new property context to a close. But in terms of privatization, the Court has new choices: It can begin defining the state action requirement in ways independent of *Jackson* and it can embrace fair procedure alternatives that might arise in contractual or statutory form independent of *Goldberg*. The privatization setting is a ripe one for the application of the public-private distinction.

## C. THE NEW DUE PROCESS AND PRIVATIZATION

What process will now be due for new property? Richard Pierce predicts that due process protections will remain in only two circumstances: "The jobs of academics and the jobs of government employees whose skills are not transferable to private sector jobs."[101] These two categories offer compelling claims to constitutional consideration either because of First Amendment implications (in the case of academics) or because of the monopoly characteristics of certain types of government employment. Still, Pierce's due process world sounds ominous. It potentially excludes government employees, state and federal, whose interests are not elevated to special status.[102]

But there is no necessary reason why the courts must end up on this limb.[103] Due process should ensure nonarbitrary treatment by government, as William Van Alstyne long ago proposed[104] and Professors Shapiro and Levy recently have advocated.[105] Whether the government acts directly or through its private delegates, it should be subject to this condition.[106]

Pierce's due process world is not entirely bleak; it presupposes "private" hearing rights that can ameliorate its effect.[107] As is discussed in Chapter 8, the ability to contract for procedural requirements applies both to government and the private sector. Due process can be afforded to parties as part of the bargaining process, as Judith Resnick has suggested.[108] This alternative helps offset a right–privilege revival that otherwise would be a disastrous step backward for the administrative state.

## 1. Alternatives to Due Process

We are far from achieving a consistent theory of privatized due process,[109] but incremental private process alternatives are emerging under federal and state law. In the welfare situation, the use of block grants[110] in lieu of fixed statutory payments frees states from some of the individualized procedural requirements dictated by the Aid to Families with Dependent Children program in *Goldberg*. Although applicants may be asked to take the procedural bitter with the substantive sweet,[111] some process can still be due under state law. In fact, in some states, such as California, the notion of fair procedure has given those subject to monopolistic practices at hospitals, clubs, and associations a statutory right to due process.[112] By reconnecting the monopoly rationale to due process, these cases echo the Supreme Court's decision in *Munn*.[113]

These developments posit a regime in which procedures will be drawn from multiple sources in the future. And these procedural adjustments may already be reducing pressures on traditional state action–based due process actions. Due process cases seem not to be reaching the Court in large numbers,[114] which may indicate that alternative sources of procedures are filling the due process gap. The privatization movement, however, poses additional challenges. The more government functions are outsourced, the greater the pressure will be on those sources to respond procedurally. Either more private due process alternatives must be created or more federal procedural dictates will be needed.[115] This uncoordinated effort to provide private due process will have to be regularized.

Gillian Metzger has proposed a "private delegation doctrine" to help control activities privatized by government.[116] This doctrine shifts the focus from traditional state action and nondelegation theory to precise efforts to add procedures to delegated activities. The question for her becomes whether "grants of government power to private entities are adequately structured to preserve constitutional accountability."[117] When contractors act in behalf of government as they do in the Medicaid or nursing home situations, they exercise potentially coercive powers over members of the public. These delegatees should be required to provide sufficient process to third parties as a means of assuring constitutional accountability.

## 2. The Private Contractor Accountability Conundrum

In the variety of private contractor situations explored in Chapter 2, only some involve actions against individuals that could trigger due process protections. If, for example, the private contractors who interrogate and abuse prisoners in Iraq (the Abu Ghraib situation) were called to judgment, their status prevents them from being state (federal) actors subject to the due process clause under traditional theories.[118] In this situation, for an abused plaintiff to prevail against the private interrogator, he would need to rely on contractual due process alternatives described earlier.[119]

But sometimes the private contractors are doing work that does not injure individuals in a tort or property sense. For example, if a private contractor fails to do an adequate hurricane prevention plan for FEMA or provides a deficient statement of basis and purpose to EPA, there are no individuals who are injured. Rather this is an offense against the government or the public as a whole. Even if due process applied, it does not speak to such matters.[120] The "procedural" protections are different here – they consist of the public's right to know whether the private contractor is performing properly. This right may not be addressable under the Constitution, although "We the People" sovereignty gives it a conceptual legitimacy.

The clearest statutory expression of this right is the Freedom of Information Act (FOIA),[121] which mandates transparency in government. As the Supreme Court noted early on: "The basic purpose of FOIA is to ensure an informed citizenry, vital to the functioning of a democratic society, needed to check against corruption and to hold the governors accountable to the governed."[122] While the salutary purposes of the act have eroded due to the concerns with government secrecy after 2001,[123] it is still a force for public legitimacy.

For present purposes, it is sufficient to note that this provision applying as it does to government records (or to records held by government) does not reach documents in the hands of private contractors who are doing the work of government. By analogy to the state action requirement, the FOIA "agency" requirement has an exempting force that makes it harder for the public to learn what its private agents are doing. Given the perceived need for secrecy that is sweeping the executive branch in the wake of 9/11, the ability to keep private contractors out of FOIA makes transparency and accountability harder to achieve.[124]

## NOTES

1. *General Theory of Law and State* at 207.
2. Moe, *Governance Principles* at 37.
3. The dividing line between democracy and fascism consists of some limits upon the merger of the public and private sectors. *See* Paxton, *The Anatomy of Fascism* at 11 (stating that in fascism, "an individual had no rights outside [the] community interest").
4. *See* Dicey, *Introduction to the Study of the Law of the Constitution*. In the United States the law of the Constitution includes the vast field of administrative law. *See* n. 10.

5. *See* Rodin & Steinberg, *Introduction: Incivility and Public Discourse* at 7–11. *See generally* Jean L. Cohen & Andrew Arato, *Civil Society and Political Theory* (describing civil society).

6. Smelser, *A Paradox of Public Discourse and Political Democracy* at 179.

7. Taggart, *The Province of Administrative Law Determined?* at 4.

8. Justinian's Digest read as follows: "There are two branches of legal study: public and private law. Public law is that which respects the establishment of the Roman commonwealth, private that which respects individuals' interests, some matters being of public and others of private interest." Dig. 1.1.1.2 1 The Digest of Justinian 1.

9. *See generally* Faulkner, *Public Services, Citizenship and the State: The British Experience 1967–97* at 36–37 (discussing how civil law tradition connected the public interest to public law); Freedland, *Law, Public Services, and Citizenship – New Domains, New Regimes?* at 33–34; Harlow, *Public Service, Market Ideology, and Citizenship* at 49.

10. Public law in common-law America and England is far less well developed than in civil law Europe. However, various public law doctrines have been incorporated in our system of administrative law. *See* Pierce et al., *Administrative Law and Process* at 1.1. *See generally* Tomkins, *Public Law* (describing the development of English public law).

11. *See* Verkuil, *Separation of Powers, the Rule of Law and the Idea of Independence* at 340–41 (connecting the public interest to the rule of law); Verkuil, *Understanding the "Public Interest" Justification for Government Actions* at 142 (describing various formulations of the public interest and seeking to define it in rule of law terms).

12. *See, e.g.*, Silver & Cross, *What's Not To Like About Being a Lawyer?* at 1479 (arguing that private sector lawyers, by pursuing their self-interest, make an "enormous economic contribution to social welfare").

13. *See* Schlesinger, *The Coming of the New Deal* at 87–102, 319–34 (describing the creation of the National Recovery Administration and the Tennessee Valley Authority).

14. *See* Verkuil, *Reverse Yardstick Competition* at 4–5 (describing how Reaganomics challenged assumptions behind the New Deal).

15. *See, e.g.*, Krugman, *The Fighting Moderates* at A19 ("It takes an act of willful blindness not to see that the Bush plan for Social Security is intended, in essence, to dismantle the most important achievement of the New Deal.").

16. Sunstein, *Free Markets and Social Justice* at 271–82 (regulatory paradoxes involve regulations that fail to produce a net benefit to society).

17. Professor Sunstein argues for a "cost-benefit state" that tests the effectiveness of regulations, but does not displace them. *See id.* at Ch. 13.

18. *See* Dig. 1.1.1.2–4 1 The Digest of Justinian 1 (noting that some matters of private law can be of public interest and dividing private law into a tripartite structure, including natural law, the law of nations, and civil law).

19. Indeed, even in France, which has always embraced the public-private distinction, the dividing line between the ordinary and administrative courts sometimes has to be adjudicated by the Tribunal des Conflits. *See* Brown et al., *French Administrative Law* at 144–45.

20. For a good discussion of the public-private distinction as it relates to English common and public law, *see* Loughlin, *The Idea of Public Law* at 6, 77–80.

21. Because much of the common law has become statutory, the work of legislatures amounts to the publicization of private law. And of course, contracts are only enforceable through public acts. *See* Hayek, *The Constitution of Liberty* at 230–32; Calabresi, *A Common Law in the Age of Statutes* at 135–38. *See also* Ripstein, *Private Order and Public Justice: Kant and Rawls*, (private ordering reforms public justice).

22. *See, e.g.*, Age Discrimination in Employment Act (ADEA) (displacing "private" tort remedies with government regulatory programs).

23. *See Lawrence v. Texas*, 539 U.S. 558 (sodomy laws), overruling *Bowers v. Hardwick.*

24. For example, the First Amendment in separating church and state ensures a "private sector" for religion. And the Due Process Clause also covers even larger notions of privacy. *See Lawrence v. Texas*, 539 U.S. at 567, 578–79 (holding that consensual and private sex acts may not be reached by sodomy laws); cf. Franke, *The Domesticated Liberty of Lawrence v. Texas* at 1401–04 (asserting that the case announces a "privatized liberty right").

25. *See* Ryfe, *Deliberative Democracy and Public Discourse* at 40, 42–45 (comparing deliberative democracy to individual rights and social choice theories and noting that many Americans prefer "political privatization"). *But see* Posner, *Law, Pragmatism, and Democracy* (expressing generally critical views of deliberative democracy).

26. The question of privatization becomes the political one of how far "the individualization of judgments about what constitutes public value" can or should go in our society. *See* Moore, *Introduction to Symposium, Public Values in an Era of Privatization* at 1218 (discussing the left–right politics of the privatization debate).

27. *See* Ayres & Braithwaite, *Responsive Regulation* (introducing concept of enforced self-regulation).

28. Hampshire, *Justice Is Conflict* at 4. Hampshire makes a powerful case for "adversarial thinking" as a constraint on human nature. *See id.* at 12. In the privatization setting, this adversarial posture is retained when procedures are transferred along with delegated duties. *See* nn. 148–49 and accompanying text.

29. Social contract theorists from John Locke to John Rawls have understood the role of government in civil society to be a limited and consensual one. For Locke, the purpose of government (commonwealth) was the preservation of

both private property and the civil society. But he talks about the need for the ruler to act for the "public good." Locke, *Two Treatises of Government* 124–25; *see* Rawls, *A Theory of Justice* at 11–17. One difference between Locke and Rawls, however, is that Locke accepts that there is a "public body" that has a right to preserve itself, whereas Rawls's liberalism rejects the notion of political society as a community. *See* Josephson, *The Great Art of Government – Locke's Use of Consent* at 11–12.

30. *See* Lovejoy, *The Glorious Revolution in America* at 235–70 (describing how the colonies responded to the 1688 Glorious Revolution in England). Locke's influence on the Constitution and the Declaration of Independence is well established. *See* Wood, *The Creation of the American Republic, 1776–1787* at 14 (showing how American colonists "borrowed promiscuously" from John Locke, among others); *see also Mistretta*, 488 U.S. at 420–21 (Scalia, J., dissenting) (quoting John Locke on nondelegation of legislative powers). *See generally* Hayek, *The Constitution of Liberty* at 169–71 (placing Locke at the center of the Glorious Revolution's creation of the rule of law).

31. Underpinning Locke in this regard was Benedict de Spinoza, who relied on a public-private dichotomy as a way to protect the rights of religious minorities. *See* Nadler, *Spinoza's Heresy* at 19–22. The motivation for Spinoza's political philosophy was the "theologico-political problem," the resolution of which required the separation of church and state. Smith, *Spinoza, Liberalism, and the Question of Jewish Identity* at 1–27; Smith, *On Leo Strauss's Critique of Spinoza* at 751–52. Spinoza was probably read by Locke and Thomas Jefferson. *See* Goldstein, *Reasonable Doubt* at A13.

32. *See generally* Von Humboldt & Burrow, *The Limits of State Action*. Von Humboldt's classic work, which inspired John Stuart Mill's *On Liberty*, focused on the need to restrain government activity in order to preserve individual freedom.

33. The Constitution uses the word "public" in several ways: "public money," U.S. Const. art. I, § 9, cl. 7; "public acts," U.S. Const. art. IV, 1; "public danger," U.S. Const. amend. V; "public debt," U.S. Const. amend. XIV, 4. Although the word "private" is not attached to "property" in the Due Process Clause of the Fifth and Fourteenth Amendments, its presence can be assumed. The phrase "private property" is used in the Just Compensation Clause of the Fifth Amendment. It should be noted that the word "property" may not mean the same thing in these different constitutional contexts. *See* Merrill, *The Landscape of Constitutional Property* at 893, 954–56; *see also E. Enterprises*, 524 U.S. at 557 (Breyer, J., dissenting) ("[Property] appears in the midst of different phrases with somewhat different objectives, thereby permitting differences in the way in which the term is interpreted.").

34. This is the purpose of the Ninth and Tenth Amendments which speak of rights "retained by" or "reserved to" the people. *See* U.S. Const. amends. IX & X; Barnett, *Restoring the Lost Constitution* at 354–57 (rejecting the social contract theory but urging protection of liberty through application of the Ninth and Tenth Amendments).

35. *See generally* Dicey, *Introduction to the Study of the Law of the Constitution* at 179–201, 324–401 (providing the classic description of the role and limits of constitutional law and administrative law in England).

36. U.S. Const. amend. V ("Nor shall private property be taken for public use, without just compensation.").

37. The Court has left it largely to Congress or state legislatures to decide what is a public use. *See, e.g., Midkiff*, 467 U.S. at 239–43 (state); *Berman*, 348 U.S. at 32–33 (federal). *See generally*, Meidinger, *The "Public Uses" of Eminent Domain: History and Policy)* (discussing shifting definitions of public use).

38. *See Kelo*, 843 A.2d 500 (holding economic development by private entities an acceptable public use under federal and state constitutions over strong dissents), aff'd., 545 U.S. 469; *Hathcock*, 684 N.W.2d at 788 (holding condemnation for a business park fails the public use test).

39. *County of Wayne v. Hathcock*, 684 N.W.2d 765.

40. *See* id. at 786–87 (overruling *Poletown Neighborhood Council*, 304 N.W.2d 455).

41. The *Hathcock* court limited the condemnation of private property for transfer to private hands under the public use doctrine to situations where there was: (1) public necessity; (2) public oversight; and (3) a public concern. *See id.* at 781–83. These limitations give meaning to a concept of public use that respects public limits and also accountability (oversight).

42. 843 A.2d 500, *aff'd*, 545 U.S. 469 (5–4); *see* discussion n. 38 and accompanying text.

43. *Kelo*, 843 A.2d at 561–62.

44. *See* Sterk, *The Federalist Dimension of Regulatory Takings Jurisprudence* at 222–26 (explaining the confused results in takings cases as an (overlooked) function of federalism).

45. *Kelo*, 545 U.S. at 506 (Thomas, J., dissenting).

46. *Id.* at 488 (rejecting a bright line rule against transfers of private property to private developers and eschewing "empirical debates over the wisdom of takings").

47. Justice O'Connor identified three categories of takings: transfers of private property to public ownership (e.g., for roads); transfers to common carriers (e.g., railroad rights of way); and limited transfers to satisfy public purposes. *Id.* at 497–98 (O'Connor, J., dissenting). Although *Kelo* involved the third category, with its still unresolved dimensions, the second category reflects the "affected with a public interest" test, discussed in the next part.

48. *Id.* at 505.

49. *Id.* at 506–09. Justice Thomas also referred to the common law background of the Constitution as reinforcing a narrower (Blackstone-inspired) definition of public use. *Id.* at 505–06.

50. *See* Epstein, *Supreme Folly* at A14 (calling the majority opinion "a new low point in the Supreme Court's takings jurisprudence").

51. *See* discussion nn. 33–36 and accompanying text.

52. *See Charles River Bridge*, 36 U.S. at 549–52 (holding that the Contract Clause cannot be used to protect existing state-chartered bridges from new competition); *see also* Butler, *Nineteenth Century Jurisdictional Competition in the Granting of Corporate Privileges* at 138–42 (discussing abuses of the special charter system).

53. *See Trustees of Dartmouth Coll. v. Woodward*, 17 U.S. (4 Wheat) at 707–12 (explaining that the State cannot abrogate a grant to a private corporation by the public action of reincorporation).

54. Epstein, *Bargaining with the State* at 107 (emphasizing importance of limited liability to the growth of the economy).

55. 94 U.S. 113.

56. *Id.* at 123–25; *see also* Loughlin, *The Idea of Public Law* at 77–80 (describing the emergence of the public-private distinction in English law).

57. The common law had always subjected "common carriers" to absolute liability when they exercised their economic powers to raise prices and restrict output. Hackmen, ferrymen, wharfmen, innkeepers, and the like had economic control over commerce that rendered them common rather than private carriers. *See generally* Hale, *The History of Common Law of England* (providing an overview of English law). The category of common carriers became loosely tied to the exercise of monopoly power.

58. Holmes questioned whether there should be special liability rules for all common carriers but reserved some room for special cases, such as railroads, which clearly possessed monopoly power. *See* Holmes, *The Common Law* 155–62; Verkuil, *Privatizing Due Process* at 670–71; *see also The Civil Rights Cases*, 109 U.S. at 37–38 (Harlan, J., dissenting), focusing on the public use aspects of *Munn*.

59. 198 U.S. 45.

60. Of course, the regulation of monopoly had been granted statutory status by the Sherman Act after the *Munn* decision. This statutory power provided direct regulation to support, if not supplant, the need for public interest regulation. *See* Sherman Act of 1890. Also, in 1887, the Interstate Commerce Commission established rate regulation. *See* Nelson, *The Roots of American Bureaucracy* at 130–33.

61. *See* Strauss, *Why Was Lochner Wrong?* at 374–75 (arguing that *Lochner's* error was in exalting liberty of contract). *But see* Epstein, *The Perils of Posnerian Pragmatism* at 654–55 (challenging Strauss' views on *Lochner*); Posner,

*Pragmatic Liberalism Versus Classical Liberalism* at 661 (assailing Epstein's desire to make "freedom of contract the supreme constitutional principle").

62. *See* Barnett, *Restoring the Lost Constitution* at 211–18, 222–23 (extolling the virtues of *Lochner* and theorizing about its revival); *see also* Morrison, *Lamenting* Lochner's *Loss: Randy Barnett's Case for a Libertarian Constitution* at 840–45 (critiquing the libertarian constitution).

63. *See Lochner*, 198 U.S. at 74–76 (Holmes, J., dissenting) ("The Fourteenth Amendment does not enact Mr. Herbert Spencer's Social Statics.").

64. *See Nebbia*, 291 U.S. at 538–39 (permitting state regulation of retail milk prices and effectively undermining the monopoly-based limitation upon the "affected with a public interest" concept). *But see Mayflower Farms, Inc.*, 297 U.S. at 274 (striking down a New York milk regulation designed to freeze out competitors). *See generally* Cushman, *The Great Depression and the New Deal* (describing post-*Nebbia* New Deal cases that preserved the monopoly distinction).

65. *See* Horwitz, *The History of the Public-Private Distinction* at 1426–27; *see also* Kennedy, *The Stages of the Decline of the Public-Private Distinction* at 1351–57 (discussing the merger of public and private). *But see* Sunstein, *Lochner's Legacy* at 874–75 (reaffirming *Lochner's* assumption about neutrality of the common law in the state action context).

66. *See* Buchanan & Tulloch, *The Calculus of Consent* (applying public choice theory to the self-interested decisions of administrators). *See generally* Harrison, Morgan, & Verkuil, at 56–120, 250–421 (describing public choice critiques of regulation); Verkuil, *Understanding Public Interest* at 146–50 (discussing ways in which the public interest is still evoked).

67. Interestingly, if *Lochner's* substantive due process approach is to be revived, as Professor Barnett has suggested, *see* Barnett, *Restoring the Lost Constitution* at 120–24, the public interest justification could be attacked directly through the reemergence of its monopoly-based rationale. *See also* Ackerman, *Social Justice in the Liberal State* at 264–66 (comparing laissez-faire to "an active, yet principled, conception of governmental regulation").

68. *See, e.g.*, Schlesinger, *The Age of Jackson* at 45–47 (describing President Jackson's doctrine of "rotation in office," also known as the spoils system).

69. *See* Nelson, *The Roots of American Bureaucracy*, at 119–25 (providing a thorough analysis of the civil service reform period of the late nineteenth century).

70. *See* Civil Service (Pendleton) Act, 22 Stat. 403 (1883).

71. In England, the notion of civil service predated our own. *See* Dicey, *Introduction to the Study of the Law of the Constitution* at 384–87 (describing servants of the Crown and distinguishing the English Civil Service under the rule of law from the French *droit administratif*).

72. Professor Nelson attributes the creation of the term "civil service" to British reformers. *See* Nelson, *The Roots of American Bureaucracy* at 119. The

connection of "civil service" to "civil society," mentioned earlier, *see* discussion nn. 13–14 and accompanying text, is also of significance.

73. *See* Verkuil, *Understanding Public Interest* at 146–49 (explaining the historical concept of public interest in rule of law terms).

74. *See* Hampshire, *Justice is Conflict* at 4–5 (connecting procedural justice to adversary reasoning); *see also* discussion at n. 28 and accompanying text.

75. After *Nebbia*, challenges to the substance of the regulation were virtually foreclosed. *See* Karl, *The Uneasy State* at 131–39 (describing the heights of New Deal social legislation).

76. *See* Verkuil, *Understanding Public Interest* at 142 (listing the Federal Communications Commission as a New Deal agency whose mandate was to regulate in "the public interest, convenience and necessity"); *see also* Landis, *The Administrative Process* at 40–41 (describing the virtues of regulatory agencies); Sandel, *Democracy's Discontent* at 250–55 (comparing the National Recovery Administration to other New Deal regulatory initiatives).

77. The New Deal made the bureaucracy a challenging profession precisely because its powers could be exercised so creatively. *See* Irons, *The New Deal Lawyers* (documenting the career paths in government of top law school graduates); *see also* Lilienthal, *The Journals of David E. Lilienthal – The TVA Years, 1939–1945* at 10–13, 549 (discussing author's years at Harvard Law School and his relationship to Felix Frankfurter).

78. *See Lebron*, 513 U.S. at 394 (Scalia, J.) (describing the New Deal as the "heyday of those corporations").

79. *See* Harrison, *Yardstick Competition: A Prematurely Discarded Form of Regulatory Relief* at 466.

80. *See generally* Lilienthal, n. 77 (describing the TVA experience).

81. Roscoe Pound, as chair of the American Bar Association Committee to Create the Administrative Procedure Act, was a most outspoken advocate of the New Deal's penchant for "administrative absolutism." *See 63 A.B.A. Rep. 339–46* (1938); *see generally* Verkuil, *The Emerging Concept of Administrative Procedure* at 268–70 (discussing the New Deal's challenges to established notions of the rule of law).

82. *See* Verkuil, *The Emerging Concept of Administrative Procedure* at 270–72 (describing the battle between procedural conservatives and regulatory liberals that led to the compromise of the Administrative Procedure Act).

83. 5 U.S.C. §§ 551–559, 701–706.

84. *See generally* Pierce, Shapiro, & Verkuil, *Administrative Law and Process* at 2.3 (describing the APA's role).

85. 321 U.S. 649.

86. 326 U.S. 501.

87. *See Marsh*, 326 U.S. at 506 (finding that a "company" town performs public functions and is subject to First Amendment control); *Smith*, 321 U.S. at

663–64 (noting that conduct of elections is a public functions); *see also Terry*, 345 U.S. at 469 (same); Metzger, *Privatization as Delegation* at 1422–24 (describing public functions).

88. *See The Civil Rights Cases*, 109 U.S. at 25–26 (declaring a federal statute that would have prevented certain private businesses from discriminating unconstitutional under the Fourteenth Amendment); *see also* Verkuil, *Privatizing Due Process* at 670 (discussing how the "Supreme Court limited the potential reach of the Due Process clause in the Civil Rights Cases").

89. The monopoly point was raised by the Court in *Flagg Bros.*, 436 U.S. at 162, when it distinguished the private monopoly in *Marsh* from the wide number of choices debtors and creditors have under the state self-help statute in *Flagg*. Professor Metzger also has connected the state action cases to the Court's earlier concerns with private delegations in cases such as *Carter Coal*. *See* Metzger, *Privatization as Delegation* at 1444 (noting this as a link the Court itself has failed to make).

90. *See, e.g., Jackson*, 419 U.S. at 348 (regulation of private utility is not "state action" under the due process clause of the Fourteenth Amendment); *see also* Verkuil, *Privatizing Due Process* at 674–75 (describing the state action pullback led by *Jackson*).

91. Intriguingly, those members of the Court who hesitate to give these open-ended terms legal content have in their *Kelo* dissents embarked on a comparable attempt to define "public use" under the Fifth Amendment. *See* discussion nn. 49–53 and accompanying text.

92. 419 U.S. 345.

93. 436 U.S. 1.

94. *See Munn*, 94 U.S. at 130 (holding state regulation of private elevators as a business "affected with a public interest"). In Justice Rehnquist's majority opinion in *Jackson*, the Court rejected the affected with a public interest test that historically placed private monopolies under state regulatory control. 419 U.S. at 353–54. *See, e.g., Pollak*, 343 U.S. at 462 (explaining that, in finding that the case invoked the Due Process Clause, the Court did not rely on the fact that the party conducted a public utility business or the fact that the party enjoyed a monopoly on the public transportation system in the District of Columbia). The majority in *Jackson* cited *Nebbia* for the proposition that businesses need not be monopolistic to justify regulation. It ultimately decided that *Jackson* fell on the private side of the state action debate, relying on *Moose Lodge No. 107*, 407 U.S. 163.

95. Justices Brennan and Marshall, in separate dissents, sought to avoid the merits in *Jackson* by dismissing the writ as improvidently granted. *See Jackson*, 419 U.S. at 365–74 (Brennan, J. & Marshall, J., dissenting) (arguing that the petitioner did not have a basis for the claim of entitlement). Justice Marshall also postulated a narrow procedural duty on the utility that involved only notice and someone to contact before service was cut off. *Id.* at 373 (Marshall, J.,

dissenting) (explaining the requirement to provide notice before termination of service). This duty was similar to what the utility already provided in its tariffs. *See id.* at 345 n.1 (illustrating the language of Rule 15 of the tariff that allows the company to terminate service on reasonable notice).

96. Justice Powell's opinion for the majority in *Craft* required only notice and the availability of some person at the utility to hear a challenge to a bill as due process procedures. 436 U.S. at 12–13.

97. *Id.* at 22 (Stevens, J., dissenting).

98. Compare *Sandin*, 515 U.S. 472 (finding that there was no liberty interest in prison disciplinary segregation for the use of foul and abusive language), with *Goss*, 419 U.S. 565 (holding that minimal procedures were due in a school suspension situation).

99. *See* 339 U.S. 33 (equating administrative due process in the immigration setting with APA formal adjudication). Although that decision was reversed by Congress, it had the virtue of using an available procedural code as a template. *See Marcello*, 349 U.S. 302 (upholding legislation exempting procedures from APA formal adjudication). In the *Goldberg* new property context, there is no available template because informal adjudication procedures under the APA are virtually nonexistent.

100. 397 U.S. 254 (finding due process applicable to the pretermination phase of welfare benefits denials).

101. *See* Pierce, *The Due Process Counterrevolution of the 1990s* at 1996 (predicting a revival of the rights–privilege distinction). Pierce limits procedurally protected government jobs to those without private sector analogues, not to government jobs generally. He believes the latter will be covered only by civil service or contract claims in the future. *Id.* at 1992–94; *see also Bd. of Educ. of Paris Union Sch. Dist.*, 466 U.S. 377, *aff'g* 706 F.2d 1435 (upholding a state employee's right to a due process hearing with reservations expressed in Judge Posner's dissent.)

102. For example, what happens to Rachel Brawner, the cafeteria worker? Because she has neither academic nor other unique skills that would trigger Pierce's two exceptions, she can be arbitrarily denied access to her job site. *See Cafeteria & Rest. Workers Union*, 367 U.S. 886 (deciding a case that was a precursor to Goldberg and affirming the lower court's decision to deny Rachel Brawner's due process claim). Perhaps the answer is that she will be adequately protected procedurally through her union or through arbitration agreements that employees are increasingly required to accept as a condition of employment. *See* nn. 118–21 and accompanying text. Private due process, in other words, must come to the rescue if Pierce's right-privilege distinction is revived.

103. The recent decision in *Town of Castle Rock v. Gonzales*, 545 U.S. 748, in denying a property interest in a state restraining order raises questions about the due process direction of the Court in the future.

104. *See* Alstyne, *The Demise of the Right–Privilege Distinction in American Con-stitutional Law* (arguing that the right-privilege distinction is not effective in protecting individuals against arbitrary treatment by the government and proposing an alternative due process control).

105. *See* Shapiro & Levy, *Government Benefits and the Rule of Law: Towards a Standards Based Theory of Due Process* at 148–49 (comparing the Van Alstyne approach to the authors' standards-based approach).

106. *See* Metzger, *Privatization as Delegation* at 1394–1400 (describing privatized functions of government that retain procedural controls).

107. *See* Pierce, *The Due Process Counterrevolution of the 1990s* at 1996 (acknowl-edging private procedural alternatives to due process).

108. *See* Resnick, *Procedure as Contract.*

109. *See* Verkuil, *Privatizing Due Process* at 987–89 (describing a patchwork quilt of alternative private procedures through contract (arbitration, state contract, and tort law and federal substantive mandates).

110. *See* The Personal Responsibility and Work Opportunity Act 110 Stat. 2105 (1996) (codified at 42 U.S.C) (expressly declaring that "no individual enti-tlement" exists); *see also* Farina, *On Misusing "Revolution" and "Reform": Procedural Due Process and the New Welfare Act* at 608–09 (rebutting the due process demise theory in welfare).

111. *See Arnett*, 416 U.S. 134 (Rehnquist, J.) (holding that the posttermination procedures at issue adequately protected the federal employee's liberty inter-est).

112. *See, e.g., Unnamed Physicians v. Bd. of Trade*, 113 Cal. Rptr. 2d 309 (due process rights delegated to private sector); *see generally* Verkuil, *Privatizing Due Process* at 676–78 (discussing cases and statutes).

113. *See* nn. 55–58.

114. In the 1970s (the ten terms beginning with October 1970) there were 293 U.S. Supreme Court cases addressing due process, compared with only 109 in the ten-year period starting with the October 1994 term. The trend continues throughout the 1990s and beyond. In the October 1992–93 terms, there were thirty-four due process cases, but only twenty-two in the 1994–96 terms, and nineteen in the 2002–03 terms.

115. *See* Verkuil, *Privatizing Due Process* at 690–92 (recommending the develop-ment of a new APA to apply to privatized functions of government).

116. Metzger, *Privatization as Delegation* at 1437–42.

117. *Id.* at 1456.

118. The private interrogators are not subject to punishment under the Uniform Code of Military Justice, which regulates conduct of the military.

119. Of course, Iraqi prisoners make unlikely plaintiffs for many reasons, including the military setting.

120. *Bi-Metallic Investment Co.*, 239 U.S. 441 (Holmes, J.) (where all are "equally concerned" no due process claim can be made).

121. 5 U.S.C. § 552.

122. *Robbins Tire & Rubber Co.*, 437 U.S. at 242.

123. In October 2001, Attorney General Ashcroft issued a memorandum to agencies restricting disclosure, reversing an earlier Clinton administration memorandum that admonished agencies to adopt a "presumption of disclosure." *See Ashcroft Memorandum to Heads of All Departments and Agencies* (Oct. 12, 2001).

124. *See* Shapiro & Steinzor, *The People's Agent: Executive Branch Secrecy and Accountability in an Age of Terror* (describing how secrecy is replacing transparency in government).

# 5 THE CASE FOR CONSTITUTIONAL GOVERNANCE

The buck stops here.

– Harry S Truman[1]

Our structural Constitution is all about governance or, more precisely, democratic governance, as Justice Breyer has recently reminded us.[2] This insight vindicates the "We the People" view of sovereignty. The People, by delegating her sovereign powers to the political branches, expects democratic governance. The Constitution was designed to provide it. And chief executives like the redoubtable Harry Truman understood how to implement it.

Separation of powers helps to ensure democratic governance by assigning duties to separate political branches, and by preventing those branches from transferring or reassigning those duties. Much of the duty to govern is assigned to the Executive under Article II.[3] The Executive power and the Commander-in-Chief power ensure that the military remains subject to civilian control.[4] Other clauses ensure executive control of the administration. The president does not act alone, of course; he works through a network of constitutionally defined deputies.[5]

These officials, designated "Officers of the United States" under Article II, conduct all significant public duties not performed directly by the president. Presidential control of these officers is ensured through the ability to require "the Opinion, in writing, of the principal Officer in each of the executive Departments."[6] And the president's duty to "take Care that the Laws be faithfully executed"[7] is a constitutional obligation. Like the oath itself, it is a promise to Congress and the people that the laws (including the Constitution) will be defended and enforced. The president is the Constitution's most duty-bound actor.[8] He must delegate with care to public officials and he has no express authority to delegate to private officials.

The only reference in the Constitution arguably relevant to delegation to private parties is the Marque and Reprisal Clause.[9] That clause at one time contemplated using "privateers" to act for the government. It has important limitations. The Constitution requires congressional approval for its implementation (Art. I, Section 8) and it forbids states from issuing them (Art. I, Section 10). Privateers have not been considered a policy option since the administration of Andrew Jackson,[10] but the Clause was brought up in connection with the Iran–Contra investigation.[11] It is connected to an accountability theory of government because the president cannot act on his own to privatize; she must secure congressional approval to do so. By analogy, when it comes to the outsourcing of government duties to private contractors, modern "privateers", Congress has a comparable obligation to act.

## A. CONSTITUTIONAL RESTRAINTS ON DELEGATION

The president appoints officers pursuant to the Appointments Clause. Congress, through the Senate, advises and consents to many of the appointments. This clause provides horizontal protections (the executive is protected against congressional usurpation) and vertical protections (both political branches are "protected" from delegating to private actors).[12] The former protections prevent Congress from aggrandizing power by exerting control over the appointment and removal of executive officials.[13] The latter protect against delegations to those not under the oath requirement. Although issues still arise related to this horizontal effect of separation of powers,[14] they are not the main concern here. It is the vertical effect that is directly implicated in the privatization setting.

If the president assigns duties to private contractors that are normally performed by either principal or "inferior"[15] officers of the United States, the vertical dimension of separation of powers is triggered. Officers of the United States "exercis[e] significant authority"[16];

this is authority inherent in the executive function. Transfer of this function to private hands potentially violates authority delegated to the executive. For example, the president appoints military officers, and they are within the constraints of this requirement.[17] These officers exercise command authority that cannot devolve to private contractors. Thus, when private contractors interrogate prisoners in Iraq or particulate in military actions involving the use of force, they usurp public authority, unless Congress has approved. The exercise of this authority is a public function, which makes the phrase "private military"[18] an oxymoron offensive to our Constitution.

On the civilian side, the vertical dimension is not as clearly defined. The Office of Legal Counsel Memorandum discussing the horizontal/vertical dichotomy cites only two "vertical" cases, *Northern Pipeline* and *Schechter Poultry*, neither of which is really applicable to the private contractor situation.[19] Cases that directly forbid delegations by the president of significant government authority to private hands are not easy to find. This may be due to any one of three factors: the absence of any instances of policy delegations to private hands (a factual question); the assumption that such delegations are within the executive power (a legal question explored here); or, more likely, procedural limitations such as justiciability and standing[20] that inhibit such precedents from emerging.

The theory of nondelegation to private hands derives from agency law. According to Justice Story: "The general rule is that a delegated authority cannot be delegated."[21] Since under our Constitution the president already has been delegated powers by the People, attempts to delegate further (beyond the limits of the Appointments Clause) are without constitutional authority. Agency cost theory, explored in Chapter 8 confirms the economic importance of honoring this principle.

The principle of public responsibility for public acts is thus a constitutional rule that requires explanatory force. What is needed is a corollary to the "antiaggrandizement" principle, which limits Congress's ability to usurp the president's appointing and removal authority.[22] Such a principle (the "antidevolution principle") would prevent the president from aggrandizing power at the expense of Congress by privatizing what would otherwise be executive functions under Article II.

The current urge to privatize encourages the development of such a principle. In the military setting, the president is overseeing unprecedented delegations of combat authority to private hands[23] in situations where Congress has not acted to authorize such delegations.[24] The president's authority is at its "lowest ebb"[25] when he acts without congressional authorization. Similar concerns arise from the use of private contractors to implement domestic programs.

To make matters worse, privatized actions are often nontransparent. FOIA is inapplicable to private contractors, a deficiency of democratic control.[26] The desire for secrecy may be one of the motivations for executive delegations of significant authority to private contractors, at least for some presidents. During Iran–Contra, the Reagan White House in effect ran a private war in Nicaragua against Congress's instructions. Harry Truman is said to have been appalled by such actions.[27]

The antidevolution principle employs the Appointments, Opinion in Writing and Take Care clauses to prevent the president's transfer of policy making authority to private hands. The goal is to protect Congress and the people from the loss of democratic accountability. But the principle also insulates the president from the inadvisable and uncontrolled use of private contractors.

The lack of direct precedents on vertical restraints is not surprising. However, related theories and cases can be employed to establish boundaries on the delegation of public power to private hands.

## 1. Due Process Limits on Private Delegations

*Carter v. Carter Coal*[28] provides one avenue. Under the Bituminous Coal Conservation Act[29] district boards elected by coal operators and unions would set wages binding on all coal producers and enforceable without public review. The Court set aside this grant of private decision-making power on nondelegation and due process grounds. Although the nondelegation doctrine has waned in influence,[30] the due process dimension has enduring explanatory power. What offended the Court then and would do so now is that the public interest was nowhere represented in this arrangement. As Lawrence Tribe has noted, "[t]he judicial hostility to private lawmaking represents a persistent theme in American constitutional law."[31]

In *Carter Coal*, the private decision arrangement could only be cured by the inclusion of a public decider in the process.[32] It was different from the pure *Schechter*-type nondelegation challenges that require Congress to write adequate standards. Of course, vertical delegations of governmental power to private contractors do not always involve private decision making in the *Carter* sense. But the requirement of a public actor, even if not a decider, is still the relevant consideration. In requiring in a public decider, due process "publicizes" the grant of power by making it transparent to the public.[33]

This transparency principle is reflected in statutes that apply openness requirements to private groups. The Federal Advisory Committee Act (FACA) ensures some measure of transparency when private persons participate in actions of the government.[34] Private parties can be exempted from FACA because of executive privilege concerns[35] which reflect countervailing constitutional interests. The accountability principles expressed in FACA and *Carter Coal*[36] reflect a commitment to democratic governance in Justice Breyer's active liberty sense.[37] They should be compromised only for the strongest of reasons.

## 2. Appointments Clause Limits on Private Delegations

The Appointments Clause can be viewed as a democracy-forcing requirement. Part of its purpose is to check the exercise of private power on government. Due process deters private delegations of significant government authority by preventing conflicts of interest. But it cannot do the job alone. The Appointments Clause anoints public officials to conduct the business of government. The Clause covers principal and "inferior" Officers of the United States who are defined as those who exercise "significant authority."[38] They are contrasted with "employees," who do not. But this concept only begins the inquiry. If significant authority were the only criterion, many private contractors, including not only employees of the private military and contractors in Katrina relief but also peer review panels and even RAND consultants, might be within its terms. The sole question would be whether private contractors exercised significant authority, or "insignificant" authority, that is, whether they performed duties of officers rather than employees.[39]

But whether that one criterion is a sufficient definition of officers under the Appointments Clause is debatable. The *Buckley* Court also staked out two other criteria for officer status: duration of employment and the permanent nature of the duties assigned.[40] Because *Buckley* itself involved members of the Federal Election Commission, there was no doubt that all three criteria were satisfied (nor indeed any likelihood that their duties would be outsourced to private contractors). The question for Appointments Clause purposes is whether these criteria are independent or alternative.

This debate has divided two presidential administrations. The first Bush administration (through its Office of Legal Counsel [OLC]) argued for the unconstitutionality of *qui tam* actions[41] on this ground.[42] In asserting that the criterion of significant authority under the Appointments Clause stood alone, the OLC reached the conclusion that the private relator who initiated an action on behalf of the government would be exercising constitutional authority reserved to the Attorney General.[43]

This strict reading of the Appointments Clause has direct application to the private contractor situation. It makes it more likely that outsourcing decisions could be held to violate that clause. Private contractors delegated "significant authority," would, like *qui tam* relators, *ipso facto* become unconstitutional actors. If *qui tam* relators were to fall, private contractors exercising significant authority would not be far behind.[44] The Supreme Court has addressed but not completely resolved the constitutionality of *qui tam* actions.[45] So where does that leave privatization decisions? The second Bush administration has been encouraging such delegations to their constitutional limits. But under the Bush I OLC interpretation, any delegation that devolves "significant authority" is suspect. If the Bush II administration does not accept this position, which interpretation should carry the day?

Fortunately for the privatization movement, the Clinton administration intervened between Bushes I and II. President Clinton's OLC expressly disavowed the earlier Bush OLC opinion. It argued instead for the independent status of each of the three Appointments Clause criteria considered by *Buckley*.[46] In doing so, of course, it sought to preserve *qui tam* actions, not to opine on private delegations. The Bush II administration has not weighed in on the *qui tam* debate. Perhaps the administration's reluctance to disturb the Clinton view reflects doubts about the independant counsel statute (now expired) rather than with *qui tam* actions specifically.[47]

The Clinton position is convincing in its analysis. In recognizing the three criteria in *Buckley* that expand the definition of officers beyond the lone criterion of significant authority, it justifies *qui tam* relators. But the opinion helps preserve private contractors. This may be fitting since the False Claims Act can also be used to control private contractors. Given the increased use of single-sourced, noncompetitive bid contracts and the shortage of contracting officers,[48] contractual oversight by private relators, especially in Iraq, fills an accountability need. Ironically, the Clinton position, by implicitly facilitating private contractors, helps make relators available to control them.

One might think that those who believe in a unitary executive[49] would press against the Clinton administration view. But that may not be the case. Those who believe in the unitary nature of executive power may be potential allies against the delegation of policy making to private hands. If the executive power belongs to the president, the argument would go, then it is the president who exercises it, not Congress, congressionally assigned officials or privately contracted ones. Professor Sai Prakash has indirectly reinforced the Clinton position in finding the single criterion argument of Bush I less persuasive in the *qui tam* context as a matter of original constitutional intent.[50] If the Clinton interpretation survives an originalism critique, the Bush II OLC might be less inclined to opine against it.

This position will not, however, help stem the outsourcing tide. The more expansive single criterion view of the Appointments Clause would make it easier to sustain a constitutional claim against excessive delegations of government functions. All the president (or a Head of Department) would have to do by this theory is delegate duties of an Officer of the United States to a private contractor.[51] In the military setting, this occurs with regularity, because the term "officers" includes the lowest ranks.[52] Ensigns or lieutenants are confirmed just like admirals and generals; they exercise significant authority when they carry out battlefield engagements or interrogate prisoners.[53]

When Blackwater, CACI International, and other private military contractors are delegated these tasks, they clearly encroach on the duties assigned to "officers." To satisfy the other two criteria of *Buckley*[54] in the private contractor setting, contracts of long duration with established roles and titles would have to be found. Some contractors might rise to this level, RAND for example, but those criteria are far harder to establish on a general basis. Of course, a constitutional violation of the Appointments Clause in the military context hardly assures judicial intervention.[55] The president's Commander-in-Chief power is so pervasive, especially in wartime, that excessive delegations are unlikely to be resolved judicially.

On the civilian side, improper contracting out to private parties enjoys less judicial deference. It is already controlled by Congress legislatively and by OMB administratively. If one takes the definition of officer as involving significant authority alone, challenges to private delegations in the civilian setting are more readily established. There are many instances where principal officers, if not the president directly, have delegated such power to private hands. Consultants to agencies often do work that government would characterize as policy making. For example, those who advise FEMA officials to contract for services or make payments in disaster relief situations or those who prepare hurricane evacuation plans would seem to fall into this category, as would those who conduct peer review processes for agencies or those who review, summarize, and report on submissions in rulemaking.[56]

These contractors satisfy the significant authority, if not for the duration and permanency criteria, of *Buckley*. But they are still formally overseen by government officials. When contractors exercise authority does it remain "governmental" because an official oversees their work? A government official who signs off on significant private work retains some measure of authority over private delegatees. But should this be enough to defeat a constitutional challenge?

## B. THE DISTINCTION BETWEEN "SIGNIFICANT" AND "AUTHORITY" – WHERE DOES THE BUCK STOP?

Parsing "significant authority" is a necessary next step. Private contractors clearly do "significant" work, but do they exercise the "authority" to implement that work? If final authority remains with the government official, the decision is in a formal sense still governmental. The question becomes: Should the exercise of government authority by officers of the United States involve more than rubber-stamping the work of private contractors? Consider the actions of FEMA in the aftermath of the events surrounding Hurricane Katrina. When private consultants prepare the Hurricane Relief Plan[57] and let contracts to private construction firms, the federal officials who employ them are shunted aside.

There is little learning on what it means to *exercise* significant authority.[58] Initially, *Morgan v. United States*[59] established the requirement that the one who decides also must hear. This principle called government officers to account if significant work was delegated to government employees with only the sign off power remaining in the officer's hands. *Morgan* involved the Secretary of Agriculture, Henry Wallace, who delegated adjudicative decision power to subordinates, either employees or "inferior" officers.[60] Wallace was acting in a judicial capacity, not a policy-making one, when he delegated decision-making power to subordinates. Adjudication raises due process issues as well as Appointments Clause considerations. Obviously, his position would have been even weaker if he had delegated decision authority to a private contractor.[61]

But the requirement that those who adjudicate also must be the ones who preside was later abandoned.[62] The *Morgan* principle had rejected the notion of an institutional decision. But it was just too intrusive from a separation of powers perspective for the courts to question officials as to their actual knowledge of the decision being made. Earlier cases endorsing a "presumption of regularity" over administrative decisions were expanded to protect officers exercising official duties from being second-guessed (and potentially embarrassed) in the reviewing courts.[63]

Still, the principle of decisional responsibility has continuing appeal if private deciders are used in the context of adjudication.[64] And even in the rulemaking setting, record and analysis requirements[65] place on the agency official an enhanced duty to decide. Delegation to private contractors of the record compilation function in informal rulemaking is one thing. But when the analysis function or indeed the drafting of the concise statement of basis and purpose are involved, transfer of significant decision analysis powers to private hands has occurred.[66] Even though the final signature remains with the government official, thereby triggering the principle of regularity, significant authority under *Buckley* has been transferred. Analysis and drafting are surely significant if not inherent government functions.

Congress and the president create constitutional officers to ensure responsible decision making. These officers have commitments to the political branches, and to the judiciary as well. The courts require reasoned decision making as a function of judicial review.[67] The expectation is that reasoning will be done by the public official responsible, not some private contractor who hands the decision off for signature.

In the era of *Chevron*,[68] during which deference to agencies has, in the words of Cass Sunstein, taken on constitutional dimensions,[69] this may be a hard sell. Indeed, if one succumbs to the view that judges do politics,[70] which has empirical support,[71] the commitment to reason giving itself may be compromised. On this view, hard look review[72] sounds almost naïve. But the reasoned decision making requirement should not be jettisoned on this basis. The courts, whatever judges' political inclinations, stand for rational decision making. They (and we) cannot afford to ignore the requirement that agencies act rationally.[73]

The duty to consider and evaluate is a clear responsibility of office. Judicial intervention to test these propositions should be used sparingly, but not abandoned. The courts need not probe the mind of an administrator[74] to determine whether she engaged in a real decisional process after accepting a contractor's work. If the official simply signs off on the contractor's "decision," the *Chevron* deference bond has been broken. When reviewing courts learn of such practices they should invoke hard look review as a basic level of oversight on judicial review.

Bolder avenues to check inappropriate delegations include intervention under the Appointments Clause or through notions of due process. But to challenge excessive delegations on these bases, the principle of regularity would have to be rethought.[75] While returning to the era of *Morgan I* is unrealistic, using hard look review to signal that public officials have decision responsibilities may be enough to end the practice of excessive contractor delegation. Agencies do not want to be embarrassed before the courts.

Significant authority has now become a concept that needs to be defined if the privatization movement continues at its current pace. The Bush I view of *Buckley* is more hospitable to Appointments Clause challenges, at least as they apply to *qui tam* actions. But these challenges might be knocked out by the independent Clinton OLC requirements of duration and scope of appointment,[76] to say nothing of the *Morgan* cases and the presumption of regularity.

It is hard not to think of President Truman. Despite the sign on his desk, Truman did not expect his subordinates to pass the buck.[77] He decried it. In situations where agencies, such as FEMA, employ private contractors to do important jobs on a regular and recurring basis,[78] the buck has been passed. Even the Clinton OLC requirements might be violated if significant private authority delegations are made to contractors who have what amounts to "tenure" in office.[79] The Congress (even more than the courts) has an important oversight function to perform in this regard.

## C. NOTE ON THE OATH REQUIREMENT AND THE ROLE OF CONGRESS

The Appointments Clause requires that significant authority must be exercised by officials who have taken oaths to uphold the Constitution. The oath requirement is not a mere formality. It separates public from private actors.[80] It is something government officials have in common with the justices of the Supreme Court, the president, members of Congress, and state officials. As Akil Amar has reminded us, the oath requirement "presupposed that the Constitution spoke not merely to federal judges, but rather to all branches and ultimately to the people themselves."[81]

The recent furor over President Bush's use of signing statements has its genesis in this proposition.[82] The president claimed equal power to interpret the Constitution. Whether that gives him a broad right not to follow statutes he believes are unconstitutional is the debatable point. Under *Marbury v. Madison*, the Court has final if not sole authority to interpret the Constitution. Still, the oath requirement gives all three branches the duty to uphold the Constitution; to do so they must necessarily interpret it, even though the Supreme Court has the last word most of the time.

The constitutional role of Congress in the private delegation context goes beyond ensuring that oath requirements are met. The president's Article II powers – to Appoint Officers of the United States, to Take Care that laws are faithfully executed, to require the Opinion in Writing of Heads of Departments – are grants of power to the president as well as restrictions on congressional diminution of executive authority. But these provisions are also commitments to Congress by the Executive. The Take Care requirement, for example, expresses a power of the president and also imposes a duty to Congress and the People that the laws will be faithfully executed.[83] Failure to do so is an impeachable offense.

The vertical dimensions of these Executive prerogatives are much less appreciated. Congress has a constitutional stake in the president's proper exercise of his duty to govern, since officers of the United States are confirmed by the Senate. Because the Appointments Clause involves the Advice and Consent function,[84] it reflects a sharing of power between the branches. Any officer so appointed bears Congress's imprimatur as well as the president's. When that official's duties are fulfilled in part by private contractors, congressional as well as executive prerogatives have been compromised[85] – and that official has breached a trust to all three branches and to the People.

The fact that these officers are also subject to the impeachment power gives Congress a further role in overseeing the executive branch. When duties of executive branch officials are delegated to private hands, these delegatees in effect become "unimpeachable." Congress has lost a constitutionally designed accountability mechanism.[86] In this way also, separation of powers issues are implicated in the privatization process. Congress and the president both have nondelegable responsibilities to discharge. Congress's stake in the control of privatization, though often overshadowed by the Executive's, is clearly within the constitutional plan.

Beyond Appointments Clause challenges, nondelegation theories can also constrain the privatization of significant authority.[87] A *Schechter*-type nondelegation approach to privatization of significant government functions would be hard for the courts to accept. But the *Carter Coal* nondelegation/due process approach can potentially limit privatized functions.[88] The due process approach could require at a minimum oversight procedures before significant authority could be transferred to private hands. These procedures could be imposed by Congress or incorporated into the contracting process itself, as Chapter 7 discusses in more detail. The requirement for due process should apply whether the delegated functions are civilian or military.[89]

These constitutional approaches serve to alert the political branches to the dangers inherent in the unchecked use of consultants.[90] Because it is in their interest to respond, the remedies can also be statutory or administrative, rather than constitutional, as the next chapter shows.

## NOTES

1. *See* McCullough, *Truman* at 467; Truman, *Where the Buck Stops.*
2. *See* Breyer, *Active Liberty: Interpreting Our Democratic Constitution* at 3 (public liberty means more than freedom from despotic governments; it means freedom to participate in our governing institutions).
3. U.S. Const. art. II, § 2.
4. If there was ever any doubt on this point, it was satisfied when President Truman fired General MacArthur for insubordination in seeking to expand the Korean conflict. *See* McCullough, *Truman* at 836–45. This was no easy decision: Senator Nixon demanded MacArthur's reinstatement and Senator Taft threatened impeachment. *Id.* at 844. Dean Rusk saw Truman's action as essential to "civilian control of the military." *Id.* at 855.
5. *See Myers v. United States*, 272 U.S. 52 (Taft, C.J.); *Williams v. United States*, 1 How. [42 U.S.] at 296–97 (settled usage that Secretary of the Treasury may act for the president).
6. U.S. Const. art. II, § 2.
7. *Id.* at § 3.
8. The president's oath reinforces his duties: "I will faithfully execute the Office of President of the United States, and will to the best of my Ability, preserve, protect and defend the Constitution of the United States." U.S. Const. art. II, § 1, cl. 8.
9. U.S. Const. art. I, § 8, cl. 11.
10. *See generally* Marshall, *Putting Privateers in Their Place: The Applicability of the Marque and Reprisal Clause to Undeclared Wars* at 963–64.
11. *See* John Yoo & James C. Ho, *Marque and Reprisal* at 130–31.
12. *See Constitutional Limits on "Contracting Out" Department of Justice Functions under OMB Circular A-76*, 14 Op. Off. Legal Counsel at 96 (describing horizontal and vertical effects of the Appointments Clause).

13. *See Buckley v. Valeo*, 424 U.S. 1 (limiting Congress' power to appoint officers); *Myers*, 272 U.S. 52 (limiting Senate's power to participate in removal of officers).

14. *See Humphrey's Executor*, 295 U.S. 602 (approving congressional for cause limit on presidential removal of independent agency commissioners); *see also Weiss*, 510 U.S. 163 (deciding whether congressional addition of duties for military judges are within the Appointments Clause).

15. Article II, Section 2 permits Congress to vest the appointment of inferior officers "in the President alone, in the Courts of Law, or in the Heads of Departments." U.S. Const. art. II, § 2, cl. 2. It is under this power that Congress placed some officials under the protection of the Civil Service. *See Perkins*, 116 U.S. 483 (civil service law constitutional); *Myers*, 272 U.S. at 162 (explaining inferior officer limitations under civil service); *see also Freytag*, 501 U.S. at 886 (defining "Heads of Departments").

16. *See Buckley v. Valeo*, 424 U.S. at 125–26.

17. The president appoints all military officers and the Senate confirms them. *See Weiss*, 510 U.S. at 170 (all military officers are Officers of the United States). Such officers are required to be appointed by the president. *See Perkins*, 116 U.S. at 484 (cadet engineer appointed by Secretary of Navy); *see* OLC Memo to General Counsels, May 2, 1996 at 47 n. 55.

18. *See* Singer, *Corporate Warriors* at 206–07 (describing how the drug war in Colombia is run by private armies contracted for by the Dept. of State); *see also* Avant, *The Market for Force* at 7–16 (describing various private military contracts).

19. *See Constitutional Limits on "Contracting Out"*, 14 Op. Off. Legal Counsel at 96 n. 3 (citing as examples of forbidden verticality *Northern Pipeline Constr. Co. v. Marathon Pipeline Co.*, 458 U.S. 50, and *A.L.A. Schechter Poultry*, 295 U.S. 495). Because *Northern Pipeline* involved forbidden delegations of Article III power to bankruptcy judges (who, if not constitutional judges, are at least federal employees) and since *Schechter* involved forbidden delegations by Congress to the president, neither case involves private parties or contractors. But *see Carter v. Carter Coal Co.*, 298 U.S. 238 (delegation to private groups); Verkuil, *Public Law Limitations*, at 422–24.

20. *See Flast v. Cohen*, 392 U.S. at 105–06 (taxpayer standing to challenge expenditures to parochial schools).

21. *Shankland v. Washington*, 30 U.S. (5 Pet.) at 391.

22. The antiaggrandizement principle emerges from the Framers' concern with congressional hegemony (at the time the most dangerous branch). *See Bowsher v. Synar*, 478 U.S. at 726 (Congress cannot execute the laws nor appoint or remove one who does); *Buckley v. Valeo*, 424 U.S. at 122–23 (*per curiam*) (same); *compare Mistretta v. United States*, 488 U.S. at 411 n. 35 (special counsel poses no special danger).

23. *See* Singer, *Corporate Warriors* at 20–25.

24. *See Youngstown Steel & Tube Co. v. Sawyer*, 343 U.S. at 635–37 (Jackson, J., concurring) (if the president has congressional authorization for his actions, judicial deference is granted). Attorney General Gonzales's memo justifying the president's national security intercept program also relies on *Youngstown*. *See NSA Spying Memo* at 19–20.

25. *See Youngstown*, 343 U.S. at 637. *See also* the discussion of *Carter Coal* in Chapter 7.

26. *See* Shapiro, *OMB's Dubious Peer Review Procedures* (documenting FACA's inapplicability to private contractors in the peer review setting).

27. *See* Chapter 1, Part C; Truman, *Where the Buck Stops* 96 (Margaret Truman states that her father would have fired North and Poindexter for "trying to work up a secret government").

28. 298 U.S. 238.

29. 49 Stat. 991 (1935), 15 U.S.C. §§ 801 *et seq.* (1936).

30. Professor Jaffe, writing at the time of *Carter Coal*, thought the nondelegation aspect was unnecessary and the decision could have relied on due process alone. *See* Jaffe, *Law Making by Private Groups*; *see also* Verkuil, *Public Law Limitations*.

31. Tribe, *American Constitutional Law* at 993.

32. The coal company and union representatives were in effect private adjudicators; and they were private parties that had an interest in the outcome. The problem was not with private adjudicators *per se*. The Court subsequently upheld statutory requirement that registrants submit to binding arbitration before private arbitrators. *See Thomas v. Union Carbide Agric. Prods. Co.*, 473 U.S. 568 (the government's use of a private panel of arbitrators). But *Thomas* did not involve the due process issue present in *Carter Coal* – a biased tribunal in the *Dr. Bonham's Case* sense. *See* note 36.

33. This is the import of Gillian Metzger's use of the nondelegation doctrine as a process control over private contractors. *See* Metzger, *Privatization as Delegation; see also* Freeman, *Extending Public Law Norms Through Privatization* (urging a "publicization" view of privatized activities).

34. FACA requires openness and balanced representation, both ideals of democratic decision making. *See* Croley & Funk, *The Federal Advisory Committee Act and Good Government*.

35. Executive privilege is often used to render government decisions nontransparent. *See* Lipton, *White House Declines to Provide Storm Papers* at A1, A17 (describing resistance to producing documents and witnesses in Katrina congressional oversight review).

36. The decision makers in *Carter Coal* were involved in an adjudicatory context; they were conflicted by their interest in the outcome of the wage setting and could not be neutral deciders. *See e.g. Tumey v. Ohio*, 273 U.S. 510; *Bonham's Case*, 77 Eng. Rep. 646. Most of the FACA committees do not

involve adjudications, so due process does not technically apply. But the due process interests behind open decision making are still worth noting. *See* Tribe, *Structural Due Process* (describing the due process of lawmaking).

37. *See* Breyer, *Active Liberty* at 5–6 (judicial review should emphasize the Constitution's "democratic objective").

38. *See Buckley v. Valeo*, 424 U.S. at 125–26. In contrast, "[e]mployees are lesser functionaries subordinate to officers of the United States." *Id.* at 126 n. 162.

39. Chief Justice Marshall observed that "[a]lthough an office is 'an employment,' it does not follow that every employment is an office." *United States v. Maurice*, 26 F. Cas. at 1214. The distinction between officers and employees has long been elaborated. *See e.g. Burnap v. United States*, 252 U.S. at 516–19 (landscape architect was an employee, not an officer).

40. *Buckley* cites with favor decisions that have excepted employees with intermittent and temporary duties from the definition of "officer." *See Auffmordt v. Hedden*, 137 U.S. 310 (merchant appraiser hired for special case); *United States v. Germaine*, 99 U.S. 508 (surgeon appointed to examine applicants for pensions in special cases not an officer).

41. *See* False Claims Act, 31 U.S.C. §§ 3729 *et seq.* (2006). Qui tam actions permit private relators to bring actions on behalf of the government for fraud unless the DOJ intervenes. *See generally* Caminker, *The Constitutionality of* Qui Tam *Actions*.

42. *See Constitutionality of the Qui Tam Provisions of the False Claims Act*, 13 Op. Off. Legal Counsel 249.

43. This argument created a split within the administration: OLC argued that this criterion rendered the *qui tam* provision unconstitutional; this position was contested by the Solicitor General's office. *Id.* The opinion also argued that the *qui tam* actions violated Article III standing requirements and the separation of powers doctrine. *Id.*

44. A relater is much like a private contractor (or bounty hunter) hired to help bring those committing fraud against the government to justice. The IRS recently announced that it would be outsourcing the collection of back taxes to private firms who will be performing much like bounty hunters in recovering back taxes less their retainage (which is said to exceed the government's direct costs). *See* Johnston, I.R.S. *Enlists Outside Help in Collecting Delinquent Taxes, Despite the Higher Costs*; Chapter 1 Part A n.18 (criticizing the decision by the IRS to outsource).

45. *See Vt. Agency of Nat. Resources*, 529 U.S. 765 (Scalia, J.) (supporting the Article III dimensions of the False Claims Act but reserving the question as to Article II).

46. *The Constitutional Separation of Powers Between the President and Congress*, 20 Op. Off. Legal Counsel 124 n. 65 ("We now disapprove the Appointments Clause analysis and conclusion of an earlier opinion of this Office.").

47. The debate, which arose in the context of the independent counsel, is over whether prosecution is an inherently executive function. *Compare* Lessig & Sunstein, *The President and the Administration* at 15–16 *with* Carter, *The Independent Counsel Mess. See Morrison v. Olson*, 487 U.S. 654 (upholding constitutionality of independent counsel statute).

48. *See* discussion at Chapter 7 Part B.

49. *See, e.g.*, Yoo, Calabresi, & Colangelo, *The Unitary Executive in the Modern Era, 1945–2004*; Calabresi & Prakash, *The President's Power to Execute the Laws* (arguing that the president must control prosecutions).

50. *See* Prakash, *The Chief Prosecutor*, at 575–77, 590–91 (arguing that, even though the president must exercise the prosecutorial power, *qui tam* and other private prosecution schemes are constitutional so long as the president can terminate these actions, even if by exercising the pardon power over those subject to private suits).

51. One way to avoid the Appointments Clause limitations on private contractors is to designate such delegatees as employees rather than officers. Under the independent three criteria view urged by the Clinton administration this would pass muster easily. *See The Constitutional Separation of Powers Between the President and Congress*, 20 Op. Off. Legal Counsel 124 n. 60. The Bush I rule, however, required a further inquiry into the "significant authority" dimension of the delegation.

52. *See Weiss*, 510 U.S. at 170.

53. For example, the Office of Legal Counsel has advised that only "officers" may dispose of government property. *See Constitutional Limits on "Contracting Out"*, 14 Op. Off. Legal Counsel 94.

54. *See* n. 40.

55. *See e.g. Allen v. Wright*, 468 U.S. 737; *United States v. Richardson*, 418 U.S. at 179 (no standing).

56. *See* Chapter 2 Part D.

57. *See* Innovative Emergency Management, Inc., *IEM Team to Develop Catastrophic Hurricane Disaster Plan for New Orleans & Southeast Louisiana*.

58. *Buckley* did not raise the issue because the federal officials, the FEC, did not employ private contractors to implement their work.

59. 298 U.S. 468.

60. The line between employees and inferior officers who have decisional responsibility is not easily drawn. *See Freytag v. Commr. of Internal Revenue*, 501 U.S. 868 (determining that a "special trial judge" is an inferior officer appointed by the Tax Court which the majority found to be a "court of law" under the Appointments Clause); *see also Landry v. FDIC*, 204 F.3d 1125 (determining administrative law judges at FDIC to be employees rather than inferior officers).

61. Such a delegation would have raised due process and delegation concerns under *Carter Coal. See* discussion at nn. 28–31, *supra.*
62. *Morgan,* 313 U.S. 409; *see* Gifford, *The Morgan Cases: A Retrospective View* at 238 (*Morgan IV* "placed a veil of secrecy over the 'mental process' of the decision makers").
63. *See Moffat v. United States,* 112 U.S. at 30 ("every officer . . . acting under the obligation of his oath, will do his duty"); *see also U.S. Postal Service v. Gregory,* 534 U.S. 1 (same).
64. *See Schweiker v. McClure,* 456 U.S. 188 (private contractor may adjudicate reimbursements up to a set ceiling; government employees required if claims go beyond).
65. *See* Pierce, Shapiro, & Verkuil, *Administrative Law and Process* § 6.4.6.
66. *See* discussion in Chapter 2.
67. One function of judicial review is to ensure that the agency officials who decide on a policy have actually reviewed the record before them. *See e.g. Motor Vehicle Mfrs. Assn. v. State Farm Mut. Auto. Ins. Co.,* 463 U.S. at 43 (agency required to consider alternatives to proposed rule). Congress sets this standard (under the APA) but the courts enforce it.
68. *Chevron U.S.A., Inc. v. Natural Resources Defense Council, Inc.,* 467 U.S. 837 (deference to agency's interpretation of statutes if views are "permissible" or reasonable under applicable law).
69. *See* Sunstein, *Beyond* Marbury: *The Executive's Power to Say What the Law Is* at 2607–08.
70. *See* Pierce, *Waiting for* Vermont Yankee II.
71. *See* Miles & Sunstein, *Do Judges Make Regulatory Policy? An Empirical Investigation of* Chevron (conservative judges vote to validate agency decisions less often than liberal judges).
72. *See* Verkuil, *The Wait is Over:* Chevron *as a Stealth* Vermont Yankee II.
73. *See* Peter L. Strauss, *Within* Marbury: *The Importance of Judicial Limits on the Executive's Power to Say What the Law Is* (supporting the Court's independent role).
74. *See Citizens to Preserve Overton Park, Inc. v. Volpe,* 401 U.S. at 420 (inappropriateness of putting administrator on the witness stand).
75. *See* Guttman, *Governance by Contract: Constitutional Visions* at 323 (questioning the principle of regularity when "the official workforce can no longer be presumed to possess the capacity to account for the government's operations").
76. The Opinion also notes the requirement of oath taking by executive branch officials, which further distinguishes them from private contractors. *See The Constitutional Separation of Powers Between the President and Congress,* 20 Op. Off. Legal Counsel 124 n. 9.
77. Especially, one might imagine, to private contractors.

78. *See* Lipton, *Homeland Security Chief Outlines FEMA Overhaul* (describing FEMA's failures to respond to the Katrina disaster and proposing more public controls).

79. That would be a difficult standard to meet. RAND might be an example of a "tenured" consultant, as it was created by the Department of the Air Force in 1947 and has regularly received government contracts ever since. *See* RAND Corp., *History and Mission*, http://www.rand.org/about/history/.

80. *Compare Lujan v. Defenders of Wildlife*, 504 U.S. 555 (Scalia, J.) (emphasizing importance of public officials, who are subject to the oath requirement, in the enforcement of public law).

81. Amar, *America's Constitution: A Biography* at 62–63 (describing the importance the Constitution places on oaths and affirmations); *see also* Chapter 1 Part D (on popular sovereignty).

82. *See* Task Force on Presidential Signing Statements and the Separation of Powers Doctrine, Am. Bar Ass'n, Recommendation and Report (condemning the excessive use of signing statements by presidents).

83. *See* Flaherty, *The Most Dangerous Branch* at 1788–98 (finding the historical meaning of the Take Care clause includes a duty to enforce the laws fairly).

84. *See* U.S. Const. art. II, § 2, cl. 2.

85. The Advice and Consent function may raise the issue of congressional overreaching under the removal power, which is not addressed here. *See e.g. Myers*, 272 U.S. 52 (Tenure of Office Act applied to Postmasters is unconstitutional); *Humphrey's Executor*, 295 U.S. 602 (for cause removal permitted over independent agency commissioners).

86. Of course, Congress could impeach the officer who granted the private contractor significant authority.

87. Indeed, the Clinton OLC Memorandum expressly reserves challenges to private contractor actions under "the non-delegation doctrine and the general separation of powers principle." *The Constitutional Separation of Powers Between the President and Congress*, 20 Op. Off. Legal Counsel 124 nn. 60–62.

88. *See* Verkuil, *Public Law Limitations* at 422–23; Metzger, *Privatization as Delegation* at 1440–42.

89. Due process could involve review by military tribunals as opposed to judicial review by courts. *See Hamdi v. Rumsfeld*, 542 U.S. 507. In this setting military courts serve are like administrative agencies in terms of due process hearings. *Compare Crowell v. Benson*, 285 U.S. 22.

90. One role of the judicial branch, through the mechanism of hard look review, may be to alert the political branches to the encroachment of consultants upon the analysis and judgment function required of administrative agencies. *See* discussion at nn. 68–73.

# 6  STATUTORY AND ADMINISTRATIVE LIMITATIONS ON PRIVATE DELEGATIONS

## A. NONDELEGATION, SUBDELEGATION, AND DISCRETIONARY ACTS

Once an inherent government power is identified, can it be delegated at all? The nondelegation doctrine does not go that far. In both its Article I and due process faces, the doctrine is about process. The nondelegation requirement is satisfied if Congress provides an "intelligible principle" for the Executive to follow.[1] As was discussed in Chapter 5, the constitutional constraints on delegation are exceedingly difficult to enforce.[2] *Carter Coal* does, however, call for procedural mechanisms that require government rather than private officials to exercise public power.

But certain government functions may be so fundamental as not to be transferable to private hands under any circumstances. Acts of government committed to high officials, including the president, who have taken oaths to uphold the Constitution[3] are especially sensitive. However, calling some government acts nondelegable does not identify them. What are the functions of government that cannot be privatized?

### 1. Nondelegable Duties of Government

Some duties have always been nondelegable. We can all agree with Justice Scalia that Congress cannot hand the legislative power to the president and adjourn *sine die*.[4] Congress must actually perform its constitutional duties. By a parity of reasoning, the president cannot turn the executive power over to the vice president and retire in office.[5]

These are clear examples of nondelegable duties of office under the Constitution. Important powers exercised by cabinet officials and other principal officers presumably must be exercised by those who have taken an oath to uphold the Constitution.[6] Thus, the Secretary of Defense cannot delegate the power to conduct the war in Iraq to the RAND Corporation any more than the Attorney General can leave it to private (rather than "special") counsel to decide when or how to prosecute.[7] In these situations, the core responsibility is both to exercise and to oversee the exercise of government powers. Stated more broadly, the duty to be accountable for public decisions is not a function performable by those outside government.[8]

But these are obviously farfetched scenarios. Secretary Gates is never going to outsource war planning to RAND or Blackwater. Instead, his subordinates will award contracts that peel off certain military functions and put them in private hands. The question then becomes are these functions themselves ones that must be performed by government officials. Here the issue is both statutory and constitutional. The constitutional sources were set out in Chapter 5; the statutory restrictions are discussed next.

## 2. The Subdelegation Act

Some power to delegate within government is necessary to make the system work. Even though the president embodies the executive power under Article I, he cannot carry out all duties directly. Realizing this, Congress long ago gave the president the necessary power to delegate to his subordinates. Under the Subdelegation Act,[9] initial executive delegations can be further subdelegated without specific legislation. But these delegations can only be made to officers of the United States.

This is a powerful tool of executive reorganization. The act delegates to the president the unrestricted power to subdelegate without express legislative authority.[10] Although those with a unitary view of the president's powers[11] might object to Congress limiting subdelegations, reorganization powers are well established. Moreover, as the act is permissive rather than restrictive, it does little to harm the president's inherent powers.[12] The Subdelegation Act is also consistent with the exclusive delegation theory posited by Thomas Merrill.[13]

The idea that the president needs to delegate to his cabinet officials or other officers of the United States recognizes the realities of modern government. The act was passed as part of the reorganization recommendations of the Hoover Commission.[14] It honors the president's need to organize the administration, within express limits. The act assures that delegations of significant authority will be to government officials who have been appointed by the president (and often confirmed by the Senate).

Thus, the act can be construed as both a grant and a limitation upon the executive branch's power to subdelegate.[15] By limiting delegations to government officials, indeed to high government officials, the act implicitly draws a line between public officials and outside parties, and it has been so interpreted. In *U.S. Telecom*,[16] the D.C. Circuit emphasized that "the cases recognize an important distinction between subdelegation to a subordinate and subdelegation to an outside party." So understood,[17] the Subdelegation Act becomes relevant to the outsourcing situation. When the executive tries to delegate powers to private parties, the Subdelegation Act tests whether these delegations are consistent with the exercise of executive authority. If inherent functions are being delegated to contractors, for example, the act can question whether such delegations meet statutory requirements. Congress can then decide whether to approve these subdelegations through enabling legislation. In this way, the act is a congressional early warning system to detect errant delegations.

Here is how it might work in the contractor setting. When an agency outsources important functions, as when the IRS uses contractors to collect delinquent taxes,[18] the act is potentially violated. If Congress thereafter accepts this practice, it is validated. But if it does not, the contractor action should fail.

Reading the act in this manner reflects existing practice. Congress has permitted some delegations to private contractors in statutes such as the Federal Activities Inventory Reform Act (the FAIR Act). But this act importantly incorporates limits as to inherent functions.[19] The harder constitutional question — whether, without the Subdelegation Act, the president has the inherent power to delegate duties assigned to him by Congress[20] – is not raised in the private delegation context. The president could never claim an inherent power to delegate significant duties to private hands. In fact, when viewed this way, constitutional limits on private delegations seem unexceptionable, even to those who would expand executive powers.

The Subdelegation Act does nothing to deprive the president and other executive officials of inherent and political powers that derive from Article II. Those powers are discretionary and may not be second-guessed by the courts or limited by Congress. In the words of Chief Justice Marshall:

> By the constitution of the United States, the President is invested with certain important political powers, in the exercise of which he is to use his own discretion, and is accountable only to his country in his political character, and to his own conscience. To aid him in the performance of these duties, he is authorized to appoint certain officers, who act by his authority and in conformity with his orders.[21]

The politically sensitive and discretionary nature of decision making about core decisions of government limits Congress's ability to assign most substantive delegations to executive officials and to control aspects of that power.[22] But the genius of *Marbury* is that in insulating certain political acts from judicial scrutiny, it also established principles of judicial review over other government actions affecting individuals.[23] Under this power, the courts could invoke the Subdelegation Act to police delegations to private contractors.

A further implication of *Marbury* relates to the privatization issue. The president is protected in the exercise of his political powers by subordinates, but this category is limited to public officials. Private contractors can never be public in this sense. As Chapter 5 emphasized, officials of government take an oath of office to uphold the Constitution. Only oath-takers can discharge these protected duties. Executive privilege protects "the President against judicial intrusion into 'official acts.'"[24] Official acts are those performed by "officials."

## B. CONTRACTING-OUT AND THE CIRCULAR A-76 PROCESS

Contracting-out the provision of services by the government has a long history.[25] Most of this activity takes place between agency contracting officers and selected private vendors of services; contracts are usually awarded after competitive bidding,[26] even though the number of performance-based or single-sourced contracts has been growing.[27] This is especially true in connection with DOD contracts for private military services in Iraq[28] and with FEMA contracts after Hurricane Katrina.[29] Most of these contracts are entered into between the agency involved and the contractor. But sometimes outsourcing occurs under competitive conditions, which is where OMB's Circular A-76 comes in.

## 1. The A-76 Process

This process applies when contractors are invited to challenge the government's performance of public activities. The agencies are required to list the number of commercial positions performed by their employees.[30] But under the A-76 process, "competitive sourcing" is not permitted for those functions that are "inherent."[31] A review process is required that gives the agency whose competitive functions are challenged the right to defend itself on efficiency grounds versus the private challenger. These decisions are reviewed first through agency appeals and then by GAO. If unsuccessful, private contractors can challenge the results in the Court of Federal Claims.[32]

The Bush administration, as part of its downsizing project, has expanded the conditions under which contracting-out may be employed. In May 2003, OMB's Circular A-76 was amended to encourage contracting-out (or "competitive sourcing"),[33] and in September 2003 OMB issued a report: "Competitive Sourcing and Responsible Public-Private Competition" that documented the government's success at contracting-out.[34]

Circular A-76 also recognizes limits on contracting-out. It describes certain functions as "inherently governmental" activities. These activities involve:

1. Binding the United States to take or not to take some action by contract, policy, regulation, authorization, order, or otherwise;
2. Determining, protecting, and advancing economic, political, territorial, property, or other interests by military or diplomatic action,

civil or criminal judicial proceedings, contract management, or
otherwise;

3. Significantly affecting the life, liberty, or property of private persons; or

4. Exerting ultimate control over the acquisition, use, or disposition
of United States property (real or personal, intangible), including
establishing policies or procedures for the collection, control, or
disbursement of appropriated and other federal funds.[35]

The circular connects to the FAIR Act, which requires agencies to submit annual inventories of agency-performed commercial
activities.[36] The circular also requires agencies (including independent agencies) to identify all of their activities as either commercial
or inherently governmental.[37] Agencies must appoint a "competitive
sourcing official" to centralize agency oversight and to publish annual
inventories of jobs eligible to be contracted-out.[38]

The Bush administration's goal has been to contract-out the jobs
of more than 850,000 federal civilian employees.[39] This push for privatization has produced tensions with Congress over the effectiveness
of private sourcing,[40] and focused attention on the A-76 process. In
2004, the GAO responded to requests from Senate and House members by examining the competitive sourcing practices of seven federal
agencies.[41] This progress report followed the GAO's earlier report of
its Commercial Activities Panel that set out the process agencies should
follow in implementing A-76.[42] The GAO found that the agencies had
mixed success at implementing the president's management goals on
outsourcing.

Some agencies had not allocated enough personnel to administering the process or failed to integrate the A-76 process into their strategic and human capital plans. Others were having difficulty classifying
positions as "inherently governmental" or commercial.[43] On the private side, complaints were registered over the fact that when the agency
"won" the competition (i.e., retained the jobs as public), the winner
was not held accountable for performance.[44]

Overall, the GAO found that the percentage of "competable" positions was over 26 percent of the 2002 federal workforce (including Education, where it was 62 percent).[45] It reported "significant progress"[46] in implementing A-76 and gave agencies what amounted to a vote of confidence to Congress. Still, objections to its use must be evaluated.

## 2. Critiques of the A-76 Process

Dan Guttman asks whether contracting-out under A-76 implicates the "constitutional premises of our Government."[47] The danger is that inherent government functions are often included in agency inventories with little oversight, as the review function focuses on the competitive sourcing side of the ledger. The constitutional question of outsourcing inherent functions is submerged – not highlighted – by this process.

Moreover, a separate management question is whether the push to outsource by government ignores private sector developments that challenge the effectiveness of outsourcing more generally.[48] If the administration finds itself encouraging outsourcing when the practice is questioned by private managers, the whole push to outsource becomes problematic. The private sector worries about the complexity of managing the outsourced operation. The public management dimension of the problem is much greater, especially in light of no-bid, performance-based contracts.[49]

Outsourcing exercises a centrifugal force on government. Effective outsourcing requires the capacity to oversee. This capacity is limited in government due to downsizing initiatives. The shortage of government employees to oversee outsourced functions has a cumulative effect. It pushes government even further in the direction of contracting out and increases the need for oversight. Indeed, now government requires contracting-out the duty to oversee those jobs already contracted-out. It is in these circumstances that Guttman raises constitutional concerns as inherently governmental functions, including the oversight responsibility, are themselves contracted-out. Inherent functions were once thought to be overarticulated, but they are now increasingly at risk.[50] The concern is both with the number and nature of jobs being contracted-out. When private contractors are evaluating the performance of government programs on which they may ultimately bid,[51] the system seems institutionally, if not constitutionally, unbalanced.

As a legal matter, of course, government officials remain responsible for overseeing the expenditure of public funds.[52] But when fewer and fewer federal officials are available to oversee more and more private contractors (Paul Light's 12 to 1 ratio[53]), accountability and oversight are bound to suffer. The legal responsibility cannot be discharged when public management is ineffective. Supervision implies quality control; when public officials are stretched thin or are replaced by contractors, the effective predicate to supervision is lost.

But this is not a problem with the formal requirements of Circular A-76. It defines inherent government functions[54] and tells agencies to exempt them from contracting out. However, if government managers are unavailable to make that decision, which the agencies claim to be the most difficult one to make,[55] those functions will not be protected from erroneous classifications. The agency's designation of what is "inherent" is not subject to administrative review. The procedural protections of Circular A-76 as well as the FAIR Act[56] are directed instead at the competitive sourcing process. If an agency erroneously designates an inherent function that involves policy making and decision control as competitive, review of these false positives will go undetected. The only challenges on administrative review are those over whether the choice between competitive sourcing candidates was properly made. Although officials and their unions can raise issues of who is the most competitive source, the underlying decision of what is competitive or inherent is much harder to challenge.

Under the FAIR Act each agency makes the initial determination of inherent or competitive. This decision is reviewed only by OMB,[57] which is concerned about increasing competitive jobs to meet the President's mandate to privatize 850,000 federal positions. Indeed, OMB has sought to narrow inherent government functions by changing their definition from "exercise of discretion" to "exercise of *substantial* discretion."[58] One would hardly expect the agency that lightened the definition to worry about its violation — thus, false positives many go undetected.[59]

While the FAIR Act permits "an interested party"[60] to challenge an agency's inclusion of a function as not inherently governmental, these challenges have avoided judicial review largely for standing reasons. Review remains a dimension of the A-76/FAIR Act process that has not received adequate attention.[61]

## 3. The Special Problems of Contracting-Out and the Military

The Department of Defense is by far the largest government contracting agency.[62] In addition to the procurement of equipment (weapons systems, supplies, etc.), the DOD also has become a large services contractor. Over 57 percent of the Pentagon's procurement dollars are spent on services, not equipment; services expenditures increased by 66 percent from FY 1999 to FY 2003.[63] Many of these services potentially involve significant or inherent functions of government, but they are only subject to Circular A-76 if they involve competitive sourcing.[64]

The war in Iraq has been either an outsourcing nightmare or a bonanza, depending on whether you are the government or a private contractor.[65] The war has posed enormous personnel and deployment challenges for the military. War requires the ability to bring services on line quickly which can be done only if the military contracts some services to the private sector.[66] This necessity, however, brings with it management problems of the first order.[67]

There is an obvious need for the military to contract out logistical or support services (food services, construction, etc.) to private hands. The difficulty comes when these services include military functions.[68] When force is privatized, how can the military ensure that the private exercise of power is circumscribed by public values and controls?[69] Military discipline is assured by training, by obedience to command, and by penalties administered under the Uniform Code of Military Justice. Private contractors are deficient in all three respects.

The abuse of detainees at Abu Ghraib prison outside Baghdad demonstrates the outsourcing dimension, as well as the challenges to military discipline and command and control.[70] Large contracts were issued to organizations such as CACI, International and Premier Technology Group, Inc. for "intelligence and technical support,"[71] which led to private contractors being employed as interrogators.[72] Unlike military translation services provided by contractors such as

Titan Corp.,[73] which might well be "commercial" in the Circular A-76 sense,[74] interrogation of prisoners is clearly an inherently governmental function. Interrogation involves "military action and matters significantly affecting life, liberty and property."[75] When interrogation leads to prisoner abuse, the result is an embarrassment for the military and its civilian leadership.[76] The Abu Ghraib abuses cannot be blamed solely on private contractors, of course. But when civilian contractors assume military roles, the public accountability function suffers.

The public management question is how did these contracts happen. Objections to interrogation contracts were not raised under DOD contracting rules or in the A-76 process.[77] In general, military privatization reveals gaps in oversight and control. Private contractors are not subject to the Uniform Code of Military Justice for any crimes they may have committed.[78] Although they are made subject to other criminal statutes,[79] such as the Military Extraterritorial Jurisdiction Reform Act,[80] those controls are weak at best.[81] Statutory liability for the commission of criminal acts by private contractors is not as effective as public controls would be.

This accountability gap exists, of course, whether contractors are performing commercial or inherently governmental functions, but the stakes are necessarily higher in the latter situation. The Iraq invasion has put enormous pressure on the military resources of the United States,[82] and contracting-out has been a response to recruiting shortfalls.[83] The management problems privatization produces have made personnel problems worse.

Under the FAIR Act, private contractors can provide "noninherently governmental" goods and services, but they cannot fill military positions, such as those involving essential military skills or other skills necessary for career progression.[84] Even though the Circular A-76 inherently governmental function requirement, which tracks the FAIR Act, was not changed in 2003,[85] the use of military contractors in sensitive roles seems to have increased. The line between military and competitive functions has been blurred in a way that the laws have not yet responded to.[86] When private contractors are accused of participating in acts of torture,[87] there is a failure of public responsibility. Whatever else it is, torture is surely a governmental "function" that cannot be privatized.[88]

Many military contracting-out decisions are single sourced rather than competitively bid,[89] despite Circular A-76's commitment to competitive sourcing.[90] When the A-76 process is not employed, this potential check on military contracting is unavailable. Chapter 7 shows how competitive sourcing can be a check on irresponsible outsourcing.

This is not a problem of which the DOD is unaware. The Department of the Army reviewed its use of military contractors on the battlefield by commissioning a report from the RAND Corporation.[91] The RAND Report analyzed the Army Field Manual (#3−100), which instructs military officers on how and when to hire private contractors. The report was designed to sharpen the Army's risk assessment procedures,[92] and it did a remarkable job of laying out the options and challenges.

In an appendix to the report, RAND researchers focused on principal-agent problems with the use of contractors on the battlefield.[93] The Report noted that private contractors pose unusual "loyalty" problems because of their profit incentives;[94] however, it concludes that *properly overseen* contractors can still be effective.

The report also noted a concern about the long-term effect of outsourcing. Once a function is outsourced, the Army loses the capability to perform that function in house: "Over the long run, once the Army gives up a capability, the start-up costs may simply become too high to justify bringing it back in-house, even if it should never have left in the first place."[95] This wise observation makes it essential that the Army decide carefully in the first instance whether the function proposed to be contracted out is an inherent function of government. Not enough attention is given to this preliminary question.

The report, however, did not address the larger question of whether the type of job being outsourced on the battlefield was the kind that should not be contracted out under any circumstances. When the DOD issued final rules on the use of contractor personnel, it also ignored this overriding issue.[96] The question of whether some government jobs – especially combat ones – are not delegable at all seems not even to be on the horizon. Until the DOD faces up to what is driving decisions in this area – the lack of adequate military personnel to perform combat assignments – it will continue to outsource missions that are military in nature. When the military has to contract-out the plan to deal with contracting-out on the battlefield, it shows how limited its "inherent" policy-making resources really are.

## NOTES

1. *J. W. Hampton, Jr & Co.*, 276 U.S. 394 (Taft, C. J.) (upholding tariff setting power to President).
2. A rigorously enforced nondelegation doctrine might end up forbidding delegations simply because Congress may be unable politically to respond. In this way, nondelegation could transmute itself into a form of substantive due process that forbids delegations altogether. *See* Pierce, Shapiro & Verkuil, *Administrative Law and Process* at 48–49. Still, there are articulate advocates for its revival. *See* Larson, *The Rise and the Rise of the Administrative State* at 1239 (must determine when delegation has "crossed the line").
3. *See* U.S. Const. art. VI, cl. 3 (requiring oaths or affirmations to support the institution of all federal and state legislative, executive, and judicial officers); *see also Webster*, 486 U.S. at 613 (Scalia, J., dissenting) (concluding that taking the oath to uphold the Constitution sometimes allows executive officials "to perform that oath unreviewed").
4. *See Mistretta*, 488 U.S. at 415 (Scalia, J., dissenting) ("Our members of Congress could not, even if they wished, vote all power to the President and adjourn sine die."). Justice Scalia's *Mistretta* dissent also noted that some duties of legislators, such as voting on bills, cannot be delegated. *Id.* at 425. He calls the Sentencing Commission a "junior-varsity Congress." *Id.* at 427. One wonders whether the same pejorative might apply to private legislative delegatees such as standard setting organizations. *See also* Tribe, *American Constitutional Law* at 982 (the legislative power as a whole is not transferrable).
5. *Cf.* Strauss & Sunstein, *The Role of the President and OMB in Informal Rulemaking* at 190 (questioning the vice president's role in overseeing the rulemaking process).
6. Duties of principal officers are nondelegable both because of the oath or affirmation requirement, *see* n. 3, and because of the Senate's advise and consent function in Article II. Any officer confirmed by the Senate owes a duty both to the president and to the Congress to perform her responsibilities directly; the Senate is consenting to the exercise of duties by the officer confirmed, not by some unconfirmed private subdelegatee. Moreover, the impeachment power is also compromised because Congress cannot hold the private subdelegatee responsible through its exercise. *See* Chapter 5.
7. *See Young*, 481 U.S. at 802–09 (finding the Attorney General's duty to be nondelegable and disqualifying a private attorney from presenting a violation of a court order).
8. The Attorney General's constitutional control over litigation for the United States must be reconciled with *qui tam* suits that permit private parties to

represent the government. *See, e.g.,* discussion in Chapter 5. These actions have been available since the beginning of our constitutional period, but their anomalous nature still raises nondelegation questions under Article II's Appointments and Take Care clauses. *See Vermont Agency of Nat. Res.,* 529 U.S. at 778 n.8 (Scalia, J.) (upholding the False Claims Act against an Article III challenge, but reserving the question as to Article II); *see also FEC v. Akins,* 524 U.S. at 34–37 (Scalia, J., dissenting) (noting that citizen attorney general provisions of the act may violate the president's Article II requirement of "faithful execution" of the laws).

9. 3 U.S.C. §§ 301–302 (2000) (permitting delegation by the president to any official required to be appointed by and with the advice and consent of the Senate, unless affirmatively prohibited by Congress).

10. Even though the act permits broad delegations, it has never been challenged on nondelegation grounds. *See* Posner & Vermeule, *Nondelegation: A Post-Mortem* at 1335 ("But to our knowledge, no one has ever suggested that the Subdelegation Act violates the Constitution. . . . "). And because the subdelegations are limited to public officials, they would not involve the *Carter Coal* variations on the nondelegation doctrine.

11. *See, e.g.,* Calabresi & Prakash, *The President's Power to Execute the Laws* at 571 (advocating an expansive reading of Article II). Conceivably, unitarians would object to any statute that channels, if not limits, the president's powers as the Subdelegation Act does. However, the view expressed by Professor Stack asserts that the president has both statutory and constitutional powers. *See* Stack, *The Statutory President* at 541–46 (describing how Congress has long delegated power directly and exclusively to the president and other executive officials).

12. Unless, of course, delegations to private contractors are considered part of the president's inherent powers. The unitarian approaches appear not to have gone that far. *See* Chapter 5 at n. 47.

13. The virtue of Professor Merrill's exclusive delegation approach is that it removes any concerns about standardless delegations under the Subdelegation Act. *See* Merrill, *Rethinking Article I, Section I: From Nondelegation to Exclusive Delegation* at 2179. But under the exclusive delegation theory, the existence of some statutory delegation, rather than implied executive authority to subdelegate, is essential. *See id.* at 2175–76.

14. The Subdelegation Act dates to the Reorganization Act of 1951, which in turn was based on the Hoover Commission reorganization plan. *See The Hoover Commission Report on Organization of the Executive Branch of the Government* at 433–39.

15. Over the years the courts have limited subdelegations under this act. *See Cudahy Packing Co.,* 315 U.S. at 788 (amending an earlier decision); *U.S. Telecom Ass'n v. FCC,* 359 F.3d at 567–68 (limiting independent agency delegations to state authorities).

16. 359 F.3d at 565.

17. Admittedly, this gives the act some clout it did not have originally, since its concerns were more permissive than restrictive. *See* 3 U.S. C. § 302 (the president's power to delegate is absent only from the functions vested by those laws that "affirmatively prohibit delegation of the performance . . . or specifically designate the officer or officers to whom it may be delegated."). But the logic of the act surely cuts in the direction of limitations to private parties.

18. *See* Johnston, *I. R. S. Enlists Help in Collecting Delinquent Taxes, Despite the Higher Costs* at A1 (pointing out that IRS employees could have done the job at much lower cost).

19. *See* discussion of Circular A-76, Chapter 6 Part B.

20. The president cannot ignore congressional decisions to place political power in the hands of specific cabinet officers. *See* Strauss, *Presidential Rulemaking* at 986 (arguing that the president wields executive power within congressional constraints); *see also* Schubert, *Judicial Review of the Subdelegation of Presidential Power* at 684–89 (describing cases limiting presidential powers to subdelegate).

21. *Marbury*, 5 U.S. (1 Cranch) at 165–66.

22. The appointment and removal cases plumb the depths of what is both inherent and not subject to congressional control. *See Humphrey's Executor*, 295 U.S. at 629 (permitting congressional removal restrictions for quasi-judicial officials); *Myers*, 272 U.S. at 176 (holding even inferior executive officers – i.e., postmasters – free from congressional removal); *see also Perkins*, 116 U.S. at 484–85 (stating that civil service restrictions are constitutional).

23. *See* Monaghan, *Marbury and the Administrative State* at 15–17 (describing the judicial review imperatives of *Marbury*).

24. In *Cheney v. U.S. Dist. Ct.*, 542 U.S. at 375–77, Vice President Cheney claimed that receiving advice from the private sector for energy policy is protected by executive privilege. And this position was upheld. *See* In re *Cheney*, 406 F.3d at 728 (en banc) (holding that the vice president need only certify that decision authority on energy policy was not delegated to the private sector).

25. *See* Guttman, *Governance by Contract* at 326–29 (documenting earlier efforts to contract out during the Eisenhower and Kennedy administrations).

26. *See* discussion in Chapter 7.

27. *See* Palmer, *Performance-Based Contracting "Not Working," Industry Leader Says* (stating that "in fiscal 2004, $41.66 billion worth of procurements were noncompetitive").

28. *See* Swain, *Making a Killing* at 40–45 (documenting contracts for private military services in Iraq that have made the private military the second largest force in Iraq after the U.S. military itself).

29. *See, e.g.*, Shane & Lipton, *Stumbling Storm-Aid Effort Put Tons of Ice on Trips to Nowhere* at A1 (describing contracting errors in FEMA's provision of supplies to storm victims).

30. *See* Commercial Activities Panel, *Improving the Sourcing Decisions of the Government, Final Report* at 15 (listing the number of commercial positions by agency, e.g., Defense 412,756; Veterans Affairs 189,399).
31. *See id.* at 7.
32. *See id.* at 19.
33. *See* Office of Mgmt. & Budget, Executive Office of the President, OMB Circular A-76, at Attachment A, pt. B, 1(a) (Circular A-76) (2003) (narrowing nondelegable functions by changing "requiring the exercise of discretion" to "requiring the exercise of substantial discretion"); Vernon, *Battlefield Contractors: Facing the Tough Issues* at 376. Circular A-76 defines commercial functions as:

> Commercial Activities. A commercial activity is a recurring service that could be performed by the private sector and is resourced, performed, and controlled by the agency through performance by government personnel, a contract, or a fee-for-service agreement. A commercial activity is not so intimately related to the public interest as to mandate performance by government personnel. Commercial activities may be found within, or throughout, organizations that perform inherently governmental activities or classified work.

Circular A-76 at Attachment A, pt. B, 2.
34. Circular A-76 and the reports are *available at* http://www.whitehouse.gov/omb/index.html. In May 2004, OMB issued a report on competitive sourcing for the prior year, which indicated that agencies had completed 662 "competitive assessments" with a net estimated savings of $1.1 billion (over three to five years) or about $12,000 per full-time employee competed with a total cost avoidance of about 15 percent. *Competitive Sourcing: Report on Competitive Sourcing Results Fiscal Year 2003* at 2.
35. Circular A-76 at Attachment A, pt. B, 1(a).
36. Federal Activities Inventory Reform Act, 31 U.S.C. § 501 note.
37. Circular A-76 at Attachment A, pt. A, 1 ("An agency shall prepare two annual inventories that categorize all activities performed by government personnel as either commercial or inherently governmental.").
38. The agency lists appear in the Federal Register. *E.g., 69 Fed. Reg. 30,341–02* (May 27, 2004); *69 Fed. Reg. 3401–02* (Jan. 23, 2004). In its 2004 report, the GAO lists only some agency contracting out data and it is from 2002. U.S. Gen. Accounting Office, *Competitive Sourcing: Greater Emphasis Needed on Increasing Efficiency and Improving Performance* [hereinafter GAO Competitive Sourcing].
39. In November 2002, President Bush announced that the White House intended to let the private sector compete for 850,000 out of less than two million civil service jobs. Guttman, *Governance by Contract* at 330, n.23 (citing Stevenson, *Government May Make Private Nearly Half of Its Civilian Jobs* at A1. *See generally* Office of Mgmt. & Budget, *The President's Management*

*Agenda* at 17–18 (2002) (committing the administration to the cost saving objectives met by competitive sourcing).

40. Guttman, *Governance by Contract* at 332 n.33 (explaining that "in the mid-1990s, promised reforms led to congressional inquiries regarding hundreds of millions, even billions, in actual or projected cost overruns on various M&O contracts" (citing DOE's Fixed Price Cleanup Contracts: Why Are Costs Still Out of Control?: Hearing Before the Subcomm. on Oversight & Investigations of the House Comm. on Commerce, 106th Cong. 27–28 (2000) (prepared statement of Gary Jones, GAO))).

41. *See* GAO Competitive Sourcing at 2 (the agencies surveyed – USDA, DOD, Education, HHS, DOI, Treasury, and VA – represented 84 percent of all commercial positions being outsourced).

42. Comm. Activities Panel, n. 30, at 10.

43. *See id.* at 3.

44. *Id.* at 5.

45. *Id.* at 6.

46. *Id.* at 7.

47. Guttman, *Governance by Contract* at 327.

48. *See* Deloitte Consulting, *Calling a Change in the Outsourcing Market* at 4 ("Instead of simplifying operations, outsourcing often introduces complexity, increased cost and friction into the value chain. . . . ").

49. *See* discussion at Chapter 7, Part B.

50. *See* Guttman, *Governance by Contract* at 327.

51. *See* Chris Strohm, *TSA Examines Conflict of Interest Charges Against Contractor* (describing Lockheed Martin's contract with the Transportation Security Administration to evaluate airport screening operations, some of which may be contracted out to Lockheed at a later date); *see also* nn. 91–96 and accompanying text (discussing RAND Report on the use of private contractors on the battlefield).

52. *See* Guttman, *Governance by Contract* at 332–34.

53. See Light, *The True Size of Government* at 1 (providing numbers as of 1996).

54. *See generally* Nash & Cibinic, *Contracting Out Procurement Functions: "The Inherently Government Function" Exception*, at 45 (analyzing the definition of "inherently governmental function" and its application to the government's procurement activities).

55. *See* n. 53.

56. The FAIR Act codified the preexisting definition of "inherently governmental" contained in Circular A-76 and the OFPP Policy Letter. *OMB Transmittal Memorandum #20* (explaining that "the FAIR Act codified the pre-existing requirement for agencies to inventory their commercial activities, as well as the pre-existing definition of 'inherently governmental function'"). 10 U.S.C. § 2464(b) dictates that the "performance of workload needed to maintain a logistics capability [by DOD] may not be contracted for performance by

non-Government personnel under the procedures and requirements of [OMB] Circular A-76."

57. *See* nn. 35–36.

58. Office of Mgmt. & Budget, Executive Office of the President, OMB Circular A-76, at A2.

59. OMB issued a clarification to its revised circular that permitted challenges both to existing and "reclassified" agency positions. *See* 68 Fed. Reg. 48961 (Aug. 15, 2003). But these challenges are administrative only.

60. Federal Activities Inventory Reform Act, 112 Stat. 2382 (1998), 31 U.S.C. §501 (2003).

61. *See* Verkuil, *Public Law Limitations on Government Functions*, at 452–54 (outlining limits and possibilities of judicial and administrative review).

62. In FY2005, DOD issued $272.9 billion in contracts, which was 71.5 percent of all contracts issued by government. *See* OMB Watch, *OMB Watch Launches FedSpending.org.*

63. U.S. Gov't Accountability Office, *Contract Management: Opportunities to Improve Surveillance on Department of Defense Service Contracts* 1 [hereinafter GAO Report on Improving Surveillance].

64. *See* discussion n. 34.

65. Of course, it can sometimes also be a nightmare for private contractors who bear the brunt of poorly articulated contractual requirements that, when violated, make them look bad to the public.

66. *See* Bergner, *The Other Army* at 29, 30 (placing the number of armed military contractors in Iraq at 25,000, the second largest force after the U.S. military).

67. *See* Avant, *The Market for Force*, at 1.

68. *See* Singer, *Corporate Warriors* (documenting private military deployments in the Balkans, Colombia, and Africa in addition to Iraq).

69. *See* Avant, *The Market for Force* at 5–7.

70. *See* Schmitt, *Abuse Panel Says Rules on Inmates Need Overhaul: Command Chain Faulted* at A1 (summarizing the *Final Report of the Independent Panel to Review Department of Defense Detention Operations*); *see also* Schooner, *Contractor Atrocities at Abu Ghraib* at 555–57 (discussing the problems caused by using contractor personnel).

71. *See* Harris, *Technology Contract Used to Purchase Interrogation Work* (documenting CACI, Inc. and Premier Technology Group, Inc. contracts for "intelligence advisors" and "intelligence and technical support").

72. The military has been investigating ten homicides at Iraqi detention centers including at least one by a private contractor. *See* Graham, *Army Investigates Wider Iraq Offenses* at A1. At Abu Ghraib, several of the challenged interrogators were private contractors. Schmitt, *Abuse Panel Says Rules on Inmates Need Overhaul: Command Chain Faulted.*

73. *See* Lococo, *Titan Competing with Northrup, L-3 To Keep Its Largest Contract.*

74. *See* n. 33.

75. *See* n. 35.
76. Secretary of Defense Donald Rumsfeld, in hearings before the Armed Services Committees of the House and Senate on May 7, 2004, said: "These events occurred on my watch as secretary of defense. I am accountable for them. I take full responsibility." Graham, *Rumsfeld Takes Responsibility for Abuse* at A1. Secretary Rumsfeld also alerted Committee members that "there are a lot more photographs and videos that exist. If these are released to the public, obviously it's going to make matters worse." *Id.*
77. There have been few challenges to the contracting-out of military functions. When the Army tried to bypass A-76 altogether and deny federal employees any opportunity to retain their jobs (even if they could do them more cost-effectively), the debate became whether or not agencies could waive the requirements of A-76. In only one of those cases, dealing with a challenge to outsourcing army logistics jobs, was the challenge brought under A-76 for contracting out "inherently governmental" functions. *See Federal Employees Union Appeals Decision to Outsource Logistics Jobs.*
78. The Uniform Code of Military Justice does not apply to civilians. *See Grisham,* 361 U.S. at 279–80; *Gatlin,* 216 F.3d at 220–23.
79. The Department of Justice has indicted a private contractor, employed by the CIA, for beating a detainee in Iraq who later died. *See* Oppel & Hart, *Contractor Indicted in Afghan Detainee's Beating* at A1. Other statutes that may apply are the War Crimes Act of 1996, 18 U.S.C. § 2441 (2000); The Torture Act of 2000, 18 U.S.C. § 2340 (2000); and the Torture Victim Protection Act of 1991, 28 U.S.C. § 1350 (2000).
80. *See* Perlak, *The Military Extraterritorial Jurisdiction Act of 2000: Implications for Contractor Personnel* at 95 (discussing the ambiguity of the act as it relates to contractors oversees).
81. The Military Extraterritorial Jurisdiction Act, for example, only applies to civilians working for the DOD, not other federal agencies such as the CIA. *See* Singer, *War, Profits, and the Vacuum of Law* at 523–24 (discussing the difficulty of regulating a private military firm).
82. Iraq presents many challenges to the military, not least of which is its failure to meet recruiting targets, thereby increasing the pressure to contract out. *See* Shanker & Schmitt, *Rumsfeld Seeks Leaner Army, and a Full Term* at A1.
83. Private contractors also affect casualty figures, as they are not counted in military lives lost or wounded. Informed estimates put contractor deaths between two hundred and five hundred. Conversation with various parties.
84. *See* Vernon, *Battlefield Contractors: Facing the Tough Issues* at 376–77.
85. *See* nn. 33–35 and accompanying text.
86. This gap is potentially widened in Iraq by a June 2003 order that protects civilian contractors from Iraqi prosecution. *See* Mariner, *Private Contractors Who Torture*; *Coalition Provisional Authority Order Number 17 (Revised)* ("Contractors shall be immune from all Iraqi legal process with respect to

acts performed by them pursuant to the terms and conditions of a contract or any sub-contract thereto.").

87. *See* nn. 71–72, 79, and accompanying text.

88. *See The Torture Act* of 2000, 18 U.S.C. § 2340A (listing those individuals covered by the act).

89. *See* discussion nn. 27–28 and accompanying text.

90. Circular A-76 at Attachment A, pt. B, 1(a)(3).

91. Camm & Greenfield, *How Should the Army Use Contractors on the Battlefield?* at iv. *See* discussion at Chapter 5.

92. *See id.* at 125–28 (summarizing relevant risks in choosing between military or private personnel).

93. *See id.* at 146–49.

94. For one thing, the Report notes that a field commander cannot simply order a contractor to perform as he could a military subordinate. It also notes that a chaotic battlefield (the fog of war) can allow contractors to avoid effective oversight. *Id.* at 152–53.

95. *Id.* at 170.

96. *Defense Federal Acquisition Regulation Supplement; Contractor Personnel Supporting a Force Deployed Outside the United States*, 70 Fed. Reg. 23,790 (May 5, 2005) (to be codified at 48 C. F. R. pts. 207, 212, 225, and 252).

# 7 OUTSOURCING GOVERNMENT SERVICES: CONTRACT THEORY AND PRACTICE

Given the necessity and inevitability of outsourcing, a better understanding of government contracting is essential to overcoming the crisis of public control. A recent congressional report[1] sets out the scope of the outsourcing problem. During the period FY 2000 to FY 2005, the value of federal contracts increased by 86 percent (from $203 billion to $377 billion) and the value of noncompetitive contracts increased by 115 percent (from $67 to $145 billion).[2] The largest contractors received over 20 percent of these contracts and Halliburton's totals increased by 600 percent.[3] Iraq is undoubtedly a principal cause of these increases in the growth of noncompetitive contracts, but government has also been turning more generally to contractors during this five-year period.

This chapter approaches the contract problems inherent in private delegations by comparing contract theory with constitutional theory. It then utilizes agency cost theory to explain the current contracting out process at key agencies such as the DOD and the DHS. Sole sourcing has become a significant accountability issue. Government often relies on competition as a defense against inappropriate contracting. Rampant sole sourcing compromises the process. But even when contracts are competitively bid, the shortage of contract personnel to oversee the contracts that are awarded is itself an accountability concern.

## A. A CONTRACTARIAN APPROACH TO DELEGATION OF PUBLIC AUTHORITY TO PRIVATE HANDS: CARTER COAL MEETS BOSTON ICE

Contract theory underpins both public and private law. But public law concepts of delegation, which derive from the separation of powers doctrine, have not often been connected to the common law contract theory of nondelegation.[4] During the *Lochner* period, contract theory virtually merged with constitutional theory.[5] But the difficulties of managing private and public law concepts through the courts ultimately led to the demise of substantive due process review.[6] Still, as we live in a (social) contract state,[7] the connection of public nondelegation limitations to the private law of contracts continues to be relevant.

Contract theory illuminates a notably dark corner of delegation practice – the transfer of power from a principal to an agent. By posing limits on transfers of this authority, the law of contracts reinforces constraints upon delegations of public power to private hands. In effect, the words "delegation" and "nondelegation" have two meanings – contractual and constitutional. These meanings intersect and mutually reinforce one another. They also help set limits on the government contracting function.

### 1. Nondelegation, Due Process and *Carter Coal*

Government, through the Executive branch, has been delegating to private contractors an increasing number of services previously performed directly. This includes certain military functions (outsourced to the "private military"[8]) and civilian functions relating to homeland security and disaster relief.[9] These contracts by government do not involve simple "make or buy" choices[10] where procurement is straightforward and the products can be readily identified. Often the contractual delegations outsource services that transfer authority to private hands without adequate descriptions of the services to be provided. When that happens, the danger that government functions involving "significant authority" are also transferred is heightened and control of the public enterprise is threatened. Distinguishing between appropriate and inappropriate delegations of public power to private contractors is a crucial assignment for our legal system, as was taken up in Chapter 5. That chapter introduced *Carter v. Carter Coal* and the nondelegation/due process doctrine it supports.[11] Several cases from the *Lochner* era structure the limits on delegation to private hands of significant authority,[12] but *Carter Coal* is a better precedent for two reasons: First, it focuses on delegation to private partners, and, second, its core concern was due process–based.[13]

When Justice Sutherland labeled the delegation to private persons (who by majority and supermajority vote set prices for coal binding on the minority) a violation of due process, he cited *Schechter*.[14] But to him, it was delegation not to an official body "presumptively disinterested," but to "private persons," that made this "delegation in its most obnoxious form."[15] *Schechter* involved an industry code that fixed prices with government approval, a step that the court found lacking in *Carter Coal*.[16] Private parties in effect implemented government policy without the approval of public officials; those sworn to uphold the Constitution were excluded from the decision process. Such public protections were important to Justice Sutherland in *Carter Coal*. Although the point was not stressed by the parties,[17] it gave the Court a further reason to strike down the offensive statute.

This distinction between nondelegation and due process theories has survived in the post-*Lochner* era and the eclipsing of *Panama* and *Schechter*. *Carter*-type facial challenges to private adjudicators are not reached by federal due process,[18] but they remain viable under some state constitutions.[19] Applied due process challenges based on biased private adjudicators, however, continue to be successful in federal and state courts.[20] To this extent, due process continues to police the exercise of public power by private groups.

But due process challenges have not yet been brought in the outsourcing setting. To succeed, they would have to satisfy several conditions: first, the government function delegated would have to involve "significant authority" in the *Buckley* sense; second, the exercise of that authority would have to affect the property or liberty interests of an individual subjected to the privatized action; and third, restraints on justiciability or immunity from suit would have to be overcome.[21]

These three obstacles reduce the probability of successful litigation. If the actions were based on conduct of the private military (such as abusive interrogation practices), the proper plaintiff could be hard to find. Similarly, if the issue related to actions by private contractors working for FEMA during Katrina, which are not difficult to imagine, the issue of government immunity for their actions would figure prominently.[22] If the question was whether nursing home contractors improperly transferred, dismissed, or otherwise dealt with a nursing home patient, the question would be whether the state action requirement operates to constrain suits against the government.[23]

Absent a due process claim, striking down on a structural basis the use of private contractors who exercise significant authority would require the revival of the nondelegation doctrine. This will not likely happen at the federal level, where *Lochner*'s period of judicial activism remains vivid in the Court's mind.[24] Even applying structural due process challenges to decisions by private groups who exercise public power would produce echoes of the *Lochner* era. The problem with nondelegation or due process challenges is that they make it hard for the Court to create a decision rule that limits its authority.[25] Alternative, non-constitutional, theories may have a better chance at addressing the contractor devolution problem.[26]

## 2. Contractual Nondelegation and *Boston Ice*

A contractarian analysis of delegation implicates the social contract and the liberal political theory that connects public and private law.[27] Contract theory has much to offer. The nondelegation doctrine in private law provides interesting analogies to its constitutional counterpart. Contract theory has the great advantage of operating on an incremental basis;[28] it can be employed without jeopardizing the entire practice of outsourcing.

In contract law, the law of assignments and delegation evolved to overcome the difficulties of imposing on third parties what was essentially a personal relationship between contracting parties.[29] The modern law of contracts favors assignments and delegations, much like our constitutional law favors delegations; but contract law also poses limits relevant to the public setting.

The Restatement of Contracts and the Uniform Commercial Code both express reservations about delegations to third parties.

Section 318 of the Restatement 2d of Contracts reads as follows:

(1) An obligor can properly delegate the performance of his duty to another unless the delegation is contrary to public policy or the terms of his promise.
(2) Unless otherwise agreed, a promise requires performance by a particular person only to the extent that the obligee has a substantial interest in having that person perform or control the acts promised.

The UCC §2–210 reflects a similar approach:

(1) A party may perform its duty through a delegate unless otherwise agreed or unless the other party has a substantial interest in having his original promisor perform or control the acts required by the contract.

These provisions are the product of an evolution in delegation theory at common law, whose starting point is *Boston Ice Co. v. Potter*.[30] The defendant Potter contracted with Citizens to deliver ice. He did so to avoid dealing with the plaintiff (the competing ice provider in Boston). The plaintiff purchased Citizens and later presented to the defendant a bill for services. Potter refused to pay and the Massachusetts Supreme Judicial Court upheld his position (by sustaining his demurrer) on privity of contract grounds. Modern assignment cases have rejected privity of contract as a defense,[31] and *Boston Ice*'s restrictive nondelegation theory has been rejected as well.[32] When it comes to the delivery of ice – the ultimate fungible product – restricting the contracting parties from delegating the supply requirement to a third party (even an offensive one) makes little sense. Indeed, since one doubts that Potter even knew who was delivering the ice until he received a bill from Boston Ice rather than Citizens, his defense to payment seemed entirely self-serving.

But contractual delegations still have limits – the Restatement and U.C.C. provisions expressly state them. For Professor Corbin, a duty cannot be delegated if it is of a personal nature – Caruso, he says, cannot delegate his duty to sing.[33] Some courts hold that "personal services" can never be delegated.[34] The notion of personal services includes both "rare genius or extraordinary skill" in a Caruso sense[35] and also "best efforts" situations in which a party is placed in a compromised position by rendering services to a competitor.[36] Moreover, if there is a nonassignment or nondelegation clause in the contract, its presence reinforces the need for assent to personal delegations.[37]

Contractual nondelegation theory relies on principles of trust, judgment, and accountability to shift the presumption in favor of delegation. If the contracting parties have established a duty-bound relationship, it cannot be transferred to strangers without permission.[38] Allowing the parties to control risks relating to relationships of trust and discretion is a continuing purpose of the delegation doctrine in contract law.

## 3. Constitutionalizing the Contract Analogy

Constitutional nondelegation theory is concerned with matters of trust, judgment, and accountability as well. Contract theory supports constitutional theory in a way that would make the *Lochner* majority proud. In fact, it can be viewed as a metaphor for constitutional government.

Does the duty to govern, which is a contract between the People and its representatives (the Executive and Congress),[39] serve to limit delegation to third parties? When the duties are personal in a performance or governing sense – duties, in other words, that involve the exercise of significant authority – contract and constitutional delegation theories merge. To play out the analogy, think of the president as Corbin's Caruso, a virtuoso in the performance of government. When the "executive power" is delegated it must be given to those government officials who have the capacity to exercise the president's responsibilities. These are officials who are vetted by Congress.

The People "employ"[40] the president through the Constitution to exercise authority directly under Article II or indirectly through congressional grants under Article I.[41] Under agency theory, the people are the principal and the president is their agent.[42] When Congress delegates "legislative" powers to the president, the traditional nondelegation doctrine is triggered.[43] Whatever one feels about the traditional view, however, the president also delegates when he exercises executive powers.[44] When his Article I duties are subdelegated, Congress plays a direct role (on behalf of the people). It has a stake in the character of subdelegatees and in limiting those delegations to officers of the United States. Indeed, a purpose of the Subdelegation Act is to facilitate delegations within constitutional limits. In effect, the act becomes a nonassignment clause that impliedly forbids delegations to private contractors. Its purpose is to reduce the potential for faithless agents to exercise government functions. In this way it also honors the people's role as principal.

The relationships of personal confidence and trust that prevent delegations under contract law also preserve the relationship between the president and the people.[45] Nondelegation doctrine, when understood in terms of contract theory, helps illuminate reasons behind the limits on delegation to private parties. The statutory basis for limiting outsourcing of significant authority – matters of trust and judgment – is captured in the Subdelegation Act or indeed in any statute where the president or agency officials are granted authority to enforce the laws.[46] These statutes, like nonassignment clauses, can be read to restrict the further subdelegation of significant authority. This is how contract law informs public law. Thus when *Carter Coal* meets *Boston Ice*, these cases still have much to tell each other.

## B. CONTRACTS AND COMPETITION

Contract law is also a tool of government. Government contracts should help protect the public against abuses from outsourcing. Even without a nondelegation doctrine, substitute theories of public control pose constitutionally based process limits and statutory and administrative requirements. One of these is the institution of contract itself. This section explores the framework of government contracting, especially as it relates to the DOD.

Given its monopoly over force – it is the only buyer of military equipment and services – the United States is in an enviable position as a buyer of goods and services. DOD has the market power to dictate terms and conditions of service.[47] In fact, this leverage led Congress to provide rights to government contractors through procedural protections in the Competition in Contracting Act.[48]

### 1. An Overview of DOD Contracts with Private Providers

Since the 1980s, executive agencies have been governed by the Federal Acquisition Regulation (FAR),[49] which requires acquisition decisions that deliver the "best value" to the customer. The FAR is managed by the Office of Federal Procurement Policy, a White House–based office that reports to the OMB. The FAR has been amended several times[50] but its basic purpose- to deliver value to the government- remains unchallenged. A vast and complicated system of procurement and appeal accompanies the study of government contracting,[51] but this section will focus on the outsourcing of government services that arguably involve significant authority.

The procurement system relies to a great degree on contracting officers to manage the relationship with private contractors.[52] These officials act under a careful set of regulations that control conflict of interest problems[53] and help assure faithful agents. The use of competitive bidding and sealed bids produces what the FAR labels "full and open competition." This process itself is a method of achieving the best value for the customer.

But, increasingly, contracts are not awarded after competitive bidding. Sole-sourced contracts have almost become the norm. For example, Lockheed Martin, the largest government contractor in FY 2005 with $24.8 billion in awards, received only one-third of its contracts through full and open competition.[54] While spending on federal contracts has increased by 83 percent since FY 2000, no-bid and other noncompetitive contracts have increased by 115 percent.[55] The war in Iraq is the primary cause for this growth.

## 2. Single Sourcing in Government Contracts – The Iraq Effect

The situation in Iraq reveals the DOD's inability to dictate contract terms. In need of logistical services in the runup to war, the DOD felt itself in no position to bargain. It succumbed to a rash of single-sourced, no-bid contracts that are continuing years after the invasion. As Congressman Henry Waxman recently reported: "38 percent of federal contract dollars were awarded in 2005 without full and open competition, a significant percentage increase from 2000."[56]

The CACI contract to provide intelligence services at Abu Ghraib has become an embarrassing example of this practice.[57] Open-ended contracts are the rule in Iraq,[58] and have been extended more broadly by the DOD.[59] Even in the context of Iraq, once the initial surge to prepare for war was over, it is hard to understand why government should continue to award contracts that place it at an oversight disadvantage.

This question is at the heart of the government-contract dilemma. The rules on competitive bidding have been largely set aside and private contractors such as Halliburton and its subsidiaries have become indispensable players.[60] Some contracts have been cost-effective,[61] but there are those who claim outsourcing actually increases DOD expenditures.[62] Currently, over fifty contracts are being challenged by congressional overseers, who ask why, "instead of competition, the Administration has awarded monopoly cost-plus contracts to favored contractors like Halliburton."[63]

There is little doubt that these contracts permit or even encourage fraud and abuse.[64] Incompletely negotiated agreements can undermine the purpose of the contracting function. They are temptations in themselves, and they also lead to legitimate misunderstandings between contractor and government that take years to resolve. Iraq is an environment where, in the words of one experienced observer, it is often hard to tell whether the contractors are patriots or crooks, or perhaps "crooked patriots."[65]

Overseeing these contracts is a demanding and complex task. To do the job correctly contracting officers must be readily available and in a monitoring mode. In fact there are too few contracting officers in Iraq. And, in general, the oversight problem is exacerbated by a shortage of DOD contract administrators. Pentagon contracting officials were trimmed by 38 percent in the past five years. Again, observers believe some contractors "may have exploited the new freedom" from oversight.[66] The DOD knows this. A report to the Secretary of Defense on contract management issued by the GAO noted that contractual surveillance was deficient in twenty-six of the fifty DOD contracts reviewed.[67] The report noted that declining personnel levels was a factor influencing the inadequacy of oversight.[68] The inevitable question is why more has not been done to protect the public sector from the exploitative effects of inadequate contracting practices.

## 3. The Governance Virtues of Competitive Contracts

Competition is an ideal constraint on overreaching. Where it is possible to achieve, it creates a self-enforcement regime. Competition sets up winners and losers who themselves serve as checks against each other. Even when competition is limited, big entities such as Lockheed Martin or Boeing, repeat players with much to lose, are also potential critics of each other's performances. Competition therefore sets the baseline for government contracting.[69] It provides a process dimension that can help ensure better contracting on the government's part. In fact, viewed from a perspective of public law values,[70] competitive contracting procedures are essential.

But not all contracts can be competitively sourced. Situations arise, such as Iraq, where immediate needs trump competitive bidding. Sole sourcing then becomes an important contracting tool, so long as it is viewed as an exceptional one. But sole-sourced contracts encourage opportunistic behavior and hold up problems by the contracting parties.[71] Engaging in sole-sourced contracting usually leads to incomplete contracts (cost plus arrangements) and places a powerful negotiating tool in the hands of contractors. They are on the scene, often without adequate oversight, and free to make changes whether or not conditions on the ground call for them. This "freedom" leads to self-interested and arbitrary behavior. It undermines most of the protections the public contracting process is meant to achieve.[72]

The public law values of process, openness, and fairness are at risk in the single supplier situation. Moreover, in the military setting, the contracts themselves are often secret or severely circumscribed in disclosure,[73] making them difficult for the public to monitor. Indeed, even government itself has difficulty in monitoring contracts with open-ended terms and cost-plus assurances. The need for close supervision requires additional staff. With current personnel limitations, this function cannot even be performed in house and has been outsourced. When oversight becomes a commodity, its status as a public value has been diminished, if not eliminated. Outside monitors may do acceptable work, but they must themselves be monitored.

The problem of who guards the guardians is further exacerbated in these circumstances. Moreover, given the limited number of eligible companies, conflicts of interest inevitably emerge.[74] Even the well-intentioned contractor can be compromised, as it tries to comply with government requests for services and oversight. Although services can be competitively sourced, the oversight function itself should remain an inherent function of government. The problem with Iraq, or with other situations requiring exceptionally fast responses, like Katrina, is that the exceptional becomes the norm. At that point, protective contract provisions that should be restored or reinstated are largely forgotten.

Laura Dickinson has suggested some general additions to Iraqi contracts that would help ensure public law values. Contractor requirements for appropriate training, monitoring (self or third party), performance benchmarks (and, where applicable, self-evaluation), and strengthened enforcement mechanisms can be drawn from other public contract settings.[75] These practical suggestions to establish parameters around the broad discretion provided Iraqi contractors are surely feasible now even if they were not at the outset of the conflict. In a war zone some five years old, the provisions should become part of the "exceptional routine" of Iraqi reconstruction.[76] To the extent that government ignores them, the contracting process will remain fraught with inefficiencies, failures to perform, and fraud.

Contracting rules are meant to ensure that government gets what it pays for. How contracts are constructed and administered determines their public value. Proper contract administration does not guarantee success. But the failure to use competitive bidding, combined with the inability to enforce contracts effectively, virtually guarantees deficient results. Ultimately, government contracting should ensure that the private parties government chooses to fulfill its needs are faithful agents. Agency cost theory helps make this connection more explicit.

## C. CONTRACTS AND AGENCY COST THEORY

Agency theory is a branch of transactions cost analysis.[77] Transaction costs arise in the contractual setting in which the "behavioral attitudes of human agents" determine the level of costs involved.[78] It is the job of contract law to govern or order the relationships among the parties so as to avoid agency cost problems.

In general, the agent, whether it be a corporate manager or a government contractor, has and will serve his or her own interests rather than those of the principal. Contract is one way[79] to reduce the agency costs associated with this deviant behavior. If contracts are properly employed they can reduce agency costs; competitive bidding, careful drafting, and effective oversight are all methods for achieving this reduction in agency costs by private contractors.

Moreover, government itself exhibits agency cost problems, labeled bureaucratic drift.[80] To reduce these costs, and to satisfy the nondelegation doctrine, Congress sets directions that agencies implement by rules and standards. Statutes with vague delegations invite government agents (the agencies) to pursue their own interests by emphasizing discretionary acts. Occasionally, the adventurous bureaucratic behavior that results is celebrated,[81] but in general loss of legislative control is decried. In some circumstances, private contractors, properly instructed and supervised, can be as effective in implementing instructions as the bureaucracy itself. They have financial incentives to please their employers that may offset the loyalty requirements of government officials.

Viewed from the perspective of agency costs alone, it is possible to construct a contractor regime that is more true to the principal's needs and goals than is the direct exercise of the same power by public officials. As John Donahue has shown, this would require comparing careful contracting (an agency cost-reduction device) to loosely instructed and managed public officials.[82] Careful instructions, in other words, can deliver reliable services whether the provider is private or not. But, of course, in many private contracting situations, such as in Iraq, care in contracting is absent.[83] Left adrift in a sea of discretion and no-bid contracts, private contractors are more likely than their government counterparts to produce agency cost problems.

Principal-agent theory takes us back to the definition of sovereignty in Chapter 1.[84] If the principal (the sovereign) under our Constitution is the People, her agents are the Congress and Executive. To protect the principal's interests, these agents swear loyalty to the Constitution. The question is whether the subdelegatees are also loyal to the people. Loyalty is harder to achieve the further removed the agent is from the principal. When Congress delegates to the president under

Article I, this loyalty is assured through careful instructions ("intelligible principles"). When the president subdelegates to officials under Article II, loyalty is achieved through oaths the agents have taken. Since private contractors have not taken oaths, their loyalty is harder to monitor. Careful drafting of contracts is the main device both for reducing agency costs and achieving loyal service.

Contract theory can only hope to substitute for oath taking as a means of avoiding faithless agents so long as principles of careful drafting and oversight are honored. When they are not, the burden on contracting officials to achieve accountability is heightened. One way to answer the loyalty question is simply to conclude that if the agent's service requires an oath, that is, if the job is assigned to an officer of the United States, it can never be outsourced to those for whom oath-taking is a constitutional impossibility. In all other arrangements, private delegates must be controlled by contracting requirements and overseen by public officials.

## NOTES

1. Comm. on Gov. Reform, Min. Staff, Special Invest. Division (Henry A. Waxman) (June 2006).
2. *Id.* at 3, 8.
3. *Id.* at 6.
4. *But see* Guttman, *Inherently Governmental Functions and the New Millenium* at 62–64, drawing the analogy.
5. *See* Chapter 2, *supra*; *Lochner*, 198 U.S. 45 (incorporating contract into the liberty and property rights expressed in the due process clause).
6. *See Nebbia*, 291 U.S. 502.
7. Social contract theorists from Locke and Rousseau to Rawls have wrestled with the question whether private law defines or is only part of public law, but all would accept a relationship between the two regimes. *See, e.g.*, Ripstein, *Private Order and Public Justice: Kant and Rawls* at 15–16.
8. *See, e.g.*, Singer, *Corporate Warriors*.
9. For example, the Department of Homeland Security, which includes FEMA and its disaster relief obligations, is a major delegator of public functions to private contractors. Sometimes former department officials who are now in the private sector are the beneficiaries. *See* Lipton, *Former Antiterror Officials Find Industry Pays Better*.
10. *See* Williamson, *Public and Private Bureaucracies: A Transactions Cost Economics Perspective* (tying outsourcing to reduction in transactions costs).
11. 298 U.S. 238; *see* Chapter 5.

12. The classic nondelegation cases are *A.L.A. Schechter Poultry Corp.*, 295 U.S. 495 and *Panama Refinining Co. v. Ryan*, 293 U.S. 388.

13. *See* Jaffe, *Law Making by Private Groups* at 248 (suggesting that *Carter Coal* could have dropped delegation as a constitutional category and relied exclusively on due process); Chapter 3.

14. Justice Sutherland's majority opinion in *Carter* relies on *Schechter Poultry* to support its lack of interstate commerce and nondelegation points. *See Carter Coal*, 298 U.S. at 306–09. Justice Cardozo's dissent, for himself and Justices Brandeis and Stone, focused on interstate commerce and noted that *Nebbia v. New York*, decided in the prior term, had accepted the validity from a delegation standpoint of maximum and minimum price regulation. *Id.* at 327–30. Cardozo did not address (or contest) Sutherland's enduring point - that as a matter of due process a grant of rate fixing power to a private group is "delegation in its most obnoxious form." *Id.* at 311.

15. *Id.*

16. Under § 3 of the NIRA, a trade association could propose to the president a "code of fair competition," provided he found that the group adequately represented the interests of the industry at large and that the proposal did not favor monopolistic practices. *A. L. A. Schechter Poultry Corp.* 295 U.S. at 521–23.

    The majority in *Carter Coal* found especially pernicious the provisions of the Bituminous Coal Act (BCA), by contrast, which automatically imposed on all coal producers the hours and rates agreed to by two-thirds of the producers and half of the workers. *Carter v. Carter Coal Co.*, 298 U.S. at 283–84. In Sutherland's eyes, "[t]he power conferred upon the majority is, in effect, the power to regulate the affairs of an unwilling minority. This is legislative delegation in its most obnoxious form; for it is not even delegation to an official or an official body, presumptively disinterested, but to private persons whose interests may be and often are adverse to the interests of others in the same business." 298 U.S. at 311. Thus, under the BCA the few safeguards that existed in the NIRA scheme (an intervening executive branch) were not even present; of course those protections were found insufficient in *Schechter Poultry* on nondelegation rather than due process grounds.

17. Counsel for defendants in the *Schechter* and *Carter* cases did not argue this distinction. *See* Swaine, *The Cravath Firm* Vol. II at 556–67, 697–700 (describing the firm's efforts as counsel in both cases).

18. *See Friedman v. Rogers*, 440 U.S. 1 (rejecting a due process challenge to a state appointed board of independent optometrists).

19. *Compare Texas Boll Weevil Eradication Foundation*, 952 S.W. 2d 454 (striking down on *Schechter* grounds a private body under Article II of the Texas Constitution).

20. In *Gibson v. Berryhill*, 411 U.S. 564, the Court applied the Due Process Clause to bias in the adjudication of an optometrist's application to do

business in Alabama. *See* Bonham's Case, 77 Eng. Rep. 646 ("No man can be a judge in his own cause.").

21. *See Oil, Chemical and Atomic Workers Int'l Union*, 214 F.3d 1379 (holding DOE's failure to enforce labor provisions of its contracts precluded from review under 5 U.S.C. § 701 (a) (2)).

22. Under the Stafford Act, federal government intervention is upon request of state governments. The act contains a discretionary exception to the waiver of sovereign immunity which operates much like the Federal Tort Claims Act exception. 42 U.S.C. § 5148 (applying the discretionary function exception of the Federal Tort Claims Act); *see* 28 U.S.C. § 2680 (a).

23. *See* discussion in Chapters 2 and 5.

24. *See Whitman v. Am. Trucking Ass'ns*, 531 U.S. 457; discussion in Chapter 4.

25. *See* Scalia, A Matter of Interpretation at 41–46 (discussing the indeterminacy of the "Living Constitution").

26. Still, nondelegation and due process theories could be distinguished and the latter preserved in the form of an applied challenge on *Carter Coal* grounds.

27. *See* Locke, *The Second Treatise of Government* (using the "social contract" to preserve individual freedoms). Locke's influence on our founders, particularly Thomas Jefferson in the Declaration of Independence, has long been acknowledged. *See* Becker, *The Declaration of Independence* at 27 ("The very phrases [of Locke's Treatise] reappear in [Jefferson's] writing").

28. *See* Freeman, *The Private Role in Public Governance* at 548–49.

29. *See* Grismore, *Effect of a Restriction on Assignment in a Contract*; Cook, *The Alienability of Choses in Action*.

30. 123 Mass. 28.

31. *See Lawrence v. Fox*, 20 N.Y. 268 (rejecting privity defense).

32. *See Macke Co. v. Pizza of Gaithersburg, Inc.*, 270 A.2d 645 (permitting delegation to a third party of vending machines placed in defendants' stores; *Boston Ice* disapproved).

33. Corbin, *Corbin on Contracts*, Vol. 9 §865 p. 386. Or, if you prefer the analogies to the duty to paint portraits *à la* Sir Joshua Reynolds or to write dramas per Shakespeare, consult *Taylor v. Palmer*, 31 Cal. at 247–248, cited in *Macke*.

34. *See, e.g., Sally Beauty Co. v. Nexxus Prods. Co.*, 801 F.2d at 1008 (personal services, such as distribution of plaintiff's product by a competitor, are "per se nondelegable").

35. *See* Hillman, *Principles of Contract Law* at 341–42.

36. *But see Sally Beauty*, 801 F.2d at 1009–10 (Posner, J. dissenting) (rejecting the best efforts argument in a competitor situation).

37. *See* Restatement (First) of Contracts § 160(3) (1932); *see also* U.C.C. § 2–210(2).

38. *See Valley Smelting Co. v. Belden Mining Co.*, 127 U.S. at 387–88; *Humble* v. *Hunter*, 12 Q. B. at 317.

39. *See* Chapter 1 Part C for a discussion of how sovereignty in the people defines our Constitution.

40. *See* Shapiro & Steinzor, *The People's Agent* ("employing" agency cost theory to connect the president to the public).

41. The implications of the president's exercise of direct authority under Article II (e.g., commander in chief powers) or indirect delegated power under Article I (e.g., enforcement of statutes) from an agency cost perspective are pursued in Part C of this chapter.

42. *See* Posner & Vermeule, *The Credible Executive* at 9–10 (viewing public as principal and President as agent).

43. *See A. L. A. Schechter Poultry*, 295 U.S. at 553 (Cardozo, J., concurring) ("delegation running riot"); *see also* Lawson, *Delegation and Original Meaning* (supporting traditional view).

44. A unitary approach to executive power makes it easier to justify delegations to public officials, but would not necessarily justify delegations to private hands. *See* Calabresi & Prakash, *The President's Power to Execute the Laws*.

45. *See Arkansas Valley Smelting Co. v. Belden Mining Co.*, 127 U.S. at 387–88.

46. *See* Stack, *The President's Statutory Powers to Administer the Laws* (describing various statutory limitations on the president's powers).

47. *See* Blair & Harrison, *Monopsony* 5–7.

48. 98 Stat. 1175 (1984), 10 U.S.C. §§ 2304–305 (2000); 41 U.S.C. §§ 253–253a (2000). CICA establishes procedures for disappointed bidders in contracts with executive agencies to file bid protests before GAO.

49. 48 C.F.R. Chapter 1.

50. *See, e.g.,* the Federal Activities Inventory Reform (FAIR) Act.

51. *See, e.g.,* Keyes, *Government Contracts in a Nutshell.*

52. *See also* Competition in Contracting Act (requiring agencies to appoint a "competition advocate").

53. Keyes, *Government Contracts in a Nutshell* at 58–62.

54. *See* OMB Watch, *OMB Watch Launches FedSpending.org.*

55. *Id.*

56. *See* Comm. on Gov. Reform, Min. Staff, Special Investigation Div. (prepared for Henry A. Waxman) (June 2006), *Dollars, Not Sense: Gov. Contracts under the Bush Administration*; discussion at n. 2.

57. *See* Center for Public Integrity, *Contracts and Reports* (listing the CACI contracts). *See also* Schooner, *Contractor Atrocities at Abu Ghraib*. CACI states on its website that it no longer provides interrogation services.

58. *See generally* Dickinson, *Public Law Values in a Privatized World* at 403–04 (documenting numerous Iraq contracts).

59. Kopecki, *When Outsourcing Turns Outrageous.*

60. The top Iraq contractors are KBR, Parsons Corp., Fluor Corp., Washington Group Int'l., Shaw Group, and Bechtel Group. *See* Center for Public Integrity, *Windfall of War*.

61. KBR's provision of basic services to troops, which cost over $5 billion in 2004, was found by the Congressional Budget Office to have resulted in some $2 billion in savings from an in-house perspective. At the same time, KBR is accused by DOD auditors of overcharging.

62. *See* Waste, Fraud and Abuse in U.S. Government Contracting in Iraq, Hearings before Policy Comm., 109th Cong. 10 (2005).

63. *Id.*

64. Iraqi fraud incidents are apparently not limited to private contractors. Federal auditors have found that USAID also had cost overruns in reconstruction projects. *See* Glanz, *Audit Finds U.S. Hid Actual Cost of Iraq Projects.*

65. *Id.* (quoting Jeffrey H. Smith, former Clinton CIA general counsel, now representing contractors in private practice).

66. *Id.* (quoting Frank Camm of RAND).

67. GAO, Report to the Secretary of Defense, Contract Management – Opportunities to Improve Surveillance on Department of Defense Service Contracts (GAO-05-274) (Mar. 2005).

68. *Id.* at 3.

69. The Federal Requisition Regulation (FAR) requires the use of "competitive procedures," thereby acknowledging the relationship between the two concepts. Similarly, the CICA requires full and open competition as the norm.

70. *See* Dickinson, Public Law Values at 396, 400–01 (discussing these values).

71. *See* Shapiro, *Outsourcing Government Regulation* at 430–33 (discussing hold up problems in the context of transactions cost theory).

72. *See* nn. 55 and 56, *supra.*

73. *See* Dickinson, Public Law Values, at 400–01.

74. To take one example, Bechtel Group, a top Iraq infrastructure contractor, *see* n. 60, *supra*, submitted, under the name Bechtel National, an assessment on water, ports, and airports in Iraq, *see* Iraq Infrastructure Reconstruction Program, to USAID in June 2003. *See* Center for Public Integrity, *Contracts and Reports.*

75. *See* Dickinson, *Public Law Values*, at 410–22.

76. *See* Glanz, *Idle Contractors Add Millions to Iraq Rebuilding.*

77. *See* Williamson, *The Economic Institutions of Capitalism* at 27–30 (describing agency theory).

78. *Id.* at 29.

79. Other ways include the use of information disclosure and transparency. In government, these ends are achieved through the FOIA and FACA. *See* Shapiro & Steinzor, *The People's Agent*, at 4–6.

80. *See* Gailmard, *Expertise, Subversion and Bureaucratic Discretion* at 537.

81. *See* Carpenter, *The Forging of Bureaucratic Autonomy* (documenting "entrepreneurial" achievements at the Department of Agriculture and at the Post Office in the 1920s); Mashaw, *Recovering American Administrative Law* at 1282–84 (describing early grants of power to agencies and departments).

82. Donahue, *The Privatization Decision* at 45–47 (favoring private contracts over bureaucracy where contracts involve precise requirements that can be specified in advance and noting that contracts are about ends, not means).
83. Donahue's preference scale described above requires well specified contracts in a competitive context, conditions which are surely missing in the military context in Iraq.
84. *See* Chapter 1 Part C.

# 8 STRUCTURAL REFORMS TO GOVERNMENT

This book has explored many paths to reasserting public control over government functions. In doing so, a careful line has been drawn between respecting privatization or outsourcing as a reform movement, while challenging its transformative effects. Originally seen as a way to overcome the unresponsive bureaucracy, it had many successes. But outsourcing has become so pervasive that it now operates with an unwarranted degree of acceptance. The role of the private contractor in the bureaucratic state should not be accepted uncritically. The constitutional, statutory, and regulatory options already discussed are essential to restore balance to government. But they will carry the cause only so far. A fresh look at the way the government functions – one that both utilizes and criticizes the services provided by private contractors – can help fulfill the public-private structure on which our democracy depends.

This chapter reviews and builds on established efforts to reform the bureaucracy. These efforts were not undertaken to solve the outsourcing problem, but, when so refocused, they support the ideas expressed in this book. Ultimately, inside government critiques may have the best chance to control outsourcing practices; it is surely the case that such practices will not be controlled without them. Gaining an internal perspective[1] on the problem is an indispensable condition to solving it.

## A. DISTINGUISHING PUBLIC SERVANTS FROM PRIVATE CONTRACTORS: OF FOXES AND HEDGEHOGS

The job of government is to steer, not to row the boat.

– E. S. Savas[2]

Before discussing ways to reform and improve the civil service, some goals should be identified. If the job of government has changed as a result of its reinvention, as Osborne and Gaebler concluded, finding people who can function best in this setting is crucial. This "new bureaucratic person" has more, not less, responsibility under a public-private regime. In a privatized world, the government official must manage and direct a smaller bureaucracy but a larger contractor community in which oversight and accountability are key factors.

To give but one example, government agencies are doing more contracting with private parties to establish or enforce regulatory standards.[3] This is a prevalent practice in environmental regulation. These sophisticated agreements require agencies to judge and evaluate alternatives to command and control regulation.[4] They require government officials who are up to that task.

It is more complicated to steer than to row. Steering requires adjusting. To a sailor, taking into account the prevailing winds as well as unexpected gusts is the required skill. Rowing, by contrast, is a determined, singly focused, straight ahead affair for the crew. These are distinctly different talents. Isaiah Berlin's famous metaphor of the fox and the hedgehog[5] comes to mind. The fox, facing an eclectic set of responses, is the one who steers; the hedgehog, the persistent plodder, is the one who rows. If this analogy holds, then the new bureaucrat must be a fox, not a hedgehog. What we want from him or her is judgment and management skills more than the ability to execute routine assignments. Routine assignments can be outsourced under this new regime.

Phillip Tetlock recently underscored the benefits of this distinction.[6] In a fascinating study using Berlin's metaphor,[7] he determined that foxes make better political judgments than hedgehogs.[8] "What experts *think*," he found, "matters far less than *how* they think."[9] This testimonial to relativism may strike some as insidious. Politicians who are determined and dogged are often the most highly regarded: "Stay the course," "Full speed ahead," and so forth. But that is Tetlock's point – hedgehogs, though more admired, are the ones less likely to exercise good political judgment. Even though foxes have a mixed reputation (for guarding henhouses, that is), they seem better prepared to govern.

Steering the reinvented government requires bureaucrats of good judgment. Their challenge is to manage systems and programs that are themselves the product of diverse sources. The elected political leaders must have trust in the bureaucracy, which consists of foxes and hedgehogs; increasingly consultants are doing the rowing. Ideally, these consultants are the hedgehogs – the experts who know one big thing. Management of these experts requires bureaucrats who can adjust their thinking to the challenges posed.[10]

But bureaucrats have multiple responsibilities – they are principals over consultants and subordinates to Congress. To lower agency costs, Congress wants faithful servants, not necessarily creative thinkers. As Professors Epstein and O'Halloran have taught us, in a time of divided government, Congress is reluctant to transfer broad powers to executive agencies, due to hold-up problems caused by agencies with too much discretion.[11] Operating as both principals and agents is a challenging assignment for senior bureaucrats (who are also agents of the executive). It takes a talented public servant, with a taste for the relativity of power, to perform these roles well.

These qualities argue for generalists who can implement programmatic goals in a world of shifting priorities. The Senior Executive Service (SES) originally captured this idea,[12] although it has not been realized in practice. This is one of the distinguishing characteristics of public servants that a reinvigorated SES ought to revive. In an era where consultants are leaving their burrows to become foxes, creative public leadership is essential. The preservation of inherent government functions in the hands of public officials means retaining public control of matters of discretion and judgment. The formulation and execution of public policy are for the elected and appointed branches of government.

## B. PUBLIC SUPPORT FOR IMPROVING GOVERNMENT FUNCTIONS: VOLCKER AND BEYOND

A variety of recent studies on the need to improve the government offer relevant prescriptions. The National Commission on the Public Service, chaired by Paul Volcker, issued two reports: one in 1989[13] and one in 2003.[14] These reports bracketed three Administrations (Bush I, Clinton, and Bush II), which themselves produced other relevant reports and analyses.

The Clinton-Gore "reinventing government" era highlighted (and heralded) the privatization movement. The Clinton-Gore National Performance Review (NPR) built on Bush I ideas for encouraging competition and competitiveness, and succeeded in significantly reducing the size of the federal government.[15] President George W. Bush, riding this wave, has suggested that government employment should be further reduced by 850,000.[16] As discussed earlier,[17] this would reduce the civilian federal government to about 1.2 million officials. These officials, in turn, must manage a force of twelve to fifteen million contractors,[18] a ratio of 1 to 12 or 15. However, only some government employees are managers, which makes the magnitude of the management problem far greater.

As John DiIulio has observed, in practice this means that policy level government officials will increasingly be acting solely as contract administrators over the outsourced bureaucracy.[19] Professor DiIulio's earlier work[20] on the Clinton-Gore initiatives emphasized "deregulating" the public sector, by which he meant freeing the public sector to do its job better. Further downsizing inhibits the ability of public servants to function effectively. At some stage, the ability of government officials both to act and oversee is overwhelmed by the sheer scope of their responsibilities. Very little attention seems to be paid to the costs associated with tying the bureaucracy down, so that it can neither steer nor row. The greater fear is that the importance of public service has been lost in the era of privatization.

Volcker II is concerned with aspects of this problem. This report benefits from a decade of experience and learning on governmental reform, deregulation and privatization. Paul Volcker starts with a critical question – public trust in government – which connects to the larger problem of creative public officials. There has been a deep decline in trust since World War II. To some extent, this decline is a function of government inefficiencies that have been highlighted by the deregulation movement. It is also a result of the "running against Washington" attitudes of the Reagan presidency that sought to enlist the public in bureaucracy bashing.[21]

But a remarkable thing happened after 9/11. Volcker notes that levels of trust went from 29 percent just before September 11 to 57 percent just after, reaching a level not seen since the 1960s.[22] This remarkable revival of trust was a reaction to the terrorist threat and to the performance of many civil servants in the face of that threat.

The trust levels dropped back to 40 percent thereafter,[23] and Volcker considers that fact an opportunity missed. What was missed, he believes, was the chance to organize government in a more coherent manner so as to lock in these gains in public trust. The key for his commissions was to use senior bureaucrats more effectively.

The 9/11 period was indeed a dramatic one for government at all levels. Images of New York fire and police risking (and giving) their lives at the World Trade Center helped restore the public sector to prominence.[24] Would private contractors have entered the Twin Towers that day in a vain but heroic attempt to rescue the inhabitants? The service of our military in Afghanistan and Iraq has produced a similar respect for the loyalty and sacrifice of public officials. But public sector prominence is not assured by these events; Volcker is right to urge government to take advantage of reforms necessary to solidify it.

Doing so will not be easy, however. At the federal level, personnel ceilings and retirements are leading to a "vanishing talent" problem.[25] More than 50 percent of the members of the SES are eligible to retire. A brain drain on federal service is on the horizon. To offset this threat, Volcker searches for better ways to utilize senior officials. He places the emphasis on reorganization: "Without government reorganization, it will be very difficult to revitalize the public service."[26] The Commission recommendations for reorganization fall into two broad categories: organization and operational effectiveness.[27] Both have some connections to the outsourcing problem.

## 1. Organization of Mission-Oriented Agencies

The Volcker Commission proposes to reorganize government around a "limited number of mission-related executive departments."[28] For historical and political reasons missions of agencies are so disbursed that "no coherent management is possible."[29] Unlike earlier commissions (such as the Hoover Commission in the 1950s), the Volcker Commission rejects "one-size-fits-all management" and looks for "organization, leadership and culture that fit the mission, not just a single theory of administration."[30]

This search for an appropriate level of mission orientation leads Volcker to the newest executive agency – the Department of Homeland Security. As we have seen, this is an agency that has been active in utilizing private contractors and has had difficulties with the revolving door.[31] But the report commends its mission orientation and sees it as a model to be followed throughout government.[32] The DHS was established by Congress in 2002 at the request of President Bush to move a "confusing patchwork of government activities into a single department whose primary mission is to protect our homeland."[33] The agency combines disparate functions of separate agencies such as Customs, the Immigration and Naturalization Service, the Federal Protective Service (Secret Service), FEMA, and many others under a single mission-driven directorate.[34]

The Volcker Commission's view of the DHS as a new mission-oriented agency is not without problems, however. One can accept that by reforming agency missions and purposes the public service is able to develop and perform better. But reorganization itself has problematic dimensions, especially as they relate to the DHS. There are real doubts that the creation of DHS through the massive reorganization of twenty-two disparate agencies has been or even can be a success. It has been attacked for a disastrous performance during Hurricane Katrina and more broadly for a failure to achieve accountability over its mission.[35] Indeed, Professors Cohen, Cuellar and Weingast believe that the only "success" of DHS reorganization was to frustrate the legacy mandates of the separate agencies that it replaced.[36] These authors conclude that the transactions costs involved in the reorganization were not offset by any security gains achieved through the creation of the new agency.[37]

This is a sobering study of the effects of reorganization. It also makes a point relevant to the Volcker Commission's connection of reorganization to the revitalization of the public service. The DHS reorganization disrupted the public servants involved. It caused many top officials of the key agencies, such as FEMA, to leave; more than 40 percent of high-level staff positions at the agency are vacant.[38] Surely public service has not been revitalized at this agency. Indeed, on a more general level, it stands to reason that agency officials who find themselves reorganized are likely to lose rather than gain positions of influence. As top positions contract, leadership opportunities become more remote. Because expertise favors career bureau chiefs over political appointees,[39] this contraction is likely to jeopardize the public service as much as a new mission invigorates it. Thus, while the Volcker Commission argues for it, reorganization by itself cannot be relied on for the revival of government officialdom. Something more is needed.

## 2. Political Versus Career Officials – The Need for Professional Managers

Beyond mission, the Volcker Commission focuses on another needed change – the ratio of political appointees to the number of senior career managers. Volcker notes that President Kennedy had 286 political leadership positions to fill, President Clinton 914, and President George W. Bush 3,361.[40] This fifteenfold expansion of political appointees, remarkable by itself, has been occurring, of course, at the same time that the overall government head count contracts (or remains flat at the SES level). Volcker argues that this large number of political appointees paralyzes government both because it diminishes the civil service and because the appointment and confirmation process itself is so cumbersome. By delaying the confirmation of presidential appointees, Congress has limited their availability to serve; the Commission seeks to alleviate these problems as well.[41]

The Commission also notes the demoralizing effect of political appointees on professional managers.[42] In the era of privatization, that is not a compelling argument by itself. Without knowing whether political or career managers perform better, however, government can't decide if by demoralizing SES members it is producing a cost to society or only to the individual official involved. Better performance is, after all, what the privatization movement is about.[43] Volcker does not ask the politically difficult bottom line question – which category of managers is superior? But others have.

### a. *Comparative Performance Data on Political and Career Officials*

An assumption of the Volcker Commission is that a commitment to career bureau chiefs and managers over political ones is justified if it yields better managers. This implicit proposition has recently been made explicit by Professor David Lewis. In a study comparing career SES, politically appointed SES, and Senate-confirmed appointees, Lewis used the Bush administration's own Program Assessment Rating Tool (PART), to compare performances. He found that "politically appointed bureau chiefs get systematically lower management grades than bureau chiefs drawn from the civil service."[44] This finding makes an important point of public administration and comes at a crucial time in the debate over the use of private contractors versus government officials.

It also confirms the wisdom of the Volcker Commission's proposal to cut back on the number of political appointees. At a time when downsizing has eroded the number of career leadership positions in the federal government, politics, by shifting the mix of appointees, may be further eroding effective management. The underlying logic of the merit system and the career civil service endorsed by the Volcker Commission is supported by the conclusions of Lewis's research. This research also supports the Commission's call to reduce delays and paperwork in political appointments because these obstacles may dilute the quality of those willing to be appointed.[45]

### b. *Political Appointees at FEMA*

Professor Lewis's work also has precise application to FEMA, an agency with a high number of political appointees.[46] Lewis notes that "apart from the director and his staff, many of the major divisions and all of the regional offices have historically been headed by political appointees."[47] The politicizing of bureau chiefs exceeds that of many established government agencies, and surely negatively affected the agency's preparation and performance during Hurricane Katrina.[48]

FEMA's situation also demonstrates some unintended consequences of agency reorganization. In praising the mission-oriented
reorganization of the DHS, the Volcker Commission ignored the possibility that forced integration of agencies may have negative consequences. FEMA was placed inside the DHS against its will; when that
transfer occurred, many of its top staff quit.[49] The quality of appointments connects with an agency's independence. Understandably, an
official would rather be a deputy or undersecretary of a cabinet agency
(which FEMA had become under President Clinton[50]) than a bureau
chief at the DHS. This is especially true for political appointees. They,
like ambassadors, seek status in government along with mission fulfill-
ment. Members of the SES might be more satisfied with bureau-based
positions, as their orientation is directed toward the agency's mission.
If so, this becomes another point in favor of the civil service. Reorganization to produce mission-oriented agencies must come to grips
with the prestige effects of government appointments, as well as the
performance-based superiority of career officials.

## c. *The Connection between Political Appointees and Consultants*

Certainly, the comparative inefficiency of political over career managers is an argument for reducing the number of political slots rather
than expanding them. But that is the opposite of what has been happening. The Bush administration has continued to politicize important agencies, such as FEMA.[51] But in addition to efficiency problems,
political appointees might well be having another negative effect: They
may be encouraging outsourcing. Although no studies on the use of private contractors by political versus career managers have been found,
it stands to reason that political appointees would be greater users of
consultants.

For one thing, political appointees are often selected to challenge
the bureaucracy, especially when a change in administrations occurs. In
this situation, the temptation is to rely on outsiders, not insiders. When
the Reagan administration took over for the Carter administration, the
relationship between the civil servants and political appointees became
adversarial.[52] But even if the appointee-career relationship is not adversarial, appointees may just be more comfortable with contractors than

with bureaucrats. Bureaucrats have a bad reputation among business leaders, who constitute the bulk of Bush's regulatory appointees, because of their rule-bound work habits and lack of creativity.[53] New appointees are unfamiliar with the capacities of the bureaucracy, and might be expected instinctively to turn to private contractors for support. The standard industry practice is to use consultants such as McKinsey or IBM.

But there are also problematic reasons to consider: Contractors may be part of the same team as their political bosses. Recall the situation at the DHS discussed earlier,[54] in which its former secretary and undersecretary promptly joined firms who were private contractors to the agency. Political appointees who by definition see their careers as outside government can preserve their future by keeping close ties to private contractors. Of course, when top military officers retire, they also seek employment in the defense industry, so it is not solely a political appointee phenomenon. Still, it is a situation rife with conflict of interest problems.[55] And, just to add to them, contractors are also heavy campaign contributors.[56]

A prominent example concerns Vice President Cheney's connection to Halliburton. Well before he became vice president, just after the Gulf War in 1991, then-Secretary of Defense Cheney commissioned a Pentagon study on Iraq from Brown & Root (now Kellogg, Brown & Root). Later, Cheney became Chief Executive of Brown & Root's parent company, Halliburton.[57] And, of course, Halliburton and its subsidiary KBR are primary contractors to the current war in Iraq.[58] Cheney cleared conflicts checks on his stock in the Halliburton company. And he is only the most prominent example of the political appointee-consultant connection. The list could be expanded simply by taking officials from the companies who are private contractors and tracing their appointments in government.

Vice President Cheney did not invent the cozy connections to contractors. In fact, his former boss, Richard Nixon, early perceived the political advantages of consulting. In a memo uncovered during Watergate, Nixon is reported to have said:

What the Johnson Administration did after passage [of a personnel ceiling] ... was to see that "friendly" consulting firms began to spring up, founded and staffed by many former Johnson and Kennedy Administration employees. They then received fat contracts to perform functions previously performed ... by the federal employees.[59]

So Cheney is only the latest in a long line of political appointees (and elected officials) who have taken advantage of "friendly" consulting firms.[60] But he and the Bush administration seem to have perfected the practice to a degree that would hold even LBJ in awe.

From a governance perspective, these conflicts of interest show why career officials are better situated to determine when consultants are legitimately needed to assist in the work of government. They are subject to clear rules on conflicts of interest.[61] Yet the Bush Administration continues to place political appointees in positions of power over career officials. In a recent amendment to Executive Order 12866, for example, the president has required that agency policy offices be controlled by political officials, not civil servants or scientific experts.[62] This desire to assure more political control comes at the expense of career officials. It sends a signal not conducive to the restoration of the bureaucracy.

## 3. Operational Effectiveness – Freeing Managers to Govern

The Volcker Commission realizes that federal workers are governed by personnel rules that rigidify and often hamstring their effectiveness.[63] This is no secret in government. Indeed, many of these rules were suspended by Congress when the Transportation Security Agency (TSA) was created. The Commission recommends changes in the hiring system, the compensation requirements,[64] and recruiting efforts.[65]

These reforms are already underway experimentally in some agencies under the guidance of the Office of Personnel Management. They are trying to place government recruiting on a level playing field with private sector recruiting. Currently, the difficulties government officials have in recruiting effective employees provide yet another reason why private contractors are a ready and easy alternative to hiring full time employees. Private contractors may have cost advantages as well; if they work on short time horizons and on fixed missions they do not add to permanent overhead.

The Commission deals directly with private contracting in Recommendation 14. Competitive sourcing, it says, should follow "clear preset standards and goals that advance the public interest and do not undermine the core competencies of the government."[66] This statement paraphrases what the GAO and the Comptroller have been saying for many years.[67] It minimizes the debate over the role of consultants versus the full-time government, but it makes a strategic point about core competencies. For the civil service to work effectively, it must still be in charge. It can not be relegated to contractor oversight status, as John DiIulio fears is happening.[68]

Paul Volcker is no career bureaucrat. He served in an agency (the Federal Reserve) known for its creative and effective public officials; and he made a success at private equity as well as the academy. So the report does not view private contractors from a jaundiced perspective. Still, the fact that the Commission makes key arguments in favor of reducing political appointees versus career officials is a telling and challenging point. Comparable performance evidence discussed earlier also favors the adoption of the Commission's recommendations.

It is hard to predict the success of these reforms given the political forces allied against them. How, for example, do you convince a president that it is in the public interest to reduce the number of political appointees? These positions, like ambassadorial ones, are chips to be played or chits to be collected. The connection to campaign contributions is always present. Even harder politically would be the tightening down on private contractors. Again, these are opportunities for political payoffs that flow from K Street. It may be that the Tom Delay – Jack Abramoff era has so embarrassed lobbyists that they will back off on forcing private contracts on government. But that is doubtful. Perhaps a sensitivity to outsourcing inherent functions of government will limit the scope of private contracting. If beleaguered agencies such as the DHS are ever to perform competitively, it will be as a result of a cadre of effective civil servants, not an army of consultants.

## C. GOVERNANCE, NOT GOVERNMENT – THE MARKET STATE EFFECT

Reform and revitalization of the public service are conditions that operate against a changed view of government. When the first Commission Report appeared in 1989, the Clinton-Gore NPR had not yet appeared;

by 2003, when the second Report appeared, the NPR was old news
and things had changed. We are now in an era of "market-based governance," a movement so pervasive that it "underpins civilization."[69]
These are bold statements and they help shape public policy. To some
degree, market-based governance is an extension of the concepts of
"diffused sovereignty"[70] and global governance that were introduced
at the outset of this book.[71] These ideas introduce a dichotomy between
"governance" and "government." They ask: Does it take government
to govern? Or can governance mechanisms drawn from eclectic sources
do the job better? Obviously these questions bear on the outsourcing
problem.

## 1. The Market State and Its Limits

In reacting to the Volcker Commission's proposals, Gregory Treverton, of the Pardee RAND Graduate School, has said: "The rise of the
market state and the threat of terrorism – will shape the future nature of
government and public service."[72] But these fascinating trends seem
to run in opposite directions. The market state points in the direction
of private solutions; the threat of terrorism reconnects to the public
sector. One implies governance, the other government.

Governance by market has arrived. The deregulation and privatization movements have succeeded in reducing the role of and need
for government programs both here and abroad.[73] Globalization, with
its emphasis on quasi-governmental organizations such as the World
Trade Organization, the International Monetary Fund, and so forth,
supports the efforts to limit formal governmental arrangements.[74] By
contrast, Treverton's second shaper of the future is inevitably a governmental concern. He concedes that "the exception to the drive to
privatize will be in functions, like those of TSA, where the market's drive for efficiency is regarded as simply too risky in security
terms."[75]

Airport security as a whole is an odd place to draw the public-private
line, given that Treverton seems readily to accept the private military.[76]
As we have seen in Chapter 3, airport security inspectors, properly
supervised by public authorities, can be privatized, as they have been in
Europe. Treverton, in rejecting privatization for one category (airport
security) and accepting it for the other (private military) may have

strained at the gnat and swallowed the camel.[77] Still, the confusion is understandable, since Treverton has perceptively labeled two trends: one that is away from and the other that is toward government.

The intersection of privatization and government has deposited us at a place where it is difficult to make principled arguments on either side. The governance movement challenges government to be more effective; it supports substituting private alternatives, at least when no inherent functions are involved. The Volcker II Commission reforms are pragmatic. They try to make government function more nimbly, perhaps in an effort to avoid deciding exactly what functions government should perform. If government agents do their job well, then privatized alternatives, even where feasible, become less necessary or attractive. By contrast, if they fail, then the functions they oversee are increasingly seen as candidates for privatization.

But there is another downside to regulation by the market state. Treverton notes that by devaluing government the market state raises enormous issues of legitimacy and accountability.[78] The legitimacy and accountability gap is one that only government can fill. One way to do so is with Volcker-style government managers.[79] And it is one quality that the market state cannot provide.

However, the public will tolerate change better if it is politically determined than if it appears to be the result of vague forces like "globalization." Take the example of outsourcing jobs to foreign countries. Corporations gave outsourcing a bad name, as Treverton recognized,[80] and were subject to adverse public reactions. But policies set by government, even if those policies encourage the same result,[81] are much easier for the public to accept. The legitimating function of government is something that cannot be outsourced.

## 2. Public-Private Partnerships as Alternatives

The market state does not and cannot have all the answers. The public state is still needed in many arenas, among which are warfighting and protection against terrorism. Thus, governance and government are often in false opposition to each other. Both sectors can work productively together. Inspired by the market state, public-private partnerships seek to do just that. The idea of partnership has a nice ring – it seeks accommodation, not dominance. It implies compromise, not victory. Partnerships not only keep the government in the picture, but, assuming it serves as the senior partner, keep government in control as well.[82] The private side of the partnership allows the market to do what it does best, which is to look for and incorporate flexible, creative solutions that the bureaucracy might not have considered on its own. Public-private partnerships (PPPs) can also be a means of finessing the public-private distinction. To borrow Tony Blair's (and Bill Clinton's) phrase, they offer a "third way" to view government and regulation. PPPs have the potential to reduce the tensions inherent when one or the other course is chosen. Of course, every time government contracts out it is engaging in some form of public-private partnership. This may be an example of the "new religion" that Martha Minow has both accepted and warned us about.[83]

### a. *The General Approach to Public-Private Partnerships*

PPPs are in use in many countries and in state and local governments in the United States.[84] They also have been utilized by the federal government. As Frank Camm of RAND describes them, PPPs involve "(1) a formal agreement between or among public and private parties; (2) mutual sharing of resources, information, risks, and rewards; and (3) formal links between output-oriented performance measures and the allocation of risk and reward among partners."[85] Camm explores successful PPPs[86] and identifies their advantages: better use of core competencies, flexibility and longer-term relationships, and more efficient use of assets.[87] He also restricts their use to functions that are not "inherently governmental"[88] which complies with a basic assumption of this book. Other cautions with PPPs are compromises with competitive contracting and conflict of interest principles, but after resolving these problems Camm concludes in balance that the economic advantages of PPPs exceed any regulatory costs.[89]

Camm documents accountability advantages to the use of PPPs over private contracts. He finds PPPs provide more arm's-length oversight of contracting relationships, arguing that public managers "become more attuned to communicating with the accountability-oriented language of specific performance metrics, goals and expectations."[90] As so formulated, PPPs seem to have much to offer, and their use fits in with the Volcker Commission's proposal for better and more flexible public management. It may be that the ability to govern is enhanced by cooperative as opposed to subordinating relationships. Accountability issues arising from the use of private contractors can be ameliorated by this collaborative technique. In a situation of dominant downsizing, PPPs may be a second best solution because they offer collaborative opportunities. Government needs to consider how best to integrate PPPs into its management structure.

### b. *Case Study: PPPs and Infrastructure Protection*
One area in which PPPs are vital is in the protection of the public and private investment in infrastructure.[91] September 11 and Hurricane Katrina have taught us that the social investment in America's physical resources can only be safeguarded by joint public and private action.[92] Because the assets involved, whether they be ports, airports, chemical or nuclear plants, bridges, or tunnels are owned both privately and publicly and because their protection has long involved private and public security arrangements, protection of these assets naturally falls to PPPs. John Donahue and Richard Zeckhauser call for "collaborative governance" in this circumstance.[93] This idea requires government to yield its monopoly of control over a given exercise and accept a distribution of "shared association" between the public and private collaborators.[94]

The risks inherent in such arrangements lie with the private sector's desire to lay off in government the maximum amount of security costs possible. To some extent, the Terrorism Risk Insurance Act[95] did just this by "socializing the upper range of losses for terrorism damages to property...."[96] To avoid this free-rider effect, government officials in the PPP setting must determine at the outset which security functions should be assigned to the private and public sectors.

PPPs require top-flight government managers with the capacities to negotiate favorable deals for government. The discretion involved, even if shared to some degree, must ultimately be placed on the shoulders of government. This is an inherent function, nondelegable to the private sector, for which many feel government is not well prepared.[97] Surely the Volcker Commission recommendations, evaluated earlier, calling for a stronger and more creative civil service are central to a successful transition to the use of PPPs.

## D. PROPOSALS FOR ENHANCING LEADERSHIP

Leadership studies bemoan the fact that America is "producing too few future leaders who combine substantive depth with international experience and outlook."[98] This shortage is more acute in government than in the private and nonprofit sectors.[99] The Volcker Commission recognized that senior leadership in government was suffering because of restrictive rules and muddled career initiatives.[100]

Experience bears this out. In discussing the general topic of leadership in government with a distinguished economist recently, I asked whether he was encouraging his graduate students to go into government. "No," he said, "it's the opposite – I discourage them. In fact I recently recommended that one of my best students go to Blackwater." That says it all! When students at the top graduate schools choose private contractors over the government itself, the public has lost. Has our government fallen so far behind the competition that private alternatives invariably provide better experience? Can it be that the private military is recruiting better than the public one? These are core questions for our public sector to ponder.

The military has had difficulty meeting recruiting goals for service in Iraq.[101] This problem will be exacerbated as the military expands its commitment in Iraq.[102] And it is also the case that the civilian services like the Department of State are not meeting their personnel needs for Iraq. At the same time, the service academies are not retaining many of their officers beyond their initial five-year commitment period.[103] These officers are among the best trained people in our society, and their early loss amounts to a public sector brain drain of disturbing proportions.

In seeking leaders for public service, the Volcker Commission praised the high levels of performance in the military.[104] Military leaders are adept at management under conditions of uncertainty and adversity. And they are particularly well trained. The military invests more in leadership education and training than its civilian counterparts.[105] In encouraging these leaders to remain in service rather than enter the private sector, the military should consider whether its increased use of private military contractors itself creates competition for its very best people.[106]

When our military academies, which exist to produce future leaders for the services, are having trouble retaining their graduates, public sector leadership suffers overall. The percentage of U.S. military academy graduates leaving military service after their five-year mandatory terms end reflects this problem. Whether or not they end up with Blackwater, it is in the military's interest to keep these younger officers in the public sector. Better they should be given an opportunity to serve elsewhere in government than be lost to public service entirely. But this speculation introduces the larger problem: how to make public service a desirable profession again so that the young and talented will want to have public careers.

## 1. The Bold Move – National Service

In the last two Congresses, Congressman Rangel introduced a bill to revive the draft.[107] He did this in order to make a political point, and his efforts were viewed as quixotic.[108] He asked: Shouldn't everyone have the opportunity to serve in Iraq, especially those draft-age children whose parents are supporting the war? Make no mistake about how sensitive this issue is to parents. When the "inactive" Selective Service System recently performed a routine mock draft computer exercise, its officials were inundated with concerned parents' inquiries. The Selective Service was forced to put a disclaimer on its Web site, "No Draft on Horizon!", and the White House had to issue a denial.[109]

The draft is, however, more than a political crisis. It is a serious option that must be evaluated as the volunteer ranks are further strained[110] and the military needs to be expanded. The Vietnam era taught us both how unfair the draft was, and how it could be reformed through a lottery system.[111] When the draft ended in 1973, the volunteer service took its place. It avoided the confrontations with policy makers that the draft produced and provided better quality recruits,[112] which was one reason that the Pentagon ultimately supported it and prefers it to this day.

Reinstituting a draft would be a complicated exercise. Given accepted notions in our democracy about compelled service, it is not feasible to make military service the only option. This then raises the need for service alternatives and decisions about how extensive and mandatory to make the call-up. Richard Danzig and Peter Szanton set out the options over a decade ago and they have not changed.[113] The idea of a compulsory draft or of a twenty-first-century Civilian Conservation Corps has appeal to many who see such commitments as building better citizens. But the costs associated with the idea (as a compulsory program) may make it impractical in contemporary society.[114] And it would not meet the immediate need for an increased supply of volunteers to staff the military.

But public service still has broad appeal,[115] and there are more incremental ways to respond. Expanding AmeriCorps, which currently has about sixty-six thousand volunteers, is one such course. Begun in 1990,[116] AmeriCorps members serve with nonprofits such as schools and the Red Cross and are rewarded with education grants. Thousands of members served in post-Katrina recovery efforts.[117] Seeking to support the ideal of public service in this way may be the best we can do as a society. Since the draft idea would be a political nonstarter,[118] other alternatives that can lead to greater volunteerism are worth exploring.

## 2. A Modest Proposal – Inducements to Public Education and Training

The public leadership gap identified at the outset involves both a lack of proper training and also a lack of incentives to serve. These problems can be addressed in more modest ways. Richard Posner recently wrote about protecting society against risks from bioterrorism to global warming.[119] He advocated for more scientifically literate professionals.[120] By increasing the number of lawyers and public policy students who are scientifically literate, he suggests, the prospect for good policy making can be improved. This more scientifically oriented cadre of new professionals could, in turn, help staff institutions like his proposed center for catastrophe risk assessment and response.[121] While Posner's proposal is unnecessarily elitist,[122] it develops a necessary idea about public education that could be expanded in several directions.

One source of scientific elite is already available – the service academies. These institutions turn out engineers of top intellectual quality. They already receive advanced training and education as part of their military missions. The Volcker Commission sees military training as a model for public service generally. It is not much of a step to add a "civilian" disaster control dimension to the military's postacademy educational track. Indeed, should military stresses abate in a post-Iraq world, the opportunity for these talented people to serve the government in a civilian capacity could also be explored. One way to stem the loss of academy graduates after their initial terms are concluded would be to give them options for leadership in the civilian side of the government.[123] These highly trained, patriotic, and intelligent officers have the potential to be extraordinary public servants, whether within or outside the military setting.

But limiting the focus to the graduates of military academies is still too narrow a focus. The ROTC program is another source of training and leadership. Currently, 75 percent of military officers are produced through these programs[124] that encompass many of our colleges and universities (and some high schools as well). The mission of this program, which supplies many of the military's general officers and admirals (Colin Powell famously among them), could be expanded to include civilian as well as military matters. Graduates of ROTC programs could also be offered alternatives to serve either in the military or in the public sector, including state and local as well as federal entities.

One irony in discussing these programs is that ROTC training itself has been outsourced to private contractors.[125] This is a relatively recent (post-1997) and controversial development; it replaces the military's commitment of active duty personnel to the program.[126] Whether this is another area in which private contracting has exceeded its proper boundaries is a fair question,[127] although given the demands on active duty personnel for service in Iraq it is unlikely to be changed in the foreseeable future. So if we are stuck with private contractors as ROTC teachers, perhaps we could expand their role at colleges to include training in the needs of the civilian sector of government as well. The military would not want to pay for this expanded training role, but other branches of government might be willing to do so. Nonmilitary trainers may be more flexible and able to encourage a broader view of the need for high-quality public servants. Volunteer organizations, such as the Partnership for Public Service,[128] also might be able to provide college training in the virtues of the public service.

Finally, rather than just supporting military academies, the United States might consider establishing a public service academy.[129] Such an academy would grant carefully selected students a high quality education in public policy (including the scientific agenda Richard Posner encourages) in return for a five-year government service obligation. This idea reflects a commitment to public service that would overcome many of the deficiencies highlighted by the Volcker Commission. And it would provide to the United States a cadre of talented public servants. The idea is still in its formative stages, but legislation has been proposed to Congress.[130] It describes a program that could help produce the kind of professional bureaucrats posited at the outset of this chapter. What are needed are career officials who can be flexible enough to steer government and who have the capacities and political judgment to make decisions in the complicated world of public-private governance.

## E. PRESERVING THE FALSE CLAIMS ACT

The above proposals deal with new and creative ways to reform the bureaucracy. But reforming government also requires maintaining programs that work. The False Claims Act (FCA)[131] is one of those, even though it reflects partial privatization of government functions.[132] In a way, FCA cases involve public-private partnerships.[133] Once the cases are initiated by private citizens, they can be taken over by the Department of Justice. By incentivizing private relators who retain a portion of the amounts recovered when the government has been defrauded,[134] the government adds significantly to its contract monitoring resources at a time when contracting personnel are in short supply.

Since 1986, when the act was amended, there have been over $17 billion in recoveries against those who have defrauded the government.[135] During this period, there have been over five thousand *qui tam* (relator) suits under the act and they have been growing significantly.[136] Health care and procurement fraud constitute 79 percent of FCA cases.[137] The recoveries are greater when the DOJ intervenes and takes over the case.

Practice under the act is constrained in two ways. The DOJ has not added personnel to its seventy-member fraud team as the cases have grown. It is likely that a greater investment in DOJ personnel would produce more cases and greater recoveries. Second, the DOJ by tradition relies on the agencies that were allegedly defrauded to advise it on whether to intervene. Although this is a necessary step, it seems that some agencies are less likely to want the DOJ to pursue cases on their behalf.[138] The agencies' judgment is a function both of the merits of the claims and the potential embarrassment public revelation might produce. In some circumstances, this may result in a conflict. The Department of the Interior's decision to settle or not pursue claims against companies who have oil leases on government land, which are being maintained by private relators, is an example in this regard.[139]

In a perfect world, the work of relators under the FCA would be done by government officials. But, as we have seen, those officials are in short supply in our privatized government. The FCA provides volunteers incentivized by market mechanisms. Indeed, from an agency cost perspective, their incentives are aligned with government. Financial incentives may even exceed those such as loyalty and dedication, applicable to government officials who might take their place.[140] Thus, the FCA is both a necessary institution in the short run and one that has long-run capacities to check the excesses that plague the government contracting process.

### NOTES

1. Much like the call for an internal administrative law long ago issued by Professor Felix Frankfurter, this chapter refocuses the subject away from judicial to bureaucratic solutions. See Verkuil, *The Emerging Concept of Administrative Procedure* at 266–68.
2. Quoted in Osbourne & Gaebler, *Reinventing Government* at 25 (the authors make "steering, not rowing" their reinvention theme).
3. *See* Vandenburgh, *The Private Life of Public Law* at 2037–39 (discussing "second order" regulatory agreements negotiated between agencies and the regulated community).
4. *See* Elliott, *Toward Ecological Law and Policy* at 183–84 (command and control has become command and covenant).

5. Berlin, *The Hedgehog and the Fox* at 436–98 (the fox knows many things; the hedgehog one big thing).

6. Tetlock, *Expert Political Judgment* at 3–5 (defining the elusive "it" of good political judgment).

7. *Id.* at 3–4.

8. Foxes, self identified in his survey model, bested hedgehogs on basic indicators of forecasting accuracy. *See id.* at 75, 166.

9. *Id.* at 2.

10. For example, if the assignment is to build a nuclear bomb, government wants the best physicists available. Obviously, it should not ask these experts when to use the weapon. That job, as Harry Truman knew too well, falls to the political leadership.

11. *See* Epstein & O'Halloran, *Delegating Powers* 1–3, 47–48 (Congress varies the specificity of delegations based on the potential for executive abuse of discretionary authority).

12. *See* Office of Personnel Management, The Senior Executive Service.

13. Report of the Natl. Comm. on the Pub. Serv., Leadership for America: Rebuilding the Public Service (Volcker Commission I).

14. Report of the Natl. Comm. on the Pub. Serv., Urgent Business for America: Revitalizing the Federal Government for the 21st Century (Volcker Commission II).

15. *See* Verkuil, *Reverse Yardstick Competition* (citing NPR statistics on government employment).

16. *See generally* Guttman, *Governance by Contract* (asking how far the government can be downsized).

17. *See* Chapter 2.

18. *See* Light, *The True Size of Government.*

19. Conversation with the author, Oct. 4, 2006.

20. *See* DiIuilio, Jr., ed., *Deregulating the Public Service: Can Government Be Improved?*

21. I say this as one who participated in the effort. *See* Verkuil, *Is Efficient Government an Oxymoron?*

22. Volcker Commission II.

23. *Id.*

24. *See* Natl. Commn. on Terrorist Attacks, The 9-11 Commission Report.

25. Within the next five years, one-half of senior management will be eligible to retire, though not all will. Volcker decries the "vanishing talent" this statistic reflects and does not see replacements coming into government in sufficient numbers. *See* Volcker Commission II at 20–22.

26. *Id.* at 13.

27. Within these two broad categories are fourteen recommendations, some of which are highly relevant to the concerns of this book. *See id.* at 28–55.

28. *Id.* at 28–29.
29. *Id.* at 30–31.
30. *Id.* at 20.
31. *See* discussions in Chapters 1 Part A and 2 Part B.
32. For example, Volcker mentions the twelve agencies responsible for thirty-five food safety laws and the twenty-nine agencies responsible for 541 clean air, water, and waste programs as prominent candidates for mission refocusing. Volcker Commission II at 29–30.
33. Press Release, Dept. of Homeland Security, Homeland Security Proposal Delivered to Congress.
34. Dept. of Homeland Security Home Page.
35. *See* Cohen, Cuellar & Weingast, *Crisis Bureaucracy* at 57–61 (arguing that DHS was organized for political rather than principled purposes).
36. *Id.* at 49.
37. *Id.* at 67.
38. *Id.* at 49. See Dignan, *Homeland Security Struggles with "Extraordinary" Turnover.*
39. *See* nn. 44–47.
40. *See* Volcker Commission II at 36. This dramatic expansion of presidential appointees reflects a politicalization of the executive office of the president that has largely gone unnoticed – or at least unchecked. A recent study has concluded that presidents are motivated to add more appointees when their preferences diverge from members of an agency. (This occurs in both Republican and Democratic administrations.) See Lewis, 35 Pres. Stud. Q. at 496.
41. Volcker Commission II at 34–36.
42. *Id.* at 35–37.
43. *See* Gore, *The National Performance Review*; DiIulio, Jr. et al., *Improving Government Performance – An Owner's Manual.*
44. *See* Lewis, *Political Appointments and Federal Management Performance, Policy Brief.*
45. *See id.*
46. *See id.*
47. *Id.* (noting that two FEMA programs graded prior to Hurricane Katrina received below-average management scores).
48. *See* Chapter 2 Part B.
49. When Joe Allbaugh, FEMA's director, was called on June 5, 2002 by Andrew Card to tell him of the "secret plan" to merge twenty-two agencies into the DHS, Allbaugh quit – and his deputy, Mike Brown, took over. Brown, who became the poster child for bureaucratic incompetence, then spent the next year trying to extricate FEMA from the clutches of DHS. Grunwald & Glasser, *Brown's Turf Wars Sapped FEMA's Strength* at A1.
50. *See id.*
51. *See* n. 46.

52. Stories from the time indicated that Reagan political appointees would often hold meetings at agencies that excluded civil servants, who were seen as obstacles to reform. More recently, Vice President Cheney's meetings with oil industry executives shows how much outside views are encouraged or favored. *See* Chapter 1 Part A.

53. It is also true that working with the bureaucracy can be frustrating. The level of effort may be less than with contractors who will work around the clock on projects and do not face flex time and other limitations on bureaucratic performance.

54. *See* Chapter 2 Part 3.

55. *See* Kettl, *Sharing Power: Public Governance and Private Markets* at 4–5, 164 (describing conflicts in city government).

56. Not surprisingly, the campaign contributions of the largest private contractors correlate to their contract totals. The Center for Public Integrity Web site conveniently lists the campaign contributions of postwar contractors from 1990 to 2002. The Center for Public Integrity Home Page.

57. *See* Goodsell, *The Case for Bureaucracy* at 76–77.

58. *See* Chapter 2.

59. Federal Political Personnel Manual on Presidential Campaign Activities of 1972: Hearings on S. 60 before the Select Comm. on Pres. Campaign Activities, U.S. Sen., 93d Cong. 19 (1974), cited in Guttman, *Governance by Contract*, at 35.

60. Consider only that President Kennedy had 386 political leadership positions to generate "fat" contracts, *see* text at n. 59, whereas President Bush has 3,361 who can do so. *See* text at n. 40.

61. The official is subject to discipline or even criminal liability. *See* Markon & Merle, *Ex-Boeing CFO Pleads Guilty in Druyun Case* at E1 (an Air Force procurement officer and a Boeing official pled guilty to conflict-of-interest charges).

62. *See* Executive Order 12866 Section 4(c); (amended Jan 18, 2007); Pear, *Bush Directive Increases Sway on Regulation.*

63. *See* Volcker Commission II at 47–50.

64. The Commission recommends both flexibility in compensation and an increase in compensation levels for all public officials, including judges. *See* Volcker Commission II at 46–47.

65. Simplifying the application process, permitting interviews, and publicizing announcements are only a few of the suggestions, which are obvious to the private sector. *See id.* at 62–65.

66. *See id.* at 55.

67. *See* Charles Bowsher and David Walker, Chapter 2, Part D.

68. *See* DiIuilio, Jr., ed., *Deregulating the Public Service: Can Government Be Improved? See* nn. 19–20.

69. *See* Donohue & Nye, *Market-Based Governance*; *see also* Yergin & Stanislaw, *The Commanding Heights; Bobbitt, The Shield of Achilles.*

70. The phrase was employed by the first dean of the Kennedy School. Price, *The Scientific Estate* at 75. *See* Guttman, *Public Purpose and Private Service.*

71. *See* Chapter 1 Part E.

72. *See* Treverton, *Governing the Market State* at 89.

73. Few suggest that government should return to the direct regulation of markets, for example. For the European perspective, *see* Metz, *Simplification of the Public Administration.*

74. *See* Slaughter, *A New World Order* at 33–35 (discussing the IMF and other examples of "disaggregated sovereignty").

75. *See* Treverton, *Governing the Market State* at 110–11.

76. *Id.* at 110 ("it is becoming unclear why and who should wear a uniform in the military service.... ").

77. *See* Gospel of St. Matthew, XXIII verse 24, Oxford Dictionary of Quotations.

78. Treverton, *Governing the Market State* at 103.

79. But there is a caution even here because making public managers more mission oriented and nimble gives them more discretion and, at the extreme, risks what Professor Wilson has called "mission madness." *See* Wilson, *Can the Bureaucracy Be Deregulated?* at 46. Congress, of course, as Wilson documents, is unwilling to grant agencies the freedom for mission creep, let alone mission madness.

80. *See* Treverton, *Governing the Market State* at 104.

81. For example, companies that outsource jobs to India come under public attack in the United States, but when President Bush went to India to praise the outsourcing giant (and offer nuclear concessions), hardly a word of objection was heard. *See* Bumiller & Sengupta, *Bush and India Reach Pact That Allows Nuclear Sales* at A1.

82. Government is by statute required to be in charge of most partnerships. These arrangements are reminiscent of those recommended as part of "responsive regulation," in which government delegates its regulatory authority to private entities on the condition that the delegation can be recalled if the arrangement (partnership) were to fail. *See* Ayres & Braithwaite, *Responsive Regulation* at 158–62.

83. *See* Minow, *Public and Private Partnerships: Accounting for the New Religion* (setting out pros and cons).

84. *See* Likosky, *Law, Infrastructure and Human Rights* at 17–24 (describing transnational public-private partnerships).

85. Camm, *Using Public-Private Partnerships Successfully in the Federal Setting* at 180.

86. They are DOD (Navy) contracts with Boeing to supply parts for combat aircraft; building new government buildings in national parks, including

upkeep; and programs for training and finding jobs for the unemployed. *Id.* at 183–86.

87. *Id.* at 187–89.

88. *Id.* at 189.

89. He also argues that principles of incomplete contracting and transaction cost economics support the use of PPPs. *See* Williamson, *The Economic Institutions of Capitalism.*

90. Camm, *Using Public-Private Partnerships Successfully in the Federal Setting.*

91. *See* Likosky, *Law, Infrastructure and Human Rights* at 17–24 (describing PPPs in Malaysia and Mexico).

92. *See* Auerswald et al., *Seeds of Disaster, Roots of Response* at 429–50.

93. *See id.*; Donahue & Zeckhauser, *Sharing the Watch* at 429.

94. *See id.* at 439.

95. Terrorism Risk Insurance Act of 2002 (renewed in 2005), Pub. L. 107–297, 116 Stat. 2322 (2002).

96. *See* Donahue & Zeckhausuer, *Sharing the Watch* at 446.

97. *Id.* at 455.

98. *See* Treverton, *Broadening Public Leadership in a Globalized World* at 281.

99. *Id.* In the public setting, creative ideas to develop public leaders seem to be in short supply.

100. Volcker Commission II at 35–37.

101. *See* Editorial, *America's Army on the Edge*, N.Y. Times (describing how the troop shortfall is made up by extended tours and increased use of the National Guard).

102. *See* Editorial, *The Army We Need*, N.Y. Times (noting how difficult it is to add recruits and describing cost estimates of $1.5 billion annually for ten thousand recruits, not including recruiting expenditures).

103. *See* Shanker, *Young Officers Leaving Army at a High Rate* at A1 (In 2005, "more than a third of the West Point class of 2000 left active duty at the earliest possible moment").

104. *See* Volcker Commission II.

105. *See* Robbert, *Developing Leadership: Emulating the Military Model* at 265–70 (describing the training (ROTC, military academies) and educational advantages of the military over civil service and suggesting changes for the latter.

106. Military leaders are attracted both by private military companies and the private sector more generally. Retention bonuses and early retirement opportunities are effective techniques, but the ability to do interesting and creative work in government, either in the military or civilian service, can often be the deciding factor.

107. *See* Universal National Service Act of 2006 (introduced Feb. 14, 2006). Congressman Rangel's bill "[t]o provide for the common defense by requiring all persons in the United States . . . to perform a period of military service or a

period of civilian service in furtherance of the national defense and homeland security".

108. Rangel's bill was voted down 402 to 2 in 2004. *See* Lichtblau, *Flurry of Calls about Draft, and a Day of Denials.*

109. *Id.*

110. *See* Shanker & Gordon, *Strained Army Looks to Guard for More Relief* at A1 (describing how enlistment targets have been missed, how the National Guard has been overcommitted in Iraq, and how few regulars are available).

111. *See* Gold, *The Coming Draft* at 130–38 (relating (legal) draft evasion stories).

112. It also avoided the problem of drafting women. *See id.* at 155–58.

113. They proposed and evaluated four models of service: high school-based military training programs; military exemptions; draft requiring two years of service with civilian options and expanded voluntary service; universal service with no exemptions. *See* Danzig & Szanton, *National Service – What Would It Mean?* at 10–13.

114. Depending on the size of the program(s), the costs could be prohibitive. Moreover, there does not appear to be much advantage to the military so long as the idea of an all volunteer force is not abandoned. *See id.* at 270–75.

115. *See* Moskos, *A Call to Public Service*; Gold, *The Coming Draft* at 70–75.

116. *See* 42 U.S.C. § 42501 (establishing the Corporation for National and Community Service).

117. Americorps Home Page, *National Service Responds to the Gulf Hurricanes.*

118. This is especially true in light of the Iraq situation. But also as a foreign policy matter, one wonders what the reinstitution of a draft, essentially putting the country on a war footing, would say to our allies, all of whom (except Israel) have gone to a volunteer force.

119. Posner, *Catastrophe: Risk and Response.*

120. Posner also argues for more extreme ideas like limiting foreign access to our science education and limiting civil liberties in times of stress. *Id.* at 224–44.

121. *Id.* at 213–15. This center, in Posner's view, would be private (a consortium of universities) rather than public. However, if it were made public on a PPP, this institution might help reinvigorate government along the lines Paul Volcker has suggested.

122. He considers only eight law schools that should demand scientific literacy as a condition to acceptance. *Id.* at 203.

123. Incentives would have to be offered, much like enlistment bonuses, only in this case it would be opportunities such as SES status or appointments to key agencies.

124. *See* Avant, *The Market for Force* at 116.

125. *See id.*

126. *Id.* The contractors, like MPRI, replace four to five active duty personnel with assistant professors of military science who often are retired officers.

The controversy stems from outsourcing the training function to those not necessarily steeped in the military traditions.

127. In terms of inherent government functions, *see* Chapter 6, the training function involves education, which can be competitively bid. Indeed, private contractors provide part of the training at the Army War College and other services' advanced staff schools. *See* Avant, *The Market for Force.*

128. *See* Partnership for Public Service Home Page.

129. *See* U.S. Public Service Academy Home Page.

130. *See id.*

131. 31 U.S.C. §§ 3729–3733.

132. *See* Chapter 5.

133. *See* The False Claims Act Legal Center Home Page.

134. The act provides for treble damages and civil penalties; the relator retains from 15 percent to 25 percent of the amount recovered.

135. *See* The False Claims Act Legal Center Home Page.

136. The act provides for recoveries by government directly or through the qui tam (whistleblower) provisions. In 1986, there were 66 qui tam cases; by 2005 the number had grown to 394. Fraud Statistics Overview Oct. 1, 1986 – Sept. 31, 2005 (DOJ/Civil Division).

137. *See* U.S. GAO Report to Hon. F. James Sensenbrenner, Jr., Jan. 31, 2006, at 8.

138. Conversation with James Moorman, Taxpayers against Fraud, Nov. 9, 2006.

139. *See* Andrews, *Suits Say U.S. Impeded Audits For Oil Leases* at A1.

140. *See* Williamson, *The Economic Institutions of Capitalism*, at 131–63 (describing importance of incentives).

# 9 CONCLUSIONS (WHEREIN THE PRINCIPAL INSTRUCTS HER AGENTS)

This book takes seriously the We the People form of sovereignty. With the People established as the Principal in the Preamble, her agents become the Executive, the Congress, and the Judiciary. Akhil Amar has argued for restoring the Preamble to "its proper place as the Founders' foundation."[1] Alexander Hamilton, writing as Publius in *The Federalist No. 84*,[2] emphasized the theory of "popular rights" inherent in the Constitution. Can this theory be invoked to formulate an argument against outsourcing significant government functions?

The Founders were not greatly concerned with the line between private and public. During the revolutionary period, they were delighted to receive help from wherever it originated, as the Marquis de Lafayette's presence at Washington's side testifies. But the Constitution was more careful. It might be read as endorsing private contractors in only one instance, the Marque and Reprisal Clause,[3] which authorized the long-ago repudiated practice of employing privateers to do the work of the Navy. But that Clause, even if revived, would support the arguments advanced here because it requires Congress to initiate privatizing actions. It does not leave it to the Executive or the states to do so unilaterally.

Other delegations in the Constitution by the Principal to her agents are made directly, under the assumption that those agents would themselves be the ones to act or at least would devolve their significant duties to other public officials. These are the persons generally charged with forming the administration, a concept familiar to the Founders. As Hamilton also emphasized, "... the true test of a good government is its aptitude and tendency to produce a good administration."[4]

The Constitution was careful about placing responsibility in the hands of public officials. These officials are not only required to be confirmed, but they swear oaths to uphold the Constitution.[5] The Principal (the People) as well as the president or Congress (who are both agents and principals) have the right and duty to instruct these agents. Whether at the time of the Constitution's framing or anytime since the subject of outsourcing government functions has been discussed, what might the People say to each of the branches? Here are some thoughts drawn from the arguments in this book.

## A. TO THE EXECUTIVE AND THE AGENCIES

Article II comes first. Most outsourcing or privatization decisions are initiated by the Executive Branch, since it is the branch that forms the administration. In modern times, outsourcing has been accepted as a necessary part of the governing function, especially in the military context.[6] There are many reasons why the executive has let that happen. The need for special talents not readily available in government is one reason. In addition, as a political matter, outsourcing lets the president claim to be reducing the size of government while adding to it (i.e., headcounts v. budget effect). And politics also may be a motivator when the outsourced functions devolve to loyal supporters of the president. Ultimately, although the technique has valid uses, it also can be deceptive and destructive of the common good.

### 1. On the Military Side

In Iraq, military contractors have suffered losses that are not counted as casualties; they are off the books (in a body count but not budget sense).[7] Although there is much that private contractors can legitimately do in wartime, what they should not do is exercise force in ways that are unaccountable and even uncontrollable.[8] The military has the ability to distinguish proper from improper use of contractors, even on the battlefield. The field commander is now the one on whom these decisions fall. That should be changed. He or she should not the one to make hard choices under the stress of combat. A commitment to inherent government functions, as RAND continues to remind the DOD,[9] balances the commitment to competitive sourcing and moderates the use of private power.

Military commanders find it difficult to work with contractors who are not subject to the command and control system.[10] Efforts are being made to give commanders emergency authority over contractors,[11] but that is a less than ideal situation. If commanders are adequately staffed and supported by professional soldiers, the problems of inappropriate contractor roles would not arise. But adequate staffing is the big assumption that lies behind many of the problems that the military has faced in Iraq.[12] The president, through the Secretary of Defense, is the one to determine how and when to use contractors in potentially compromising battlefield situations. This decision is tied into funding levels for personnel and strategic decisions about the use of force.

Moreover, market alternatives themselves may adversely affect the availability of military services. Private security companies (PSCs) are a $100 billion industry, which is growing to $200 billion.[13] These companies buy up top-quality professionals at two to three times their military salaries and thereby reduce the availability of experienced troops. Because that demand is largely produced by the U.S. military itself,[14] it also can be moderated by the same institution. PSCs often focus on the most highly trained members of the military (Special Forces, Seals, etc.), which are the most difficult to replace. If the military has a monopoly on force, it also has a monopoly on the market for force. The military faces competition of its own choosing and it can protect itself by reducing the desirability of nonmilitary options. P. W. Singer has urged[15] that the DOD needs to do a careful risk based analysis on the use of military contractors "at the top of the spear."[16] This analysis should limit and even consider eliminating the use of private contractors in roles that only the best trained military can perform.

It should decide how best to keep these forces in the public sector up to the time of their retirement.[17] The economics of this choice must be analyzed, as maintaining a public force is now a market-driven decision.[18] This is why the distinction between proper and improper outsourcing is so important. Support services should be market tested, but fighting forces should retain their status as a monopoly.

The DOD must reconcile the use of contractors on the battlefield with the nondelegation of military functions. The Army manual recognizes the distinction, but the field commanders are often in no position to honor it. Abu Ghraib is a scar for both the military and its consultants, and should serve as a reminder and motivator.

The DOD's broader challenge, however, is in the growth of no-bid contracts. Even assuming the war in Iraq required fast decisions when it began, after five years the contracting process should have been regularized and competitive bidding restored. The embarrassments that these contracts produce should be motivation enough to contain and to monitor them. The number of contracting officers must be augmented and they, not private contractors, should be responsible for oversight of the contracting process in Iraq.

The contracting difficulties in Iraq are inexcusable. When the special auditor assigned to Iraq is sacked, both branches should be called to account. Stuart W. Bowen Jr., the head of the Office of the Special Inspector General for Iraq Reconstruction, found his job eliminated in a military authorization bill signed by the president.[19] Mr. Bowen, a political appointee with impeccable Republican credentials, was essentially fired after successfully challenging expenditures by companies such as Halliburton, Parsons, and Bechtel.[20] The State and Defense Department Inspector Generals tried to assure dissenting members of Congress that they will assume Bowen's duties, but, given the shortage of personnel available for contractor oversight, that is a less than reassuring response. The new Congress properly reversed this decision.

## 2. On the Civilian Side

On the civilian side of government, the Executive is faced with even greater challenges. The biggest one may be confronting the risks to government inherent in a downsizing environment. Arbitrarily set personnel limits on government positions compel the use of consultants in ways that are inimical to the best interests of government. And this problem is compounded by an increase in political appointees relative to career officials. The relative performance deficit of political appointees has only recently been exposed.[21]

It is difficult to convince any president to reduce the number of political appointees, as has been proposed by the Volcker Commission. But, from the People's point of view, good administration requires talented civil servants, especially at the top. The Executive can begin restoring balance and competency to government by reinvigorating the SES.[22] An analogy to ambassadorial appointments may be helpful here. Ambassadorships are coveted by the White House as rewards for campaign contributors, but they are carefully doled out. Political appointees are sent to "safe" countries, with very strong first officers to support them. An equal effort should be made to focus career officials on those agencies where turmoil and challenge are the highest. One of the problems at DHS and FEMA was exactly this – that top flight professionals did not follow the new agency, they abandoned it. The next White House needs to send the message that public service is crucial to the proper performance of important government functions.[23]

The agencies (the traditional Fourth Branch) are ultimately the ones who hire contractors and bear responsibility for continuing them. Agencies such as DOE that have become virtual contractor shops are the most difficult to reach in this regard. It may not be possible to convince an agency this far committed to managing contractors that sovereignty transfer is a problem it can fix. But other agencies that utilize consultants in ways that encroach on inherent powers can moderate their consumption. For example, the use of consultants to read and summarize comments submitted on a rule is a reasonable outsourcing decision. But the next step of analyzing and drafting proposed rules crosses the line. Consultants who write testimony are also coming close to the inherent function line.

Here, instructions can be given to limit these practices. If new positions are necessary to do this work in-house, they should be made available. Again, cost considerations are important but not controlling in a situation involving the performance of inherent government functions.[24]

Agencies are the heart of the administration. Their career ranks both drive and implement policy for the executive and legislative branches. The use of contractors where they have expertise and can provide services not available in house is one thing, but a largely unchecked resort to contractors jeopardizes the effectiveness of government.

Viewed from the perspective of agency cost theory, the problem for the branches (and by extension, the People) is that of the non-complying agency. Political control of agencies requires a variety of techniques,[25] including political appointees and career officials who are sworn to be loyal. Consultants are less directly controlled in this regard and less easily monitored. When they act substantively, consultants are more likely to escape political and legal oversight. They cannot be called before Congress and their work is often outside the ambit of transparency devices such as FOIA. Finally, downsizing initiatives have reduced the number of government officials who can oversee contractors and hold them accountable. The limits of accountable government have been reached when contractors monitor the performance of contractors.

## B. TO THE CONGRESS

Congress, the first branch under the Constitution, has the most to lose by the excessive use of contractors. Congress already suffers an information asymmetry vis-à-vis the president and the agencies.[26] Contractors exacerbate this deficiency because their work is often outside the usual channels of review and oversight. And, in the foreign affairs arena, executive secrecy and deliberative privileges pose further obstacles to congressional information streams.[27]

Congress has three critical ways to hold government officials accountable – the appointment process, the budget process and oversight hearings. In the first two situations, consultants can cause a disconnect between Congress and the agency heads who appear before them. If consultants have prepared analyses relative to rules, for example, that fact is obscured from view. When Congress holds hearings with cabinet secretaries, it might like to know how much of the work presented has been produced by consultants. An opening question from the committee chair that asks "Who wrote your testimony?" is an impertinent but not irrelevant way to start the inquiry.

Expressed in agency cost theory, Congress might like to know who its agents really are before it delegates powers to them. And, if consultants are involved, it might like to see the contracts under which they operate.[28] It does, after all, have a choice to delegate the details of legislation or specify them itself. In times of divided government, Congress does specify details of legislation more carefully.[29] If Congress knows that an agency relies on contractors to analyze its mission, it may well feel that more direct instructions are needed. Indeed, the presence of private agents may cause Congress to retain power rather than delegate it in the first place.

The objection is not so much that the Secretary did not act personally, but that the consultants who did the work are not before the committee. Because agency testimony is vetted by the OMB or other executive officials, this problem may be manageable. Still, one purpose of oversight is to assure Congress that the agency before it is functioning properly. Proper functioning requires agency officials both to make and to understand the policy decisions before them.

To perform its role under Article I, Congress must be willing to challenge the executive. That is what the Constitution intended when it separated powers among the branches. Politically, the adversarial role of Congress is much easier when one party does not hold both houses and the presidency. As the 2006 elections show, divided government can be a source of power to the People. The quiet elimination of the Office of Special Inspector General for Iraq, for example, would likely not have occurred if the House had been in Democratic hands. Indeed, the first thing the new Congress promised was the restoration of that office.[30] Members of Congress take oaths to uphold the Constitution, not the Executive branch. Party loyalty is understandable, but branch loyalty is also expected whenever Congress acts.

Congress has other powers with regard to the outsourcing problem that it can readily invoke. The Constitution established a legislative role whenever the Executive branch privatizes. Congress has taken advantage of this opportunity by participating actively in executive reorganization. Under the Subdelegation Act, Congress can participate in the contracting-out process. That act's limiting dimensions require Congress to approve subdelegations of significant authority to anyone who is not an officer of the United States. Congress holds the key to permitting, forbidding, or challenging delegations of government functions to private contractors.

In fact, it often uses that power wisely. When it wants to delegate choices about contracting it has done so (under the FAIR Act, for example). Surely Congress does not want to micromanage the procurement process and agency (DOD) choices in this regard should be supported. But oversight hearings on the use of private contractors are entirely appropriate and necessary. Moreover, the effectiveness of the OMB's Circular A-76 process, which the GAO has explored and the FAIR Act assumes, is another area worthy of congressional study. Attention to the inherent government function side of the ledger is something Congress can require and, with the GAO's help, can calculate the results of.

Congress also has created an oversight mechanism with the enactment of the False Claims Act. By giving private parties the power to pursue government fraud, which the DOJ can ultimately control, the FCA provides an additional check on government efforts to ferret out fraud. This is particularly relevant in the context of Iraq, where many contracts have been challenged by whistleblowers.[31] In circumstances in which public inspectors general are stretched thin, this statute becomes an important tool of congressional oversight.[32]

Ultimately, the Appointments Clause gives Congress, through the Senate, the power to control the exercise of inherent government functions. When powers are delegated from these executive agents, who are also agents of Congress, to others, Congress has a constitutional stake in the process. Its job is to assure the People that the work of government stays in the hands of those responsible for its execution.

## C. TO THE COURTS

The People's expectations of the judicial branch under the Constitution are more limited. Although it is clearly the duty of the Court to say what the law (and the Constitution) means under *Marbury v. Madison*, that role has practical limitations in a democratic society. The nondelegation doctrine, when buttressed by the Due Process (*Carter Coal*) and Appointments Clauses, has precise application to outsourcing and the duty to govern. But such broad challenges to outsourcing by agencies have to be carefully justified. Few want a return to the substantive due process era characterized by the *Lochner* Court. However, it is hard to oversee delegations to private contractors without challenging current views of the constitutional role.

Moreover, this is the era of *Chevron*, where deference to the Executive has risen to the level of a counter-*Marbury* principle.[33] *Chevron* reflects a separation of powers principle that assumes the agencies are better prepared than the courts to execute legislative policy. Under *Chevron*, principles of reasoned decision making on judicial review can be invoked to challenge delegations that transfer to private contractors the duty to analyze if not govern.

At a time when the executive seeks to deprive the Court of jurisdiction over the detention policies behind the War on Terror,[34] building a constitutional case against outsourcing government functions may seem less daunting. And it reflects core values. The due process approach subjects private delegations to public oversight mechanisms.[35] The Appointments Clause approach suggests that such executive branch delegations must be connected to statutory authorizations. These limitations on the Executive's powers to delegate to private hands are not preclusive. They assume that Congress can provide adequate procedures and instructions that can be administered by following established precedents like the Subdelegation Act.

On the statutory front the courts also have a role to play. Although *Chevron* and the rule of regularity tend to insulate agency action from judicial second guessing, these doctrines must be reconciled with existing standards of judicial review.[36] Reasoned decision making and hard-look review derive from the courts' reviewing function under the Administrative Procedure Act.[37] If a court becomes aware that agencies use consultants to analyze and prepare (if not decide) important decisions (rulemaking, for example), a fair question becomes has the agency itself engaged in reasoned decision making. A few cases questioning these practices would likely put an end to them.

Finally, the courts have a role to play in agency implementation of A-76 practices. Since 1996, bid protests have been considered in the U.S. Court of Federal Claims.[38] Judicial review of decisions whether to treat a government function as inherent or not can be obtained by granting plaintiffs (government officials who lost competitions and their unions) standing to challenge results under existing law. The judicial role on the merits is limited by the arbitrary and capricious standard, so practices may not change dramatically. But, again, interest in the question by the Federal Circuit should make agencies decide the critical question of private delegation more carefully.

The People expect effective judicial review of public sector decision making. A government that operates well is a protection of citizens' interests. The Republic is better off if the courts participate in the accountability process. Contractors are vital to the provision of government services so long as they support and do not transplant the role government officials play. The courts are agents of the People, as are the two political branches. The courts can sometimes alert the other branches to institutional problems. That is one of the functions judicial review and, to a more limited extent, constitutional review serve in a democratic society.

## CONCLUSION

The People's Constitution has spoken. As faithful agents, the branches must reply. The use of contractors to displace functions normally performed by government officials who exercise significant authority can be a danger to the Republic; it should be curtailed in the future. Given its imbedded nature and the fuzzy lines between inherent and competitive functions, this cannot be done overnight. But what we require now, as Ted Sorensen asked for at a different but no less perilous time, are watchmen in the night:[39] People who can help secure and preserve our public values in an era of unprecedented delegations of power to the private sector.

### NOTES

1. Akhil Reed Amar, *America's Constitution* 471.
2. The Federalist, No. 84 (Hamilton) at 558.
3. U.S. Const. Art. I §§ 8, 10; *see* discussion in Chapter 5.
4. The Federalist, No. 68 (Hamilton) at 444.
5. *See* The Federalist No. 44 (Madison) at 297 (in discussing why state officials also had to swear to uphold the federal Constitution he said they had an "essential agency" in giving it effect).
6. *See* Avant, *The Market for Force*, at 115 (quoting the Dean of the Army War College as follows: "The U.S. cannot go to war without contractors.").

7. It is difficult to get an accurate total of private contractor deaths, but informal estimates I have heard place them between five and seven hundred.

8. Two instances described in Chapter 2 involve Abu Ghraib and Fallujah. *See* Chapter 2.

9. *See* Chapter 6.

10. *See* Douglas, *Contractors Accompanying the Force: Empowering Commanders with Emergency Charge Authority* (describing how battlefield commanders must leave direct contact with contractors to contracting officers).

11. *See id.* at 128–29.

12. The problem is, first, with an inadequate number of troops to secure the country, and, second, with knowing how many troops to leave in Iraq and for how long. *See* Gordon & Mazzetti, *General Warns of Risks in Iraq if G. I.'s Are Cut.*

13. *See* Avant, *The Market for Force* at 8 (2003 global revenue established at $100 billion; 2010 revenue at a predicted $200 billion).

14. There is a global market for security, but the United States is the desired client for firms like Blackwater. *See* Chapter 2 Part A.

15. *See* Singer, *Corporate Warriors*, at 235.

16. *See* Avant, *The Market for Force* at 16.

17. Military retirement is a big inducement to serve and stay. After retirement, the military contractors are entitled to poach all they want. Indeed, this is the practice throughout the defense industry. But it would be in the public interest to preserve our forces until that time.

18. Enlistment bonuses, for example, have recently been increased from $20,000 to $40,000. Reenlistment bonuses are equally subject to acceleration. *See* Shanker and Gordon, *Strained, Army Looks to Guard For More Relief.*

19. Glanz, *Auditor in Iraq Finds Job Gone after Exposés.*

20. *Id.* at A17.

21. *See* Chapter 8 Part B.

22. The SES constitutes the elite corps of the People's professional managers.

23. Reexamining the 850,000 civilian positions that President Bush has determined should be outsourced is a place to start. Expanding SES positions also should be considered.

24. Moreover, cost considerations may well cut in favor of government employment. The private military is much more expensive when its costs are set out against the military's needs and civilian contractors may also be less cost effective. The unfortunate fact is that GAO or DOD cannot provide comparative cost figures. This then becomes another assignment for a new administration.

25. *See* McCubbins, Noll, & Weingast, *Structure and Process, Politics and Policy: Administrative Arrangements and the Political Control of Agencies* (advocating process controls to reduce agency costs).

26. Posner & Vermeule, *The Credible Executive*, at 16–18 (showing how limited Congress's monitoring staff is (twenty-two thousand) compared to the

executive's (over two million executive branch employees). Executive branch use of consultants further widens the information gap with Congress.

27. *Id.* at 16.

28. Are they specific as to assignment and responsibility or general and open-ended? If the latter, then the problem of agency loyalty is heightened.

29. *See* Epstein & O'Halloran, *Delegating Powers* 34–39 (applying agency cost theory to determine when Congress delegates in greater detail).

30. *See* Glanz, Johnston and Shanker, *Democrats Aim to Save Inquiry on Work in Iraq* (describing Democratic bills to nullify Republican termination of the Office of the Special Prosecutor General for Iraq Reconstruction).

31. Many of these cases are under seal, but Congress could require DOJ to report on them.

32. Senator Grassley notes:

> Studies estimate the fraud deterred thus far by the *qui tam* provisions runs into the hundreds of billions of dollars. Instead of encouraging or rewarding a culture of deceit, corporations now spend substantial sums on sophisticated and meaningful compliance programs. That change in the corporate culture – and in the values-based decisions that ordinary Americans make daily in the workplace – may be the law's most durable legacy.

> *Reprinted at* The False Claims Act Legal Center.

33. *See* Sunstein, *Beyond* Marbury: *The Executive's Power to Say What the Law Is.*

34. *See* Hamdan v. Rumsfeld, 126 S. Ct. 2749 (denying the Executive the power to try a Guantánamo detainee by military commission without express congressional authorization).

35. *See* Chapter 6.

36. *See* Verkuil, *The Wait is Over:* Chevron *as the Stealth* Vermont Yankee II (discussing the viability of "hard look" judicial review).

37. *See* 5 U.S. C. § 706.

38. *See* the Administrative Dispute Resolution Act of 1996, 5 U.S. C. § 571 (2000).

39. *See* Sorensen, *Watchmen in the Night: Presidential Accountability after Watergate* (describing the effect of Watergate on the future of the presidency and urging vigilance over the executive branch).

# CASES

# BIBLIOGRAPHY

The 9/11 Commission Report (see National Commission on Terrorist Attacks upon the United States, *The 9/11 Commission Report*)

ELLIOT ABRAMS, UNDUE PROCESS: A STORY OF HOW POLITICAL DIFFERENCES ARE TURNED INTO CRIMES (Free Press 1993).

BRUCE A. ACKERMAN, SOCIAL JUSTICE IN THE LIBERAL STATE (Yale Univ. Press 1980).

ALFRED C. AMAN, JR., THE DEMOCRACY DEFICIT (N.Y.U. 2004).

Alfred C. Aman, Jr., *Privatization, Prisons, Democracy, and Human Rights: The Need to Extend the Province of Administrative Law*, 12 IND. J. GLOBAL LEG. STUD. 511 (2005).

AKHIL REED AMAR, AMERICA'S CONSTITUTION: A BIOGRAPHY (Random House 2005).

Americorps Home Page, *National Service Responds to the Gulf Hurricanes*, http://www.americorps.org/pdf/06_0305_factsheet_Katrina_rev.pdf (last visited Nov. 7, 2006).

Edmund L. Andrews, Suits Say U.S. Impeded Audits For Oil Leases, N.Y. TIMES, Sept. 21, 2006, at A1.

Army Field Manual No. 3-100.21, *Contractors on the Battlefield* (Jan. 3, 2003) *available at* http://www.globalsecurity.org/military/library/policy/army/fm/3-100-21/index.html.

*Ashcroft Memorandum to Heads of All Departments and Agencies* (Oct. 12, 2001), *available at* http://www.usdoj.gov/04foia/011012.htm.

Phillip Auerswald et al., *Seeds of Disaster, Roots of Response: How Private Action Can Reduce Public Vulnerability* (Cambridge Univ. Press 2006).

Phillip Auerswald et al., *Where Private Efficiency Meets Public Vulnerability: The Critical Infrastructure Challenge* in *Seeds of Disaster, Roots of Response: How Private Action Can Reduce Public Vulnerability* 3 (Philip Auerswald et al. eds., Cambridge U. Press 2006).

DEBORAH D. AVANT, THE MARKET FOR FORCE: THE CONSEQUENCES OF PRIVATIZING SECURITY (Cambridge U. Press 2005).

IAN AYRES & JOHN BRAITHWAITE, RESPONSIVE REGULATION: TRANSCEND-ING THE DEREGULATION DEBATE (Oxford U. Press 1992).

Susan Bandes, *Patterns of Injustice: Police Brutality in the Courts*, 47 BUFF. L. REV. 1275 (1999).

RANDY E. BARNETT, RESTORING THE LOST CONSTITUTION (Princeton Univ. Press 2004).

CARL BECKER, THE DECLARATION OF INDEPENDENCE (revised ed., Knopf 1942).

Daniel Bergner, *The Other Army*, N.Y. TIMES MAG. 29 (Aug. 14, 2004).

ISAIAH BERLIN, THE HEDGEHOG AND THE FOX, IN THE PROPER STUDY OF MANKIND (Farrar, Straus & Giroux 1997).

Vicki Bier, *Hurricane Katrina as a Bureaucratic Nightmare*, in *On Risk and Disaster* (Daniels et al., eds. Univ. of Penn. Press 2006).

Blackwater USA Home Page, http://www.blackwaterusa.com (last visited Nov. 7, 2006).

Roger D. Blair & Jeffrey L. Harrison, MONOPSONY: ANTITRUST LAW AND ECONOMICS (Princeton Press 1993).

Paul Bluestein, *Dubai Firm Cleared to Buy Military Supplier*, WASH. POST A6 (Apr. 29, 2006) (available in LEXIS, News library).

PHILIP BOBBITT, THE SHIELD OF ACHILLES: WAR, PEACE, AND THE COURSE OF HISTORY (Knopf 2002).

Tara Branum & Susanna Dokupil, *Security Takeovers and Bailouts: Aviation and the Return of Big Government*, 6 TEX. REV. L. & POL. 431 (2002).

STEPHEN BREYER, ACTIVE LIBERTY: INTERPRETING OUR DEMOCRATIC CONSTITUTION (Knopf 2005).

Joel Brinkley, *U.S. Interrogations Are Saving European Lives, Rice Says*, N.Y. TIMES A3 (Dec. 6, 2005).

John M. Broder and Robin Toner, *Report on Iraq Exposes a Divide within the G.O.P.*, N.Y. TIMES A28 (Dec. 10, 2006).

David Brooks, *How to Reinvent the G.O.P.*, N.Y. TIMES § 6, 30 (Aug. 29, 2004) (available at 2004 WLNR 5501307).

L. NEVILLE BROWN ET AL., FRENCH ADMINISTRATIVE LAW (4th ed., Oxford Univ. Press 1993).

Lynnley Browning, *I.R.S. Use of Private Debt Collectors Is Criticized*, N.Y. TIMES C3 (Jan. 10, 2007).

JAMES BUCHANAN & GORDON TULLOCH, THE CALCULUS OF CONSENT (Univ. of Michigan Press 1962).

Elisabeth Bumiller & Somini Sengupta, *Bush and India Reach Pact That Allows Nuclear Sales*, N.Y. TIMES A1 (March 3, 2006).

Henry N. Butler, *Nineteenth Century Jurisdictional Competition in the Granting of Corporate Privileges*, 14 J. LEGAL STUD. 129 (1985).

GUIDO CALABRESI, A COMMON LAW IN THE AGE OF STATUTES (Harvard Univ. Press 1982).

Steven G. Calabresi & Saikrishna B. Prakash, *The President's Power to Execute the Laws*, 104 YALE L.J. 541 (1994).

Evan Caminker, *The Constitutionality of* Qui Tam *Actions*, 99 YALE L.J. 341 (1989).

FRANK CAMM, POLICY ISSUES RELEVANT TO CIVILIANIZING BILLETS IN THE DEPARTMENT OF DEFENSE (RAND 2005).

FRANK CAMM, THINKING STRATEGICALLY ABOUT MILITARY TO CIVILIAN CONVERSION (RAND 2005).

Frank Camm, *Using Public-Private Partnerships Successfully in the Federal Setting*, in *High Performance Government* 179 (Robert Klitgaard & Paul C. Light eds., RAND 2005).

Heather Carney, *Note: Prosecuting the Lawless: Human Rights Abuses and Private Military Firms*, 74 GEO. WASH. L. REV. 317 (2006).

DANIEL P. CARPENTER, THE FORGING OF BUREAUCRATIC AUTONOMY: REPUTATIONS, NETWORKS, AND POLICY INNOVATION IN EXECUTIVE AGENCIES, 1862–1928 (Princeton U. Press 2001).

Stephen L. Carter, *The Independent Counsel Mess*, 102 HARV. L. REV. 105 (1988).

CBS News, *Coast Guard Warned of Ports Deal Gaps* (Feb. 27, 2006) (available at http://www.cbsnews.com/stories/2006/02/26/national/main1346503.shtml).

Center for Public Integrity Home Page, http://www.publicintegrity.org (last visited Nov. 7, 2006).

Center for Public Integrity, *Contracts and Reports*, http://www.publicintegrity.org/wow/resources.aspx?act=resources (accessed Nov. 13, 2006).

Center for Public Integrity, *Windfalls of War*, http://publicintegrity.org/wow/ (accessed Nov. 13, 2006).

ABRAM CHAYES & ANTONIA HANDLER CHAYES, THE NEW SOVEREIGNTY: COMPLIANCE WITH INTERNATIONAL REGULATORY AGREEMENTS (Harvard U. Press 1996).

Alan Clendenning, *Most Ports Dawdle Over Beefing Up Security; Few Nations Likely to Meet July Deadline*, WASHINGTON POST A1 (June 27, 2004).

David Cloud, Army Secretary Ousted in Furor on Hospital Case, N.Y. Times, Mar. 3, 2007, sec A, p. 1.

Coalition Provisional Authority Order No. 17 (Revised) at 4 (June 27, 2004) *available at* http://www.iraqcoalition.org/regulations/20040627_CPAORD_17_Status_of_Coalition_Rev_with_Annex_A.pdf.

Dara K. Cohen, Mariano-Florentino Cuellar and Barry R. Weingast, *Crisis Bureaucracy: Homeland Security and the Political Design of Legal Mandates* 57–61 (Aug. 2006), *available at* http://papers.ssrn.com/abstract= 926516.

Sir Edward Coke, *On the Lords' Amendment to the Petition of Right*, 17 May 1628 Rushworth's Hist. Coll. 1659, i.

Comm. on Gov. Reform, Min. Staff, Special Investigation Div. (prepared for Henry A. Waxman) (June 2006), *Dollars, Not Sense: Gov. Contracts under the Bush Administration.*

*Competitive Sourcing: Report on Competitive Sourcing Results Fiscal Year 2003* (May 2004), *available at* http://www.whitehouse.gov/results/agenda/cs_omb_647_report_final.pdf.

*Constitutional Limits on "Contracting Out" Department of Justice Functions under OMB Circular A-76*, 14 Op. Off. Legal Counsel 94 (1990) (William P. Barr, Asst. Atty. Gen.).

*The Constitutional Separation of Powers between the President and Congress*, 20 Op. Off. Legal Counsel 124 (1996) (Walter Dellinger, Acting Asst. Atty. Gen.).

*Constitutionality of the Qui Tam Provisions of the False Claims Act*, 13 Op. Off. Legal Counsel 249 (1989) (William P. Barr, Asst. Atty. Gen. to Richard Thornburgh, Atty. Gen.).

Walter Wheeler Cook, *The Alienability of Choses in Action*, 29 Harv. L. Rev. 816 (1916).

Arthur L. Corbin, Corbin on Contracts, Vol. 9 (1951) (Interim edition 2002).

Corrections Corp. of Am. Home Page, http://www.correctionscorp.com (last visited Nov. 7, 2006).

Edward S. Corwin, The President: Office and Powers (4th ed., N.Y.U. Press 1957).

Steven P. Croley & William F. Funk, *The Federal Advisory Committee Act and Good Government*, 14 Yale J. on Reg. 451 (1997).

CRS Report to Congress, Colombia: Plan Colombia Legislation and Assistance (FY 2000–FY 2001).

Barry Cushman, The Great Depression and the New Deal, in Cambridge History of Law in America (forthcoming 2007).

Richard Danzig & Peter Szanton, National Service – What Would It Mean? (Lexington Books 1986).

KENNETH CULP DAVIS & RICHARD J. PIERCE, 1 ADMINISTRATIVE LAW
TREATISE 2.6 at 67 (3d ed., Aspen 1994).

Defense Security Service, *About DSS Homepage*, http://www.dss.mil/
aboutdss/index.htm (accessed Nov. 5, 2006).

Deloitte Consulting, *Calling a Change in the Outsourcing Market* (2005).

Paul Stephen Dempsey, *Aviation Security: The Role of Law in the War
Against Terrorism*, 41 COLUM. J. TRANSNATL. L. 649 (2003).

Dept. of Homeland Security Home Page, www.dhs.gov (last visited Nov. 7,
2006).

Dept. of Homeland Security, Office of Inspector General, A Review of
Background Checks for Federal Passenger and Baggage Screeners at
Airports, OIG 04-08 (Jan. 2004).

DEREGULATING THE PUBLIC SERVICE: CAN GOVERNMENT BE IMPROVED?
(John DiIuilio, Jr., ed., Brookings Instn. Press 1994).

A. V. DICEY, AN INTRODUCTION TO THE STUDY OF THE LAWS OF THE
CONSTITUTION (10th ed., Liberty Fund 1959).

Laura A. Dickinson, *Public Law Values in a Privatized World*, 31 YALE J.
INTL. L. 383 (2006).

The Digest of Justinian (Theodor Mommsen et al. eds., Univ. of Penn.
Press 1985).

Larry Dignan, *Homeland Security Struggles with "Extraordinary" Turnover*
(June 10, 2005), *available at* 2005 WLNR 129519206.

JOHN J. DIIULIO, JR., GERALD GARVEY, DONALD F. KETTL, IMPROVING
GOVERNMENT PERFORMANCE – AN OWNER'S MANUAL (Brookings Instn.
Press 1993).

Sharon Dolovich, *State Punishment and Private Prisons*, in *Outsourcing the
U.S.* (forthcoming 2006).

John D. Donahue, THE PRIVATIZATION DECISION: PUBLIC ENDS, PRIVATE
MEANS (Basic 1989).

JOHN DONOHUE & JOSEPH NYE, MARKET-BASED GOVERNANCE: SUPPLY
SIDE, DEMAND SIDE, UPSIDE, AND DOWNSIDE 1 (Brookings Instn. Press
2002).

John D. Donahue & Richard J. Zeckhauser, *Sharing the Watch: Public-
Private Collaboration in Infrastructure Security*, in *Seeds of Disaster, Roots
of Response* (Auerswald et al., eds., Cambridge Univ. Press 2006).

Major Karen L. Douglas, *Contractors Accompanying the Force: Empowering Commanders with Emergency Charge Authority*, 55 A.F. L. REV. 127
(2004).

Editorial, *America's Army on Edge*, N.Y. TIMES A9 (Oct. 1, 2006).

Editorial, *Sharing the Riches of War in Iraq*, N.Y. TIMES A16 (July 24, 2006).

Editorial, *The Army We Need*, N.Y. TIMES §4, 11 (Nov. 19, 2006).

Dwight D. Eisenhower, President, *Farewell Radio and Television Address to the American People* (Jan. 17, 1961), *in* Pub. Papers.

Neil R. Eisner, Assistant General Counsel of DOT, communication with author (Dec. 20, 2006).

Andrea Elliot, *For Recruiter Speaking Arabic, Saying 'Go Army' Is a Hard Job*, N.Y. TIMES A1 (Oct. 7, 2006).

Elliott, *Toward Ecological Law and Policy* 183–84 (Marian R. Cherlow & Daniel C. Esty, eds., *Yale Univ.* Press 1997).

DAVID EPSTEIN & SHARON O'HALLORAN, DELEGATING POWERS (Cambridge Press 1999)

RICHARD EPSTEIN, BARGAINING WITH THE STATE (Princeton Univ. Press 1993).

Richard A. Epstein, *The Perils of Posnerian Pragmatism*, 71 U. CHI.L. REV. 639 (2004).

Richard A. Epstein, Op-Ed, *Supreme Folly*, WALL ST. J. A14 (June 27, 2005).

CLARK KENT ERVIN, OPEN TARGET: WHERE AMERICA IS VULNERABLE TO ATTACK (Palgrave Macmillan 2006).

Executive Office of the President, Bureau of the Budget, *Report to the President on Government Contracting for Research and Development* (Apr. 30, 1962).

Exec. Off. of the Pres., Off. of Mgt. & Budget, OMB Circular A-76, at A-2 (available at http://www.whitehouse.gov/omb/circulars/a076/a76_incl_tech_correction.pdf).

*The Fact Book* [see U.S. Off. of Personnel Mgt., *The Fact Book: Federal Civilian Workforce Statistics*].

The False Claims Act Legal Center, http://www.taf.org/whyfaca.htm (visited Nov. 6, 2006).

Cynthia R. Farina, *On Misusing "Revolution" and "Reform": Procedural Due Process and the New Welfare Act*, 50 ADMIN. L. REV. 591 (1998).

David Faulkner, *Public Services, Citizenship and the State – the British Experience 1967–97*, in *Public Services and Citizenship in European Law* 35 (Mark Freedland, Silvana Sciarra, eds., Oxford Univ. Press 1998).

George R. Fay, *Investigation of the Abu Ghraib Detention Facility, available at* http://www.Army.mil/ocpa/reports/ar15-6/AR15-6.pdf.

Federal Document Clearing House, *President George W. Bush Signs the Aviation Security Bill* (Nov. 19, 2001) (available at 2001 WL 1458372).

*The Federalist* (Mod. Lib. Ed. 1937).

FedSpending: A project of OMBWatch Home Page, http://www.FedSpending.org.

*Federal Employees Union Appeals Decision to Outsource Logistics Jobs*, 41 GOV'T CONTRACTOR P 275 (June 23, 1999).

Martin S. Flaherty, *The Most Dangerous Branch*, 105 YALE L.J. 1725 (1996).

Katherine M. Franke, *The Domesticated Liberty of Lawrence v. Texas*, 104 COLUM. L. REV. 1399 (2004).

Sydney J. Freedberg, Jr., *How We Fight*, NATL. J. 36 (July 1, 2006).

Mark Freedland, *Law, Public Services, and Citizenship – New Domains, New Regimes?*, in *Public Services and Citizenship in European Law* 33–34 (Mark Freedland, Silvana Sciarra, eds., Oxford Univ. Press 1998).

Jody Freeman, *Extending Public Law Norms through Privatization*, 116 HARV. L. REV. 1285 (2003).

Jody Freeman, *The Private Role in Public Governance*, 75 N.Y.U. L. REV. 543 (2000).

Thomas L. Friedman, *A New Grip on 'Reality'*, N.Y. TIMES A25 (Mar. 22, 2006) (available at 2006 WLNR 4710918).

FROM MAX WEBER: ESSAYS IN SOCIOLOGY (H. H. Gerth & C. Wright Mills, eds, Oxford U. Press 1958).

Sean Gailmard, *Expertise, Subversion and Bureaucratic Discretion*, 18 J.L. ECON. & ORG. 536 (2002).

Joe Galloway, *Army Shake-Ups Clear Path for Rumsfeld's Vision*, S.D. UNION-TRIB. A3 (April 27, 2003).

*GAO Report on Improving Surveillance* [see U.S. Govt. Accountability Off., *Contract Management: Opportunities to Improve Surveillance on Department of Defense Service Contracts*].

Daniel J. Gifford, *The Morgan Cases: A Retrospective View*, 30 ADMIN. L. REV. 237 (1978).

James Glanz, *Audit Finds U.S. Hid Actual Cost of Iraq Projects*, N.Y. TIMES § 1, 1 (July 30, 2006) (available at 2006 WLNR 13135298).

James Glanz, *Idle Contractors Add Millions to Iraq Rebuilding*, N.Y. TIMES A1 (Oct. 25, 2006) (available at 2006 WLNR 18483100).

James Glanz, *Auditor in Iraq Finds Job Gone after Exposés*, N.Y. TIMES, Nov. 3, 2006, A1.

James Glanz, David Johnston and Thom Shanker, *Democrats Aim to Save Inquiry on Work in Iraq*, N.Y. TIMES, Nov. 12, 2006, A1.

Rebecca Neuberger Goldstein, *Reasonable Doubt*, N.Y. TIMES A13 (July 29, 2006).

Abby Goodnough, *Chertoff Pushes for More Hurricane Readiness*, N.Y. TIMES A16 (Apr. 13, 2006).

CHARLES T. GOODSELL, THE CASE FOR BUREAUCRACY (4th ed., CQ Press 2004).

Daniel I. Gordon, *Organizational Conflicts of Interest: A Growing Integrity Challenge* (2005) (draft on file with author).

Michael R. Gordon & Mark Mazzetti, *General Warns of Risks in Iraq if G.I.'s Are Cut*, N.Y. TIMES A1 (Nov. 16, 2006).

AL GORE, THE NATIONAL PERFORMANCE REVIEW (Diane Books Publg. Co. 1993).

Bradley Graham, *Army Investigates Wider Iraq Offenses: Cases Include Deaths, Assaults Outside Prisons*, WASH. POST A1 (June 1, 2004).

Bradley Graham, *Rumsfeld Takes Responsibility for Abuse: Defense Secretary Warns of More Photos and Videos*, WASH. POST A1 (May 8, 2004).

FRED I. GREENSTEIN, THE HIDDEN-HAND PRESIDENCY: EISENHOWER AS LEADER (Johns Hopkins U. Press 1994).

Grover C. Grismore, *Effect of a Restriction on Assignment in a Contract*, 31 MICH. L. REV. 299 (1933).

Daniel Gross, *Why "Outsourcing" May Lose Its Power as a Scare Word*, N.Y. TIMES § 3, 5 (Aug. 13, 2006) (available at 2006 WLNR 13995021).

Michael Grunwald & Susan B. Glasser, *Brown's Turf Wars Sapped FEMA's Strength; Director Who Came to Symbolize Incompetence in Katrina Predicted Agency Would Fail*, WASH. POST A1 (Dec. 23, 2005).

Dan Guttman, *Governance by Contract: Constitutional Visions; Time for Reflection and Choice*, 33 PUB. CONT. L.J. 321 (2004).

Dan Guttman, *Inherently Governmental Functions and the New Millennium: The Legacy of Twentieth-Century Reform*, in *Making Government Manageable: Executive Organization and Management in the Twenty-First Century* (Thomas H. Stanton & Benjamin Ginsberg eds., Johns Hopkins U. Press 2004).

Daniel Guttman, *Public Purpose and Private Service: The Twentieth Century Culture of Contracting Out and the Evolving Law of Diffused Sovereignty*, 52 ADMIN. L. REV. 859 (2000).

DAN GUTTMAN & BARRY WILNER, THE SHADOW GOVERNMENT (Random House 1976).

Sir Matthew Hale, THE HISTORY OF COMMON LAW OF ENGLAND (C.M. Gray ed., 1971)

STUART HAMPSHIRE, JUSTICE IS CONFLICT (Princeton Univ. Press 1999).

RICHARD W. HARDING, PRIVATE PERSONS AND PUBLIC ACCOUNTABILITY (Transaction Publishers 1997).

Carol Harlow, *Public Service, Market Ideology, and Citizenship*, in *Public Services and Citizenship in European Law* at 49 (Mark Freedland, Silvana Sciarra, eds., Oxford Univ. Press 1998).

Scott E. Harrington, *Rethinking Disaster Policy after Katrina*, in *On Risk and Disaster* (Daniels et al., eds. Univ. of Penn. Press 2006).

Shane Harris, *Technology Contract Used to Purchase Interrogation Work*, (May 20, 2004) *available at* http://www.govexec.com/dailyfed/0504/052004h1.htm.

Jeffrey L. Harrison, *Yardstick Competition: A Prematurely Discarded Form of Regulatory Relief*, 53 TUL. L. REV. 465 (1979).

JEFFREY HARRISON, THOMAS D. MORGAN & PAUL R. VERKUIL, REGULATION AND DEREGULATION (2d ed., West 2004).

PAIGE M. HARRISON & JENNIFER C. KARBERG, U.S. DEP'T OF JUSTICE, PRISON AND JAIL INMATES AT MIDYEAR 2003 (2004).

F. A. HAYEK, THE CONSTITUTION OF LIBERTY (Routledge 1960).

Michael Hayes, *Improving Security Through Reducing Employee Rights*, 10 IUS GENTIUM 55 (2004).

SEYMOUR M. HERSH, CHAIN OF COMMAND – THE ROAD FROM 9/11 TO ABU GHRAIB (HarperCollins 2004).

Andrew Hessick, *The Federalization of Airport Security: Privacy Implications*, 24 WHITTIER L. REV. 43 (2002).

ROBERT A. HILLMAN, PRINCIPLES OF CONTRACT LAW (West 2004).

OLIVER WENDELL HOLMES, THE COMMON LAW (1881) (MARK DEWOLF HOWE ed., 1963).

JED HORNE, BREACH OF FAITH – HURRICANE KATRINA AND THE NEAR DEATH OF A GREAT AMERICAN CITY (Random House 2006).

Morton J. Horwitz, *The History of the Public-Private Distinction*, 130 U. PA. L. REV. 1423 (1982).

Spencer S. Hsu & Susan B. Glasser, *FEMA Director Singled Out by Response Critics*, WASH. POST A01 (Sept. 6, 2005).

Spencer S. Hsu, *Messages Depict Disarray in Federal Katrina Response*, WASH. POST A11 (October 18, 2005) (available in LEXIS, News library).

Spencer S. Hsu & John Pomfret, *Technology Has Uneven Record on Securing Border*, WASH. POST A1 (May 21, 2006).

Innovative Emergency Management, Inc., *IEM Team to Develop Catastrophic Hurricane Disaster Plan for New Orleans & Southeast Louisiana* (June 3, 2004) (available at http://www.ieminc.com/Whats_New/Press_Releases/pressrelease060304_Catastrophic.htm).

*Iran–Contra Report* [see *Report of the Congressional Committees Investigating the Iran–Contra Affair*].

The Iraq Study Group Report (James A. Baker III, and Lee H. Hamilton, co-chairs) (2006).

PETER H. IRONS, THE NEW DEAL LAWYERS (Princeton Univ. Press 1982).

Arthur J. Jacobson, *The Private Use of Public Authority: Sovereignty and Associations in the Common Law*, 29 BUFF. L. REV. 599 (1980).

Louis L. Jaffe, *Law Making by Private Groups*, 51 HARV. L. Rev. 201 (1937).

Douglas Jehl & David Johnston, *Rule Change Lets C.I.A. Freely Send Suspects Abroad*, N.Y. TIMES A1 (Mar. 6, 2005).

David Cay Johnston, *I.R.S. Enlists Outside Help in Collecting Delinquent Taxes, Despite the Higher Costs*, N.Y. TIMES § 1, 12 (Aug. 20, 2006) (available at 2006 WLNR 14407411).

PETER JOSEPHSON, THE GREAT ART OF GOVERNMENT – LOCKE'S USE OF CONSENT (Univ. Press of Kansas 2002).

BARRY D. KARL, THE UNEASY STATE (Univ. of Chicago Press 1983).

HANS KELSEN, GENERAL THEORY OF LAW AND STATE (1945).

Duncan Kennedy, *The Stages of the Decline of the Public/Private Distinction*, 130 U. PA. L. REV. 1349 (1982).

DONALD F. KETTL, SHARING POWER: PUBLIC GOVERNANCE AND PRIVATE MARKETS (Brookings Instn. Press 1993).

W. NOEL KEYES, GOVERNMENT CONTRACTS IN A NUTSHELL (4th ed., West 2004).

Stephen Kinzer, *The Marxist Turned Caudillo: A Family Story*, N.Y. TIMES §4, 14 (Nov. 12, 2006).

Stephanie Kirchgaessner, *Powell "Gave Warning" on Iraq Troops*, FIN. TIMES 4 (Apr. 30, 2006).

David Kocieniewski, *El Al Asks U.S. to Let It Do Extra Screening at Newark*, N.Y. TIMES B2 (May 12, 2006) (available at 2006 WLNR 8163807).

Dawn Kopecki, *When Outsourcing Turns Outrageous*, BUSINESS WEEK (July 31, 2006) (available at 2006 WLNR 12952381).

Ted Koppel, *These Guns for Hire*, N.Y. TIMES A21 (May 22, 2006) (available at 2006 WLNR 8754790).

STEPHEN D. KRASNER, SOVEREIGNTY: ORGANIZED HYPOCRISY (Princeton U. Press 1999).

Paul Krugman, *The Fighting Moderates*, N.Y. TIMES A19 (Feb. 15, 2005).

Paul Krugman, *Tax Farmers, Mercenaries and Viceroys*, N.Y. TIMES A17 (Aug. 21, 2006) (available at 2006 WLNR 14441607).

Paul Krugman, *Outsourcer in Chief*, N.Y. TIMES A27 (Dec. 11, 2006).

Howard Kunreuther, *Has the Time Come for Comprehensive Natural Disaster Insurance?* in *On Risk and Disaster* (Daniels et al., eds. Univ. of Penn. Press 2006).

JAMES M. LANDIS, THE ADMINISTRATIVE PROCESS (Yale Univ. Press 1938).

Gary Lawson, *The Rise and the Rise of the Administrative State*, 107 HARV. L. REV. 1231 (1994).

Gary Lawson, *Delegation and Original Meaning*, 88 VA. L. REV. 327 (2002).

Lawrence Lessig & Cass R. Sunstein, *The President and the Administration*, 94 COLUM. L. REV. 1 (1994).

*Letter from Charles A. Bowsher, Comptroller General, to Hon. David Pryor* (Dec. 29, 1989), in *Use of Consultants and Contractors by the Environmental Protection Agency and the Department of Energy*, Sen. Comm. on Gov. Affairs, Hearing before Subcommittee on Federal Services, Post Office, and Civil Service, 101st Cong. S. 1 (1989).

Letters to N.Y. Times, *Waging War with Private Forces*, N.Y. TIMES § 4 (May 28, 2006) (available at 2006 WLNR 9155782 through 2006 WLNR 9155788).

David Lewis, *Political Appointments and Federal Management Performance, Policy Brief* (Sept. 2005), *available at* http://www.princeton.edu/policybriefs/lewis_performance.pdf.

David Lewis, *Staffing Alone: Unilateral Action and the Politicization of the Executive Office of the President, 1988–2004*, 35 PRES. STUD. Q. 496 (2005).

Eric Lichtblau, *Flurry of Calls about Draft, and a Day of Denials*, N.Y. TIMES A11 (Dec. 23, 2006).

PAUL C. LIGHT, THE TRUE SIZE OF GOVERNMENT (Brookings Inst. 1999).

MICHAEL B. LIKOSKY, LAW, INFRASTRUCTURE AND HUMAN RIGHTS (Cambridge Press 2006).

DAVID E. LILIENTHAL, THE JOURNALS OF DAVID E. LILIENTHAL – THE TVA YEARS, 1939–1945 (Harper & Row 1964).

Alice Lipowicz, *Teams Vie for SBInet*, 21 TECHNEWS 11 (June 8, 2006).

Eric Lipton, *Billions Later, Plans to Remake the Coast Guard Fleet Stumbles*, N.Y. TIMES A1 (Dec. 9, 2006).

Eric Lipton, *Former Antiterror Officials Find Industry Pays Better*, N.Y. TIMES A1 (June 18, 2006) (available at 2006 WLNR 10517130).

Eric Lipton, *Homeland Security Chief Outlines FEMA Overhaul*, N.Y. TIMES A22 (Oct. 20, 2005) (available at 2005 WLNR 16974661).

Eric Lipton, *Seeking to Control Borders, Bush Turns to Big Military Contractors*, N.Y. TIMES A1 (May 18, 2006).

Eric Lipton, *White House Declines to Provide Storm Papers*, N.Y. TIMES A1 (Jan. 25, 2006) (available at 2006 WLNR 1333900).

Eric Lipton, *U.S. Requiring Port Workers to Have ID's and Reviews*, N.Y. TIMES A11 (Jan. 4, 2007).

Orly Lobel, *The Renew Deal: The Fall of Regulation and the Rise of Governance in Contemporary Legal Thought*, 89 MINN. L. REV. 342 (2004).

JOHN LOCKE, THE SECOND TREATISE OF GOVERNMENT (Thomas P. Peardon ed., Prentice Hall 1952) (1690).

Edmond Lococo, *Titan Competing with Northrup, L-3 To Keep Its Largest Contract*, Bloomberg News (June 7, 2004) *available at* http://quote.bloomberg.com/apps/news?pid=10000103&sid=afR4zWgUnpDo& refer=us.

MARTIN LOUGHLIN, THE IDEA OF PUBLIC LAW (Oxford Univ. Press 2004).

DAVID S. LOVEJOY, THE GLORIOUS REVOLUTION IN AMERICA (Wesleyan Univ. Press 1972).

Jonathan R. Macey, *Organizational Design and Political Control of Administrative Agencies*, 8 J. L. ECON. & ORG. 93 (1992).

Jerry Markon & Renae Merle, *Ex-Boeing CFO Pleads Guilty In Druyun Case*, WASH. POST E1 (Nov. 16, 2004).

Joanne Mariner, *Private Contractors Who Torture*, (May 10, 2004) *available at* http://writ.news.findlaw.com/mariner/20040510.html.

C. Kevin Marshall, *Putting Privateers in Their Place: The Applicability of the Marque and Reprisal Clause to Undeclared Wars*, 64 U. CHI. L. REV. 953 (1997).

Jerry L. Mashaw, *Recovering American Administrative Law: Federalist Foundations, 1787–1801*, 115 YALE L. J. 1256 (2006).

Jane Mayer, *The Hidden Power*, THE NEW YORKER, 44 (July 3, 2006) (available in LEXIS, News library).

Matthew D. McCubbins, Roger G. Noll and Barry R. Weingast, *Structure and Process, Politics and Policy: Administrative Arrangements and the Political Control of Agencies*, 75 VA. L. REV. 431 (1989).

DAVID MCCULLOUGH, TRUMAN (Simon & Schuster 1992).

McKinsey & Co. Home Page, http://www.mckinsey.com (last visited Nov. 7, 2006).

Marianne Means, *Bush's Credibility Tank is on Empty*, Seattle Post-Intelligencer B6 (May 2, 2006) (available at 2004 WLNR 3200527).

Errol E. Meidinger, *The "Public Uses" of Eminent Domain: History and Policy*, 11 ENVTL. L. REP. 1 (1980).

Thomas W. Merrill, *The Landscape of Constitutional Property*, 86 VA. L. REV. 885 (2000).

Thomas W. Merrill, *Rethinking Article I, Section I: From Nondelegation to Exclusive Delegation*, 104 COLUM. L. REV. 2097 (2004).

Emanuel Metz, *Simplification of the Public Administration: The "Lean State" as a Long-Term Task*, 4 COLUM. J. EUR. L. 647 (1998).

Gillian E. Metzger, *Privatization as Delegation*, 103 COLUM. L. REV. 1367 (2003).

Jon B. Michaels, *Beyond Accountability: The Constitutional, Democratic and Strategic Problems with Privatizing War*, 82 WASH. U. L.Q. 1001 (2004).

Thomas J. Miles & Cass R. Sunstein, *Do Judges Make Regulatory Policy? An Empirical Investigation of* Chevron, 73 U. CHI. L. REV. 823 (2006).

T. CHRISTIAN MILLER, BLOOD MONEY – WASTED BILLIONS, LOST LIVES AND CORPORATE GREED IN IRAQ (Little, Brown 2006).

Martha Minow, *Outsourcing Power: How Privatizing Military Efforts Challenges Accountability, Professionalism and Democracy*, 46 B.C.L. REV. 989 (2005).

Ronald C. Moe, *Governance Principles*, in *Making Government Manageable* (Thomas H. Stanton & Benjamin Ginsberg, eds., Johns Hopkins Univ. Press 2004).

Milton Mollen, *Report of the Commn. to Investigate Allegations of Police Corruption and the Anti-Corruption Procedures of the Police Dept* (1994), *available at* http://www.parc.info/reports/pdf/mollenreport.pdf.

Henry Monaghan, *Marbury and the Administrative State*, 83 COLUM. L. REV. 1 (1983).

Mark H. Moore, *Introduction to Symposium, Public Values in an Era of Privatization*, 116 HARV. L. REV. 1212 (2003).

Trevor W. Morrison, *Lamenting Lochner's Loss: Randy Barnett's Case for a Libertarian Constitution*, 90 CORN. L. REV. 839 (2005).

CHARLES C. MOSKOS, A CALL TO PUBLIC SERVICE: NATIONAL SERVICE FOR COUNTRY AND COMMUNITY (Free Press 1988).

STEVEN NADLER, SPINOZA'S HERESY (Oxford Univ. Press 2001).

Ralph C. Nash & John Cibinic, *Contracting Out Procurement Functions: "The Inherently Government Function" Exception*, Nash & Cibinic Report, Sept. 2000.

NATIONAL COMMISSION ON TERRORIST ATTACKS UPON THE UNITED STATES, THE 9/11 COMMISSION REPORT (W. W. Norton & Co. 2004) (available at 2004 WL 1634382).

WILLIAM E. NELSON, THE ROOTS OF AMERICAN BUREAUCRACY, 1830–1900 (Beard Books 1982).

Johanna Neuman, *Report Details Katrina Communications Fiasco*, L.A. TIMES A4 (May 3, 2006) (available at 2006 WLNR 7528229).

Alexander N.M. Niejelow, *The Derivative Effects of Don't Ask Don't Tell* (2006) (on file with author).

Floyd Norris, *In the Bush Years, Government Grows as the Private Sector Struggles*, N.Y. TIMES C1 (Sept. 3, 2004) (available at 2004 WLNR 5561431).

*NSA Spying Memo* [see U.S. Dept. of Justice, Off. of the Atty. Gen., *Legal Authorities Supporting the Activities of the National Security Agency Described by the President*]

Office of Mgmt. & Budget, Executive Office of the President, OMB Circular A-76, 68 Fed. Reg. § 2134–42 (May 29, 2003), *available at* http://www.whitehouse.gov/omb/circulars/a076/a76_incl_tech_correction.pdf.

Office of Mgmt. & Budget, Executive Office of the President, *OMB Transmittal Memorandum #20*, *available at* http://www.whitehouse.gov/omb/circulars/a076/a076tm20.html.

Office of Mgmt. & Budget, Executive Office of the President, *The President's Management Agenda* 17–18 (2002), *available at* http://www.whitehouse.gov/omb/budget/fy2002/mgmt.pdf.

Office of Management and Budget Watch Home Page, http://www.OMBwatch.org.

Office of Personnel Management, The Senior Executive Service, http://www.opm.gov/ses/.

Off. of Sen. Charles Schumer, *Press Release: Multi-Billion Dollar Company that Operates NYC Port to be Taken Over by United Arab Emirates Government-Owned Firm Today* (Feb. 13, 2006) (available at http://schumer.senate.gov/SchumerWebsite/pressroom/press_releases/2006/PR60.NYC%20Port%20Security.021306.html).

OLIVER L. NORTH, UNDER FIRE: AN AMERICAN STORY (21st Century Press 1991).

OMB Watch, *OMB Watch Launches FedSpending.org* (Oct. 11, 2006) (available at http://ombwatch.org/article/articleview/3613/1/82).

*On Risk and Disaster: Lessons from Hurricane Katrina* (Ronald J. Daniels, Donald F. Kettl & Howard Kunreuther eds., U. Pa. Press 2006).

Richard A. Oppel, Jr. & Ariel Hart, *Contractor Indicted in Afghan Detainee's Beating; First Civilian Charged in Abuses – the Prisoner Died the Next Day*, N.Y. TIMES A1 (June 18, 2004).

Alex Ortolani & Robert Block, *Keeping Cargo Safe from Terror – Hong Kong Port Project Scans All Containers; U.S. Doesn't See the Need*, WALL STREET JOURNAL B1 (July 29, 2005) (available in LEXIS, News library).

DAVID OSBORNE & TED GAEBLER, REINVENTING GOVERNMENT: HOW THE ENTREPRENEURIAL SPIRIT IS TRANSFORMING THE PUBLIC SECTOR (Addison Wesley 1992).

Kimberly Palmer, *Performance-Based Contracting "Not Working,' Industry Leader Says*, (May 17, 2005), *available at* http://www.govexec.com/dailyfed/0505/051705k1.htm.

Richard W. Parker, *The Empirical Roots of the "Regulatory Reform" Movement: A Critical Appraisal*, 58 ADMIN. L. REV. 359 (2006).

Partnership for Public Service Home Page, http://www.ourpublicservice.org.

ROBERT O. PAXTON, THE ANATOMY OF FASCISM (Knopf 2004).

Pear, *Bush Directive Increases Sway on Regulation*, N.Y. TIMES A1 (Jan. 29, 2007).

Joseph R. Perlak, *The Military Extraterritorial Jurisdiction Act of 2000: Implications for Contractor Personnel*, 169 MIL. L. REV. 92 (2001).

Alessandro Petretto, *The Liberalization and Privatization of Public Utilities and the Protection of Users' Rights: The Perspective of Economic Theory*, in *Public Services and Citizenship in European Law: Public and Labour Law Perspectives* (Mark Freedland & Silvana Sciarra eds., Oxford U. Press 1998).

RICHARD J. PIERCE, SIDNEY A. SHAPIRO & PAUL R. VERKUIL, ADMINISTRATIVE LAW AND PROCESS (4th ed., Foundation Press 2004).

Richard S. Pierce, Jr., *The Due Process Counterrevolution of the 1990s*, 96 COLUM. L. REV. 1973 (1996).

Richard J. Pierce, Jr., *Waiting for* Vermont Yankee II, 57 ADMIN. L. REV. 669 (2005).

The Port Authority of NY & NJ, *Homepage*, http://www.panynj.gov (accessed Nov. 6, 2006).

Eric A. Posner & Adrian Vermeule, *The Credible Executive* (2006) (available at http://ssrn.com/abstract=931501).

Eric Posner & Adrian Vermeule, *Nondelegation: A Post-Mortem*, 70 U. CHI. L. REV. 1331 (2003).

RICHARD A. POSNER, CATASTROPHE: RISK AND RESPONSE (Oxford Univ. Press 2004).

RICHARD A. POSNER, LAW, PRAGMATISM, AND DEMOCRACY (Harvard Univ. Press 2003).

Richard A. Posner, *Pragmatic Liberalism versus Classical Liberalism*, 71 U. CHI. L. REV. 659 (2004).

Saikrishna Prakash, *The Chief Prosecutor*, 73 GEO. WASH. L. REV. 521 (2005).

Press Release, Blackwater USA, *Blackwater Continues to Support Katrina Devastated Areas* (Sept. 13, 2005).

Press Release, DHS, *Homeland Security Proposal Delivered to Congress* (June 18, 2002), *available at* http://www.dhs.gov/xnews/speeches/speech_0039.shtm.

Press Release, DP World, Statement by H. Edward Bilkey, Chief Operating Officer, DPWorld (Mar. 9, 2006) *available at* http://www.dpworld.com/news.asp.

Press Release, Lockheed Martin, *Lockheed Martin Delivers Secure Border Initiative Proposal* (May 30, 2006).

Press Release, The White House, *President Addresses Hurricane Relief in Address to the Nation* (Sept. 15, 2005) *available at* http://www.whitehouse.gov/news/releases/2005/09/20050915-8.html.

DON K. PRICE, THE SCIENTIFIC ESTATE (Harvard Univ. Press 1965).

Dana Priest and Anne Hull, *Soldiers Face Neglect, Frustration at Army's Top Medical Facility*, Wash. Post, Feb. 18, 2007, at sec. A. p. 1.

*Private Security Firms Operating in Iraq: Hearings Before the Subcomm. on Nat'l Security, Emerging Threats, and Int'l Relations of the H. Comm. on Gov't Reform*, 109th Cong. (2006) (testimony of IPOA president Doug Brooks).

RAND, *How Should the Army Use Contractors on the Battlefield? Assessing Comparative Risk in Sourcing Decisions* (Frank Camm & Victoria A. Greenfield eds., 2005).

RAND Home Page, http://www.rand.org (last visited Nov. 7, 2006).

RAND Corp., *History and Mission*, http://www.rand.org/about/history/ (accessed Nov. 6, 2006).

Warren L. Ratliff, *The Due Process Failure of America's Prison Privatization Statutes*, 21 SETON HALL LEGIS. J. 371 (1997).

JOHN RAWLS, A THEORY OF JUSTICE (Clarendon Press 1971).

*Report of the Congressional Committees Investigating the Iran–Contra Affair*, H.R. Rpt. 100–433, Sen. Rpt. 100–216 (Nov. 1987).

*Report of the Independent Panel to Review Department of Defense Detention Operations* (2004), *available at* http://www.defense.gov/news/Aug2004/d20040824final report.pdf.

Report of the Natl. Comm. on the Pub. Serv., *Leadership for America: Rebuilding the Public Service* (Paul Volcker, Chair, Brookings Instn.1989).

Report of the Natl. Comm. on the Pub. Serv., *Urgent Business for America: Revitalizing the Federal Government for the 21st Century* (Paul Volcker, Chair, Brookings Instn. 2003), in *High Performance Government* 9–88 (Robert Klitgaard & Paul C. Light, eds., RAND 2005).

Judith Resnick, *Procedure as Contract*, 80 NOTRE DAME L. REV. 593 (2005).

Restatement (First) of Contracts (1932).

Arthur Ripstein, *Private Order and Public Justice: Kant and Rawls*, 92 VA. L. REV. 1391 (2006).

Al Robbert, *Developing Leadership: Emulating the Military Model*, in *High Performance Government* 255 (Robert Klitgaard & Paul C. Light eds., RAND 2005).

Judith Rodin & Stephen P. Steinberg, *Introduction: Incivility and Public Discourse*, in *Public Discourse in America* (Judith Rodin & Stephen P. Steinberg eds., Univ. of Penn. Press 2003).

David E. Rosenbaum, *Bush to Return to "Ownership Society" Theme in Push for Social Security Changes*, N.Y. TIMES A20 (Jan. 16, 2005) (available at 2005 WLNR 595069).

Clifford J. Rosky, *Force, Inc.: The Privatization of Punishment, Policing, and Military Force in Liberal States*, 36 CONN. L. REV. 879 (2004).

Edward Rubin, *The Myth of Accountability and the Anti-Administrative Impulse*, 103 MICH. L. REV. 2073 (2005).

David M. Ryfe, *Deliberative Democracy and Public Discourse*, in *Public Discourse in America* (Judith Rodin, Stephen P. Steinberg, eds., Univ. of Penn. Press 2003).

Robert J. Samuelson, *The Dangers of Ports (and Politicians)*, WASHINGTON POST A19 (Mar. 14, 2006) (available in LEXIS, News library).

MICHAEL J. SANDEL, DEMOCRACY'S DISCONTENT (Belknap Press 1996).

David E. Sanger & Eric Schmitt, *Cheney's Power No Longer Goes Unquestioned*, N.Y. TIMES A1 (Sept. 10, 2006).

Marc Santora & James Glanz, *Five American Security Employees Killed in Baghdad Helicopter Attack*, N.Y. TIMES A10 (Jan. 24, 2007).

Charlie Savage, *Bush Could Bypass New Torture Ban*, BOSTON GLOBE A1 (Jan. 4, 2006) (available at 2006 WLNR 169777).

ANTONIN SCALIA, A MATTER OF INTERPRETATION: FEDERAL COURTS AND THE LAW (Princeton U. Press, 1997).

ARTHUR M. SCHLESINGER, JR., THE AGE OF JACKSON (Little, Brown & Co. 1953).

ARTHUR M. SCHLESINGER, JR., THE COMING OF THE NEW DEAL (Mariner Books 1958).

Eric Schmitt, *Abuse Panel Says Rules on Inmates Need Overhaul: Command Chain Faulted*, N.Y. TIMES A1 (Aug. 25, 2004).

Steven L. Schooner, *Contractor Atrocities at Abu Ghraib: Compromised Accountability in a Streamlined, Outsourced Government*, 16 STAN. L. & POLICY REV. 549 (2005).

Glendon A. Schubert, Jr., *Judicial Review of the Subdelegation of Presidential Power*, 12 J. POLITICS 668 (1950).

Alwyn Scott, *Slipping through the Net and into Our Ports*, SEATTLE TIMES
C1 (Apr. 23, 2006) (available at 2006 WLNR 6803898).

Scott Shane, *Latest Blue-Ribbon Panel Awaits Its Own Ultimate Fate*, N.Y.
TIMES A24 (Dec. 28, 2006).

Scott Shane, *Torture Victim Had No Terror Link, Canada Told U.S.*, N.Y.
TIMES A10 (Sept. 25, 2006).

Scott Shane & Eric Lipton, *Stumbling Storm-Aid Effort Put Tons of Ice on
Trips to Nowhere*, N.Y. TIMES A1 (Oct. 2, 2005).

Scott Shane & Ron Nixon, *In Washington, Contractors Take on Biggest Role
Ever*, N.Y. TIMES, Feb. 4, 2007, at A1, A24.

Thom Shanker and Michael R. Gordon, *Strained, Army Looks to Guard
For More Relief*, N.Y. TIMES, Sept. 22, 2006, at A1.

Thom Shanker & Eric Schmitt, *Rumsfeld Seeks Leaner Army, and a Full
Term*, N.Y. TIMES A1 (May 11, 2005).

Thom Shanker, *Young Officers Leaving Army At a High Rate*, N.Y. TIMES
A1 (Apr. 10, 2006).

Sidney A. Shapiro, *OMB's Dubious Peer Review Procedures*, 34 ENVTL. L.
REP. 100064 (2004).

Sidney A. Shapiro, *Outsourcing Government Regulation*, 53 DUKE L.J. 389
(2003).

Sidney A. Shapiro & Rena I. Steinzor, *The People's Agent: Executive Branch
Secrecy and Accountability in an Age of Terrorism*, 69 L. & CONTEMP.
PROB. 99 (2006).

Sidney A. Shapiro & Richard E. Levy, *Government Benefits and the Rule
of Law: Towards a Standards Based Theory of Due Process*, 57 ADMIN. L.
REV. 107 (2005).

Deirdre Shesgreen, *Bush Offers Compromise on Aviation Security Bill;
It Stalls on Provision to Make All Screeners Federal Employees*, ST.
LOUIS POST-DISPATCH A7 (Oct. 4, 2001) (available at 2001 WLNR
11359875).

Charles Silver & Frank B. Cross, *What's Not To Like About Being a
Lawyer?*, 109 YALE L.J. 1443, 1479 (2000).

P. W. SINGER, CORPORATE WARRIORS: THE RISE OF THE PRIVATIZED
MILITARY INDUSTRY (Cornell U. Press 2003).

P.W. Singer, *War, Profits, and the Vacuum of Law: Privatized Military
Firms and International Law*, 42 COLUM. J. TRANSNAT'L L. 521
(2004).

David A. Sklansky, *The Private Police*, 46 UCLA L. REV. 1165 (1999).

ANNE-MARIE SLAUGHTER, A NEW WORLD ORDER (Princeton U. Press
2004).

Neil Smelser, *A Paradox of Public Discourse and Political Democracy*, in *Public Discourse in America*, 178 (Judith Rodin, Stephen P. Steinberg, eds., Univ. of Penn. Press 2003).

STEPHEN RATHGEB SMITH & MICHAEL LIPSKY, NONPROFITS FOR HIRE: THE WELFARE STATE IN THE AGE OF CONTRACTING (Harvard Univ. Press 1993).

Steven B. Smith, *On Leo Strauss's Critique of Spinoza*, 25 CARDOZO L. REV. 741 (2003).

STEVEN B. SMITH, SPINOZA, LIBERALISM, AND THE QUESTION OF JEWISH IDENTITY (Yale Univ. Press 1997).

THEODORE C. SORENSEN, WATCHMEN IN THE NIGHT: PRESIDENTIAL ACCOUNTABILITY AFTER WATERGATE (MIT Press 1975).

Kevin M. Stack, *The President's Statutory Powers to Administer the Laws*, 106 COLUM. L. REV. 263 (2006).

Kevin Stack, *The Statutory President*, 90 IOWA L. REV. 539 (2005).

Stewart E. Sterk, *The Federalist Dimension of Regulatory Takings Jurisprudence*, 114 YALE L.J. 203 (2004).

Richard Stevenson, *Government May Make Private Nearly Half of Its Civilian Jobs*, N.Y. TIMES A1 (Nov. 15, 2002).

David A. Strauss, *Why Was Lochner Wrong?*, 70 U. CHI. L. REV. 373 (2003).

Peter L. Strauss, *Presidential Rulemaking*, 72 CHI.-KENT L. REV. 965 (1997).

Peter L. Strauss, *Within* Marbury: *The Importance of Judicial Limits on the Executive's Power to Say What the Law Is*, 116 YALE L.J. Pocket Part 59 (2006).

Peter L. Strauss & Cass Sunstein, *The Role of the President and OMB in Informal Rulemaking*, 38 ADMIN. L. REV. 181 (1985).

Chris Strohm, *Appropriators Skeptical of Promised Secure Border Initiative*, CONG. DAILY (Apr. 7, 2006) *available at* 2006 WLNR 5903997.

Chris Strohm, *Department Moving on Massive Border Security Project*, CONG. DAILY (April 11, 2006) *available at* 2006 WLNR 6180318.

Chris Strohm, *TSA Examines Conflict of Interest Charges Against Contractor*, (May 23, 200), *available at* http://govexec.com/dailyfed/0505/052305c1.htm.

Cass R. Sunstein, *Beyond* Marbury: *The Executive's Power to Say What the Law Is*, 115 YALE L.J. 2580 (2006).

CASS R. SUNSTEIN, FREE MARKETS AND SOCIAL JUSTICE (Oxford Univ. Press 1997).

Cass R. Sunstein, *Lochner's Legacy*, 87 COLUM. L. REV. 873 (1987).

John Swain, *Making a Killing*, SUNDAY TIMES MAG. 40 (Oct. 23, 2005).

Robert T. Swaine, The Cravath Firm (1948).

Rachel L. Swarns, *House G.O.P. Planning Recess Hearings*, N.Y. Times A20 (July 28, 2006).

Matthew Sweeney, *New York Harbor "Ripe" for Al Qaeda-Style Attack*, New York Sun at 1 (Nov. 19, 2002) (available in LEXIS, News library).

Symposium, *Public Values in an Era of Privatization*, 116 Harv. L. Rev. 1211 (2003).

Michael Taggart, *The Province of Administrative Law Determined?*, in *The Province of Administrative Law* (Michael Taggart ed., Hart Publg. 1997).

Task Force on Presidential Signing Statements and the Separation of Powers Doctrine, Am. Bar Ass'n, Recommendation and Report (Aug. 2006), http://www.abanet.org/op/signingstatements/aba_final_signing_statements_recommendations_report_7_24_06.pdf.

David Teather, *Halliburton Accused of Not Justifying £1 Billion Army Bills*, The Guardian 17 (Aug. 12, 2004).

Phillip E. Tetlock, Expert Political Judgment (Princeton Univ. Press 2005).

Heather Timmons, *Dubai Port Company Sells Its U.S. Holdings to A.I.G. – Political Hot Potato Handed Off*, N.Y. Times C4 (Dec. 12, 2006).

Adam Tomkins, Public Law (Oxford Univ. Press 2003).

The Torture Papers – The Road to Abu Ghraib (Karen J. Greenberg & Joshua L. Dratel, eds., Cambridge Press 2005).

The Tower Commission Report (Bantam Books & Times Books 1987).

Transportation Security Administration, *TSA Releases Performance Report On Contract Screeners At Five U.S. Airports*, http://www.tsa.gov/press/releases/2004/press_release_0412.shtm (accessed Nov. 5, 2006).

Joseph B. Treaster, *Mollen Panel Says Buck Stops With Top Officers*, N.Y. Times A21 (July 10, 1994).

Michael J. Trebilcock & Ronald J. Daniels, *Rationales and Instruments for Government Intervention in Natural Disasters*, in *On Risk and Disaster* (Daniels et al., eds. Univ. of Penn. Press 2006).

Gregory F. Treverton, *Broadening Public Leadership in a Globalized World*, in *High Performance Government* (Robert Klitgaard & Paul C. Light eds., RAND 2005).

Gregory F. Treverton, *Governing the Market State*, in *High Performance Government* 89 (Robert Klitgaard & Paul C. Light eds., RAND Corp. 2005).

Laurence H. Tribe, American Constitutional Law (3d ed., West 1999).

Laurence H. Tribe, *Structural Due Process*, 10 Harv. Civ. Rights-Civ. Libs. L. Rev. 269 (1975)

HARRY S. TRUMAN, WHERE THE BUCK STOPS (Margaret Truman ed., Warner 1989).

U.S. Customs and Border Protection Home Page, *About SBInet*, http://www.cbp.gov/xp/cgov/border_security/sbi_net/about_sbinet.xml (last visited Nov. 7, 2006).

U.S. Customs and Border Protection, *SBI Industry Overview*, http://www.cbp.gov/linkhandler/cgov/border_security/sbi_net/library/sbi_industry_overview.ctt/sbi_industry_overview.pdf (last visited Nov. 7, 2006).

U.S. Dept. of Justice, Off. of the Atty. Gen., *Legal Authorities Supporting the Activities of the National Security Agency Described by the President* (Jan. 19, 2006) (available at http://purl.access.gpo.gov/GPO/lps66493).

U.S. General Accounting Office (GAO), *Commercial Activities Panel: Improving the Sourcing Decisions of the Government: Final Report* (2002).

U.S. Gen. Accounting Office, *GAO-04-367, Competitive Sourcing: Greater Emphasis Needed on Increasing Efficiency and Improving Performance* (2004), *available at* http://www.gao.gov/new.items/d04367.pdf.

U.S. Govt. Accountability Off., *Contract Management: Opportunities to Improve Surveillance on Department of Defense Service Contracts*, GAO-05-274 (Mar. 2005) (available at http://www.gao.gov/cgi-bin/getrpt?GAO-05-274).

U.S. Off. of Personnel Mgt., *The Fact Book: Federal Civilian Workforce Statistics* (Oct. 2004) (available at http://www.opm.gov/feddata/factbook/2004/factbook.pdf).

U.S. Public Service Academy Home Page, http://www.uspublicserviceacademy.org (last visited Nov. 7, 2006).

William Van Alstyne, *The Demise of the Right-Privilege Distinction in American Constitutional Law*, 81 HARV. L. REV. 1439 (1968).

Michael P. Vandenburgh, *The Private Life of Public Law*, 105 COLUM. L. REV. 2029 (2005).

James Varney, *Fact-Finding Senators Feel Stiffed by FEMA*, NEW ORLEANS TIMES-PICAYUNE at 1 (July 14, 2006) (available at 2006 WLNR 12145468).

Joan Vennochi, *A Military Draft Might Awaken Us*, BOSTON GLOBE A11 (June 22, 2006).

Paul R. Verkuil, *The Emerging Concept of Administrative Procedure*, 78 COLUM. L. REV. 260 (1978).

Paul R. Verkuil, *Is Efficient Government an Oxymoron?*, 43 DUKE L. J. 1221 (1994).

Paul R. Verkuil, *Privatizing Due Process*, 57 ADMIN. L. REV. 669 (2005).

Paul R. Verkuil, *Public Law Limitations on Privatization of Government Functions*, 84 N.C. L. REV. 397 (2006).

Paul R. Verkuil, *Reverse Yardstick Competition: A New Deal for the Nineties*, 45 FLA. L. REV. 1 (1993).

Paul R. Verkuil, *Understanding the "Public Interest" Justification for Government Actions*, 39 ACTA JURIDICA HUNGARICA 141 (1998).

Paul R. Verkuil, *Separation of Powers, the Rule of Law and the Idea of Independence*, 30 WM. & MARY L. REV. 301 (1989).

Paul R. Verkuil, *The Wait is Over:* Chevron *as a Stealth* Vermont Yankee II, _ GEO. WASH. L. REV. _ (forthcoming 2007).

Rebecca Rafferty Vernon, *Battlefield Contractors: Facing the Tough Issues*, 33 PUB. CONT. L.J. 365 (2004).

Volcker Commission I (*See* Report of the Natl. Comm. on the Pub. Serv., *Leadership for America: Rebuilding the Public Service*).

Volcker Commission II (*See* Report of the Natl. Comm. on the Pub. Serv., *Urgent Business for America: Revitalizing the Federal Government for the 21st Century*).

WILHELM Von Humboldt & J.W. Burrow, THE LIMITS OF STATE ACTION (Liberty Fund 1993).

Edward Walsh, *For Coast Guard, Priorities Shifted on September 11; Focus Is on Defense Against Terrorism*, WASH. POST A23 (Nov. 26, 2001) (available in LEXIS, News library).

LAWRENCE E. WALSH, FIREWALL: THE IRAN–CONTRA CONSPIRACY AND COVER-UP (W. W. Norton & Co. 1997).

White House Off. Of the Press Sec., *Fact Sheet: The CFIUS Process and the DP World Transaction* (Feb. 22, 2006) (available at http://www.whitehouse.gov/news/releases/2006/02/20060222-11.html).

White House Off. of the Press Sec., *Press Briefing by Ari Fleischer* (Nov. 6, 2001) (available at http://www.whitehouse.gov/news/releases/2001/11/20011106-8.html).

OLIVER E. WILLIAMSON, THE ECONOMIC INSTITUTIONS OF CAPITALISM (Free Press 1985).

Oliver E. Williamson, *Public and Private Bureaucracies: A Transactions Cost Economics Perspective*, 15 J.L. ECON. & ORG. 306 (1999).

James Q. Wilson, *Can the Bureaucracy Be Deregulated? Lessons from Government Agencies* in *Deregulating the Public Service* (John J. DiIulio, Jr. ed., Brookings Instn. Press 1994).

GORDON S. WOOD, THE AMERICAN REVOLUTION: A HISTORY (Modern Library 2002).

GORDON S. WOOD, THE CREATION OF THE AMERICAN REPUBLIC, 1776–1787 (U. of N.C. Press 1969).

BOB WOODWARD, STATE OF DENIAL: BUSH AT WAR, PART III (Simon & Schuster 2006).

Bernard Wysocki, Jr, Is U.S. Government 'Outsourcing its Brain'?, Wall St. Journal, Mar. 30, 2007 at A 1.

DANIEL YERGIN & JOSEPH STANISLAW, THE COMMANDING HEIGHTS: THE BATTLE BETWEEN GOVERNMENT AND THE MARKETPLACE THAT IS REMAKING THE MODERN WORLD (Free Press 1998).

Patrick Yoest, *Procurement for Secure Border Initiative Should Be Finished in September*, Officials Say, CQ Homeland Security (Jan. 27, 2006) *available at* 2006 WLNR 1791864.

Christopher S. Yoo, Steven G. Calabresi & Anthony J. Colangelo, *The Unitary Executive in the Modern Era, 1945–2004*, 90 IOWA L. REV. 601 (2005).

John Yoo & James C. Ho, *Marque and Reprisal*, in *The Heritage Guide to the Constitution* (Edwin Meese III, Matthew Spalding & David Forte eds., Regnery Publ. 2005).

# INDEX